"I loved every minute of *The Taste* Ethel, and put her in context, not shirking (or misunderstanding!) those complex aspects of her character that both pushed her to greatness, but also ultimately caused her so much suffering at times. This is an "I-can't-put-it-down" book, an historical biography that reads like a novel—an ordinary life made extraordinary through circumstance and an inordinate amount of courage."

DR. MARIE ADAMS, author of *The Myth of the Untroubled Therapist*

"The stories of what women contribute, suffer, and carry in wartime are rarely told. With original research and an elegant style, Evans allows us to see Ethel, to realize the price many women pay in conflicts, and to appreciate their resilience and grace. Such remarkable stories of Canadian women need to be told."

DR. HEATHER EATON, Professor of Conflict Studies at Saint Paul University and author of *Ecofeminism and Globalization*

"This is a story of hardship, cruelty, and disease—but also of endurance, indomitability, and friendship. Centred around a remarkable cookbook, Evans vividly recounts Ethel's resilience and commemoration of the war that marked her for life."

TIM COOK, author of *Vimy: The Battle and the Legend* and *The Fight for History: 75 Years of Forgetting, Remembering, and Remaking Canada's Second World War*

"As gripping as a novel, *The Taste of Longing* is infused with Suzanne Evans' keen sense of psychology and language. Its plot is made all the more riveting by the historical facts of the deprivation of the prisoners of war in Changi Prison. Ethel was a remarkable and fearless woman. This vivid biography is also a uniquely female history, infused with nourishment no less important for being imaginary."

NADINE MCINNIS, author of *Blood Secrets* and *Delirium for Solo Harp*

"A fascinating story that begs to be told. Ethel directs the voyage of her life from her anchor, rural Manitoulin Island, to Changi Prison, where her energy and creativity did much to sustain the bodies and spirits of the some 400 women and children interned there. Among her projects were imaginary teas and dinner parties, fashion shows and quilts, and most poignant of all, a cookbook of remembered recipes the women longed for."

ELIZABETH BAIRD, co-author of *Recipes for Victory: Great War Food from the Front and Kitchens Back Home in Canada*

"Suzanne Evans' important and compelling account of a gifted and courageous Manitoulin Island woman who wanted to make a difference is a page-turner. With sensitivity, craft, and imagination, Evans significantly expands our understanding of Canadian women's contributions to our history."

DR. LAURA BRANDON, former Historian, Art and War, at the Canadian War Museum

The
Taste
of
Longing

The
Taste

ETHEL MULVANY AND HER

of

STARVING PRISONERS OF WAR COOKBOOK

Longing

SUZANNE EVANS

Between the Lines
Toronto

First published in 2020 by
Between the Lines
401 Richmond Street West
Studio 281
Toronto, Ontario M5V 3A8
Canada
1-800-718-7201
www.btlbooks.com

Cataloguing in Publication information available from Library and Archives Canada
ISBN 9781771134897

Text design by Beate Schwirtlich

Printed in Canada

We acknowledge for their financial support of our publishing activities: the Government of Canada; the Canada Council for the Arts; and the Government of Ontario through the Ontario Arts Council, the Ontario Book Publishers Tax Credit program, and Ontario Creates.

Dedicated to all of Ethel's family
And mine too

Portrait of Ethel Mulvany while in Changi Jail by Joan Stanley-Cary, using paintbrush of human hair and paint of brick dust. Pioneer Museum, Mindemoya, Manitoulin.

The Taste of Longing

Having no reason for my scheme
Beyond the logic of a dream
To change a world predestinate
...
I'd place a table in the skies

"The Depression Ends" by E.J. Pratt

CONTENTS

ACKNOWLEDGEMENTS

This project began while I was working on a research fellowship at the Canadian War Museum in Ottawa. I was surrounded by helpful historians, librarians, and staff and was particularly fortunate to have Dr Laura Brandon as my mentor. The fellowship provided me with a fascinating learning opportunity that was further supported by a Canada Council Arts Grant for Creative Non-fiction, an Ontario Arts Council Writer's Works in Progress, an Ontario Arts Council Writers' Reserve Grant, and a City of Ottawa Arts Grant.

After I discovered the POW cookbook and told my friend Kathy Bergquist about it, she immediately said, "Oh, I know Ethel's nieces, would you like to meet them?" I will be forever grateful for this moment of serendipity and for the help Kathy has given me. She came to know of Ethel while writing a biography of Keith Greenaway, Ethel's cherished cousin. Between Keith's daughter, Brenda Greenaway-Serne, and Ethel's niece on the Cannard side, Marion King, I have had access to poignant ephemera, fascinating photos, and marvellous stories. Thanks to Bettymay Smith and April DeJong even more family tales and photos came my way. On the Mulvany side, Sally Praulitis, Denis Mulvany's daughter from his second marriage, generously shared photos and family papers.

I am so grateful to Shigeko and Isami Endo of Osaka, Japan, for contributing all their memories of Ethel which they still hold dear. Singer and songwriter Cathy Miller and author Dorothy Nixon both graciously shared their research materials on Ethel and Changi Jail. There are those up on the Manitoulin without whom this project would not have progressed. I am indebted to Patricia Costigan, Norma Hughson, Marilyn Irish, and the late Marion Seabrook. I also thank Manitoulin historian Shelley Pearen for her help.

With this project I felt the delightful pull of the past while delving into the resources of the National Library and Archives, Ottawa; the Pioneer Museum, Mindemoya, Manitoulin; the Imperial War Museum, London; the Red Cross Archives, London; the Changi Museum, Singapore; and the National Museum of Singapore Resource Centre; and, of course, at the Canadian War Museum. I appreciate all the help I received while working in these museums. I also received help at a distance from Jonathan Cooper, Singapore war historian; Jane Peek at the Australian War Memorial; Colin Gale at the Royal Bethlem Hospital Archives, UK; and from Far Eastern Prisoner of War researcher Ronald Bridge. I was touched by the assistance I received from Joyce Cummings and Vic Cole of the Cheltenham Local History Society.

I truly appreciate the work of Gwen Cumyn, Anna Cumyn, Karin Murray-Bergquist, and Lina El Samrout who painstakingly transcribed many of the 1961 taped conversations between Ethel and Sidney Katz. I am grateful to those who read and commented on the manuscript: Tom Shillington, Michael Dawson, Laura Brandon, Julie Paschkis, Wendy Evans, Carol Hunter, Ivy Lerner-Frank, Liz Hay, Marie Adams, and in particular Heather Eaton, who relentlessly pushed me in the right direction.

The recipe testers were a generous group who fed me in many ways. Thank you Dorothy Nixon, Laura Walters Baskett, Alan Cumyn,

Julie Paschkis, Jacqueline Dawson, Mary Moncrieff, Kathryn Lyons, Gates Cooney, Jane Allen, Lousia Murray-Bergquist, Kathleen Johnson, Mark Fried, Bernadette Bailey, Annie Jackson, Brenda Greenaway-Serne, Kate Preston, Gwen Cumyn, Molly Steers, Margos Zakarian, Marina Doran, Lesley LeMarquand, Amanda Lewis, Holly Lillico, Chris Elson, and Ashleigh Elson.

I must also mention the women of the Alchemy Arts Residency Program at Artscape on Toronto Island and at Hillier, Prince Edward County, Ontario. With directors Claire Tallarico and Tonia Di Risio we created our own imaginary feasts, shedding new light on Ethel's work. And thanks to producer Alisa Siegel for her fine work on the CBC radio documentary on Ethel that grew out of those feasts.

I thank Between the Lines and especially Amanda Crocker for taking on this project with such enthusiasm, and I am grateful to Mary Newberry for her keen editorial eye.

I save my greatest thanks for my husband, Alan Cumyn. Not only has he travelled the world with me on this project, he has ever so patiently shared his skills as a writer and editor each step of the way.

SETTING THE TABLE

Ethel pulled on the lumpy blue coat she'd been given by the Red Cross and glanced in the mirror before heading out to the printer's. There was nothing she could do about the coat's ugliness, but the garment was hers and not much else in the world was. Just over a year before, on an unforgettable September day in 1945 at the end of the war, she had been carried out of a Singapore prison camp on a stretcher. This five-foot-seven-inch woman had been unable to tip the scales past eighty-five pounds then, but now she was on her way back to her old size, if not her old self. When she arrived at the shop on Toronto's Danforth Avenue, she walked in with as much business in her manner as she could muster, put the two ledger books on the counter, and got on with her mission.

"The newspapers came around, several of them," she explained with some pride. "They all want my story." What she didn't say was that she hadn't been able to tell it. Her story had come out in a jumble glued together with so much venom directed at the Japanese that it had sickened even her. So she was here to try a different tack.

"You see these recipes"—she pointed out the ones with the check marks beside them—"I want you to print them up in a book. Fit as many on a page as you can." The printer started flipping through the log books while she kept on talking. "I've picked the best ones, but really they're all wonderful. Oh, how they made our mouths water when we discussed them. You see I was living in a prison camp in Singapore with a lot of other women when we wrote these and we were all starving."

He looked up in astonishment. "Really?"

"Yes. We ate bayam soup every day for three and a half years. Not much more than cooked-up buffalo grass. How would you like that?"

"Not much." He shook his head. "So all these women named in here, did they live in the camp?"

"They did and some of them died there too." She leaned in closer. "They died in the camp hospital from every disease known to man. We left many of our friends in the ground in Malaya. The soldiers, they died in battle, on firing lines, and on the work gangs of the Siam Railway." She straightened up and pounded her finger on the open books. "This is to remember the ones who died and to help those who just made it through."

The shop owner, wide-eyed, took refuge in the mundanity of his trade. "Do you want to include the women's names beside the recipes?" Ethel turned the books around and had another look. "No. There's too many of them gone already. It'd be like calling back the dead."

She handed over her one-page introduction and the sketch of Changi Jail she had for the front cover. The drawing fell short of conveying the horror of the massive concrete walls that had trapped the prisoners, but it was enough to remind Ethel. She might have guessed, though, from the way the printer kept turning the drawing around, that he wouldn't print it the right way up, but she didn't say anything. She needed to win his support and wasn't so sure of her persuasive abilities anymore. Even though the boils and the scars from her jungle sores had faded, she felt them, just as she felt the loss of her youth and charm that had so often helped her win backers for her grand schemes. She still had her smile though, so she put it on duty. "I want you to make me two thousand copies." She slapped a dollar bill on the counter. "Here's the down payment, and I'll give you my word for the rest and, as a Rogers from Manitoulin Island, my word is as good as gold."

He leaned back. "Lady, this is an interesting story, and I can see you've been through the wringer. But a dollar for two thousand copies?"

"I'll have the money to you before the year's done. I know just who I'm going to approach to sell these books, and we all know that everybody loves a cookbook." She could see he was not convinced, so she kept at it. "The money's not for me, even though I'm skint just at the moment. I'm going to buy food and send it to ex-POWs recuperating in hospital over in England. These are the men who survived the horrors I told you about. Men just like you. I'm going to send them all the tea and oranges we could only dream of when we were prisoners. You know there's still rationing over there."

"Lady—"

She held up her hand. "I'm asking a lot and you don't know me from Adam. But I raised plenty of money for good causes before the war, and this is a good cause and you'd know it if you'd ever been hungry or known anyone who suffered starvation." She could see he needed one more nudge. "Now besides all that, why would I order two thousand copies if I couldn't sell them all? I wouldn't risk being in debt for all those books when I only have eighty-six dollars to my name. Would I? I would just order maybe fifty copies for my friends and family. But I'm asking for two thousand because I—"

"Alright, alright," he interrupted. "But I won't make it longer than a hundred pages. You'll have to cut out a lot of these recipes. It'll be low grade paper too with no fancy cover and that money needs to be paid up within the month."

"Two months." She held her breath.

He shook his head and reluctantly pulled out his order pad. "Do you want your name on the cover?"

She breathed out and thought for a moment "Just my initials, E.R.M."

"And the title? *Prisoners of War Cook Book?*"

"Oh, it needs more than that. I'll call it *Prisoners of War Cook Book: This is a Collection of Recipes Made By Starving Prisoners of War...*"

"Fine."

"No, no, no! I'm not done. *Starving Prisoners of War ... While They Were Interned in Changi Jail, Singapore. Compiled by E.R.M.*"

"Well," he nodded his head, "it's a mouthful alright."

* * *

The shopkeeper was not in the business of charity work, yet, possibly daunted by a woman who could clearly out-talk a campaigning politician, he accepted Ethel Mulvany's terms. In the end, he printed 20,000 copies of the unassuming little publication with the off-kilter cover image. Ethel was none too pleased with the quality of his work, but she sold them all herself and raised $18,000 through the end of 1946 and into 1947—over $200,000 in today's dollars. Just as she had intended, she used this fortune to send food to hospitalized ex-POWs in England. These were her people. Even though Ethel wasn't in the military, she always thought of herself as a POW. There was a horror and honour attached to that term that she claimed for all civilians imprisoned within the walls of Changi Jail.[1]

More than sixty years later, when I first opened this slim cookbook with its soft green blotting-paper cover, there was no kitchen in sight and certainly not a speck of food, just stacks of books about Canadians and the horrors of war. The library at the Canadian War Museum in Ottawa seemed an appropriate spot to uncover these long-forgotten culinary stories. These were unusual wartime recipes though, not at all the practical make-do type. Instead each one gave instructions for how to shape a fantasy and, in doing so, told a tale

Prisoners of War Cook Book cover. Pioneer Museum, Mindemoya, Manitoulin.

of longing. They were packed with ingredients the prisoners had no hope of savouring in their mouths, only in their minds.

What little I knew about Ethel then had to do with one of her other prison camp projects. In my work as a research fellow at the museum, I had discovered that Ethel was known for organizing the creation of the Changi Quilts. These artful blankets, now well-known museum pieces, were fashioned by the women of Changi Jail and used as secret communication devices to send messages to military prisoners held in other Singaporean prison camps. It was an intriguing story and here was another—connected to the same woman. How could the prisoners write recipes while starving? Why did they? Who were these women? By the time I reached the last page, I needed answers to these questions and many more about war, creativity, and survival. The hunt for details and understanding began in my own neighbourhood and eventually sent me around the world.

* * *

The details of Ethel's first meeting with the printer have been pieced together based on a wide variety of sources. I have added what I imagine to be their dialogue, but for the rest of this book the words attributed to Ethel, unless otherwise noted, come from audio and visual recordings of her as well as her unpublished writings. In these sources she tells and retells many of her stories, at times from differing angles. Rather than repeating the different versions and sourcing each quote, I have edited them together for a more readable account. The sources for the words of other characters have been gleaned from both published and archival material and are all noted.

When Ethel died in 1992, two months shy of her eighty-eighth birthday, she bequeathed much of the ephemera of her life to her niece Marion King. As chance would have it, Marion, originally from Manitoulin Island, now lived ten minutes' drive from me in Ottawa and was happy to share all that she knew of her aunt. In preparation for my visit this wobbly octogenarian had headed down her basement stairs—backward, to avoid the vertigo of a forward descent—to retrieve some of Ethel's old mementoes that she thought would interest me. First there were her aunt's pictures. Carefully labelled, they trace Ethel's life around the globe from her birth on Manitoulin Island on December 22, 1904, to her death in 1992 on the same remote island in Lake Huron. Ethel's mother, Mary Jane Stirling, died just eight days after the birth. But during those short days she'd had the presence of mind to ask the Presbyterian minister Henry Rogers and his wife, Isabella McKenzie, to adopt her infant daughter. In the harsh light of mid-winter Mary Jane and her husband, Henry Cannard, realized with agonizing practicality that, as a farmer scratching out a living on the island, he couldn't alone care for a newborn as well as raise their three older children. They knew the Rogers had recently lost a baby of their own and rightly assumed the couple would be happy to take in little Ethel. Thus, rather than being an orphan, Ethel wound up with two families, both of whom she cherished.

On other visits I had with Marion, who is part of the Cannard clan, all manner of souvenirs bubbled up from her basement. Some carried a painful weight, like Ethel's prison camp bible, full of notes but missing the spine, chewed off in a moment of desperate hope that the glue, made of horses' hooves, would give her a little protein. Others Ethel had saved with a sober pride, like her Australian Red Cross Badge, promoting her to the rank of Superintendent in Singapore, just before the fall of that city to the Japanese in 1942. Marion listened carefully to all my questions and shared what stories she knew about each carefully saved treasure. Then one day she called me up to say that she had found a CD recording of Ethel. She thought it was a couple of high-school kids interviewing Ethel "up on the Manitoulin," as islanders put it.

In the beginning, Ethel's words sounded like they were coming from the bottom of a swimming pool, although her tone, full of insistence, was clear. Ever so slowly the sound improved and it became evident that this was no school project. A man was asking questions, each one articulated with care. He advised Ethel to think of this as a movie of her past. Instead of directing this film though, he found himself barely able to keep up with his subject. Listening to Ethel was like tracking a hound racing after the scent of her life's stories.

Only after many hours of interviewing did the man introduce himself. "Testing. Testing. We are now about to start a new tape. And it is a lovely and bright Tuesday morning in April, nineteen hundred and sixty-one. And this is a memorable occasion because this is the first tape that Sidney Katz has put on and threaded by himself!" At the time, Katz was a seasoned journalist working for *Maclean's* magazine. The reel-to-reel recordings were for a piece that was published on August 12, 1961, under the title "Miracle at Changi Prison: A Study in Survival."

I never met these two, but as I repeatedly eavesdropped on their conversations—fifteen hours of them—I was reminded of the tale of the Chinese artist who gave life to the dragons he painted by dotting their eyes. These tapes would be the glint I needed to awaken Ethel's stories lying dormant within dusty notes, old photos, and her collection of dream food recipes.

* * *

It was obvious, listening to the recordings, that Ethel painted her world in bold, rich colours both inside and outside the lines, and there turned out to be more to her intensity than mere enthusiasm. In 1946 she was hospitalized in Bethlem Royal Hospital, London, often known as the madhouse of Bedlam. Her medical records show a diagnosis of manic-depression, now known as bipolar disorder. They also mention that she had suffered through episodes of mania in 1935 and 1939 and then again in prison camp.

In 1958, Dr. Aldwyn Stokes, director of the Toronto Psychiatric Hospital and chair of the department of psychiatry at the University of Toronto, was asked to sum up his understanding of the disease for Ethel's medical report when she applied for compensation from the Canadian War Claim's Commission.

> The manic-depressive illness is one in which the feeling or mood is pathologically increased and maintained. When the main symptoms are depressive ... the illness is more readily apprehended than when the main symptoms are those of elation (mania). In the latter instance it is sometimes difficult to perceive that the bouncing overactivity, "not to be thwarted" over confidence, distractible discursive press of talk ... is illness and representative of overcompensation of pathological hurt.[2]

Dr. Kay Redfield Jamison, a writer and professor of psychiatry who herself suffers from bipolar disorder, describes the manic state from the point of view of lived experience. Along with the "phenomenally high levels of energy," comes "little need for sleep, a frenzied tendency to seek out others, terrible judgment, and rank impulsiveness."[3] Many of Ethel's fellow prisoners recognized this behaviour in her and were not shy to include in their diaries what it was like to be jammed into an overcrowded jail with her. Some of these long-gone souls accused Ethel, or Mul as she was often called, of lying, cheating, and stealing, yet there were others who depicted her as the heart of generosity. Either way, no one denied the intensity of her behaviour which eventually led to a breakdown and being held in solitary confinement for the final months of the war.

* * *

During Ethel and Sid's conversations of April 1961, the two spoke of plans to write Ethel's biography together. Why the book never happened may have been a function of both Ethel and the prejudices of the era. As an interviewee, Ethel was not one to fold her hands in her lap and behave. Her storytelling required a lot of pulling and tucking to bring it together. Then there was the fact of her illness. The issue was not raised in the *Maclean's* article, but in a longer work; avoiding it would be to miss out on an integral part of Ethel's story. Sid was not in the least hampered by a bias against diseases of the mind. However, the general public in Canada in the early 1960s would have been far more likely to dismiss, rather than embrace, the story of a woman who suffered from a terrifying and barely understood mental illness.

The war was long over by then, and the public gaze of the 1960s was forward-looking. Any interest of Canadians for a backward glance at the war would not have been directed at Singapore. Hong Kong was Canada's focal point of horror in the Pacific. Of the 1,975 Canadian troops who fought there, more than half never returned. For Singapore, however, the agony belonged to Britain and Australia. As for the war in general, the heroism and sacrifice of it, that was owned by men. It wasn't until the second wave of feminism of the 1960s and 1970s that interest in women's lives during both the world wars was sparked. Even then, it has taken a long time to gather what records still exist and to tell those stories. Bernice Archer, who has written extensively on civilian prisoners of the Japanese, has found many of the stories of women had simply been "erased from the public memory."⁴ Men fought, died, were brave and wise, and they saved people. They were the heroes; women were not, at least, not until we began seeing their actions differently and looking at the cost of war more holistically. Over time, traditional activities such as sewing, shopping, nursing, cooking, serving, all done under hideous conditions, became visible not only as essential activities for survival but also as bona fide acts of courage and heroism.

Ethel fought against hunger, against the tyranny of prison rules, against torture and disease, against withering boredom. The list goes on. Her battles came at a cost to her mental health and left her with a hatred of the Japanese that saturated her waking hours. Like many others who were still reeling from humanity's largest war, she knew that to find some peace she would have to loosen the oppressive grip that her bitter contempt of all things Japanese had on her. She began that process with the aid of her stories, a chance meeting, and the receptiveness of a young Japanese man.

* * *

Just up from the village crossroads in Ethel's hometown of Mindemoya, where she retired, sits the tiny seasonal Pioneer Museum, one of several proud museums on Manitoulin Island, a place where local history is honoured. Their archives hold some of Ethel's cherished belongings, including the two original ledger books filled with the handwritten recipes. Over sixty women in Changi offered up recipes of their favourite, often simple and comforting, dream foods. Elizabeth Driver, Canadian cookbook author and historian, insists that to fully understand the history contained in a cookbook, the reader must try the recipes, eat the creation, and consider the result with all senses.⁵ In telling Ethel's story, I have included a recipe from the *POW Cook Book* at the beginning of each chapter with, if available, the name and what little if any information I have found on

Rogers family. Standing: Isabella McKenzie, Margaret and Henry Rogers. Seated: Ethel and Harvey Rogers. Pioneer Museum, Mindemoya, Manitoulin.

the original contributor. If the recipes are tried, the pungent scent of a steamed sago pudding or the sharp mint flavour of humbugs made with "English Peppermint—not Japanese," may convey something of the food dreams of another time and place that sustained these women. Just as Ethel relied on others to contribute to her cookbook, a collection of women and men have tested these recipes. Their thoughts are included at the back of the book.

In her last few years Ethel made some more audio tapes. With an aging but still determined voice, she decided to fill in a few parts of her life of which she had not yet made a record. She was feeling the creaks and stresses of time by then; an eye operation, a bad back, and a fall had sent her to hospital a few times and then bound her to the house. She explained more than complained about her lot and then summed things up. "But me—I'm eighty-three in December. I'm going on with two sticks and getting around pretty well. I look after myself. I have Meals on Wheels twice a week." When her sister Margaret died in 1985, Ethel lost a friend whose companionship she had relished from their days of youthful spitting contests in the apple tree to their years of old age spent together in Margaret's Mindemoya house. Ethel now suffered not so much from her infirmities as from a dearth of companionship. As the October days got shorter and the nights grew longer she was forced to rely on her tape recorder as a witness to the stories she believed the world should hear and which she never tired of repeating—including the turn of fate that first brought her to Singapore. That is where this story begins.

Part One
Meeting the Emperor

Cool Drink

Mix 1 large bottle ginger ale,
1 pt cold tea, 1 pt water, juice of 6
or 8 limes, sugar to taste, ice. Serve
very cold.

Priscilla Hannah Jackson,
British (b. 1884)
Changi POW Cook Book

CHAPTER ONE
WHAT'S A MANITOULIN GIRL DOING IN A PLACE LIKE SINGAPORE?

Early July 1933. Ethel Rogers was exhausted and hot. On board the SS *Rawalpindi* one day out from Shanghai the twenty-eight-year-old was flattened with debilitating nausea. She was sure it had something to do with the caviar served at a party given in her honour by the Trade Commissioner in Shanghai. Her family back home on Lake Huron's Manitoulin Island would have laughed—What was she expecting eating all those fancy fish eggs? Don't they have any proper fillets there? Ethel might have laughed herself if she hadn't been feeling so wretched.

She had tried all day to deal with her condition on her own, then finally gave up and asked Auntie Rose to call for the ship's doctor. Ethel had spied Miss Rose early on in her travels and, for the sake of propriety, had asked the elderly woman if she would act as her chaperone. It wasn't as if Ethel was terribly concerned about appearances, but she was aware that as a single young woman travelling alone she had to be careful. Lila Rose, an American writer, had been delighted to oblige and had tended to her duties with a light touch and a growing fondness for her charge. But now in the worst of

Auntie Rose and Ethel on donkeys with guide at Great Wall of China, 1933. Pioneer Museum, Mindemoya, Manitoulin.

Ethel's current illness it turned out that the ship's doctor was himself indisposed. Rumour had it the cause was an overconsumption of "medicinal" whiskey. Ethel, a teetotaller, was not impressed with drinkers and might well have thought he'd had what was coming to him. Still, moral superiority was no help at the moment, so a call was put out to the passengers. Dr. Denis Mulvany, a young military doctor travelling back to his posting in India, agreed to check in on the ill Canadian.

More than half a century later Ethel, wakeful and alone in the middle of a Manitoulin October night, told her tape recorder the story. She could still see the 29-year-old Denis in her mind, as clearly as she could see to the bottom of Lake Mindemoya on a calm day. He was dressed "in his pyjamas and bathrobe and looking very chic," she recalled. After winding his way down to her tourist class quarters, he came in and sat on the side of her bunk. Her appearance shocked him.

"Why didn't you call me before?" he demanded.

Ethel, unaccustomed to his marbles-in-the-mouth British accent, was certain she had heard him say, "What did you call me for?" In spite of her weakened condition she shot back, "Well, 'tisn't for your looks. If that's what you're thinking you can just get out of here!"

"Oh, you're not going to die," Denis returned fire, "you'll be alright with a temper like that!"

He left without saying much more but had some "grog," as Ethel put it, sent down to her. She slept well that night and was out on deck the next morning. Denis found her and inquired, carefully, after her health. The light of day allowed a better view of this sharp-tongued young woman: short light-brown hair waved back off a round open face with perfectly even features, movie-star skin, and a show-stopping smile. She was almost as tall as he was, so he did not have to bend down to see that her eyes were hazel-blue. As her doctor, Denis advised her to get some exercise walking around the deck. Then, ever so cautiously shifting from medical practitioner to intrigued bachelor, he added, "I'll assist you."

From these early exchanges, Ethel could see the spark in Denis's eyes and feel her own keenness. They likely would have told each other their stories, the ones people tell about themselves when they are eager to paint an enticing self-portrait for their listener. Ethel was impressed, but not cowed, by the intelligence of this well-educated man with the posh accent. For his part, the quiet British doctor would have wondered where in the world this vivacious colonial had come from and how in God's name she came to be eating caviar in Shanghai. When he realized how little time they had together—only a few days—before Ethel was to disembark, Denis made it his mission to keep her in his sights and to listen all the more intently to her stories.

Despite this being the depths of the Great Depression, Ethel, a former teacher, was in the middle of a worldwide journey studying foreign educational systems. She had been to Japan and China and was on her way to Siam, now Thailand. The audacious plan, devised only two months before, was still being fine-tuned. But her intention was to return to Canada and give a series of lectures on what she had learned. The idea had come to her when she was working in Toronto. Having run out of money and no longer able pay for her university studies, she had appealed for help to University of Toronto professor Ned Pratt, whom she had become friends with when she was his student. Pratt, along with his teaching duties, was second vice-president of a new organization called the Canadian Society for Literature and the Arts. Their mandate was to spread the word about Canadian literature. They hired Ethel as a managing co-ordinator to arrange poetry readings and public lectures.[1] Within a few months she had talked the board into sponsoring her to do this ambitious international study trip. Likely Denis had no idea about the society or who Ned Pratt was and, even more likely, Ethel would have told him all about the Newfoundlander and his poetry and even recited some of her favourites for him.

When their ship pulled into Hong Kong harbour for a stopover, Denis saw an opportunity to have Ethel's undivided attention without having to share her with other passengers.

"Come into the city with me," he urged. "We could have tea at the Victoria Hotel and then look in the shops."

Ethel was enthusiastic and the two took their conversations ashore for the afternoon and then back again to the boat. Denis, a man of his time and of established upper-middle-class origins, would have wanted to find out more about Ethel's people and her place. Luckily, there wasn't much else in the world she loved talking about more than Manitoulin. She respected the tenacity and the cultures of the settlers, like her father, who had arrived there in the nineteenth century and had stayed, and the Indigenous peoples, the Ojibwe, the Odawa, and the Potawatomi who, for so much longer, had lived on this *Mnidoo Mnis*, Spirit Island. The settlers came to be known as Haweaters. It was island wisdom among those that had been born and bred there that the berries of the hawthorn trees growing in meadows and along old homestead fence lines provided protection from scurvy during the long winters. As for family, it would have been clear from the beginning that she adored them all, adopted and blood, especially her father. Many of his words, whether spoken in quiet bedtime conversation or as homilies from the pulpit, were carefully stored in her heart ready in an instant to be shared. Yet, in spite of her love of home, there she was very far from it, in culture and in distance, eager to explore the world.

Ned Pratt had been more than willing to help her make some useful connections for her journey, ones that led all the way to Andrew MacLean, the prime minister's private secretary. Ethel took the train down to Ottawa to meet him face to face. The flurry of letters that were sent out from his office afterwards are proof of how Ethel galvanized the man's interest. If Denis had lifted his eyebrows at this point in her story, wondering how much exaggeration was mixed into Ethel's claim, she had the paperwork to back her up. This Manitoulin girl was offered diplomatic assistance in India, France, Japan, Italy, and Russia. The best part for her, the part that "thrilled her to the nth degree,"[2] was getting to meet Prime Minister Richard Bedford Bennett—despite the fact that she was a Liberal and he was not—and tell him her plans. Bennett was taken with her proposal and promised to send her a Letter of Introduction.

The official document with its ribbons and seal, signed by secretary of state of Canada, Charles H. Cahan, had reached her just as she was stepping off the Vancouver docks onto the *Empress of Japan*. When she wrote her thank-you letter to the PM she let him know of its arrival and told him of yet another promise of assistance, that of Captain Watson-Armstrong, the Siamese Consul, who had sent introductions to the Government of Siam.

Standing on the ship's deck explaining all this to the attentive man at her side, Ethel told him her future, as far as she could see it.

Ethel and guard at main gate of Kyoto Imperial Palace, Japan, 1933. Pioneer Museum, Mindemoya, Manitoulin.

"When I get off in Singapore, I am going to Bangkok where I am going to meet the King of Siam and, you'll never guess how I'm getting there!" Of course there was no time for Denis to squeeze in a guess before she answered herself—"In a Cessna airplane!"

Herbert and Isabel Marler, with whom she had stayed in Tokyo, had helped her arrange the Siam trip. Marler, a wealthy Montrealer and former Liberal member of Parliament, was Canada's first envoy to Japan. He loved the pomp and ceremony of his office and was known for "having been born almost totally devoid of a sense of humour"— much like Isabel Marler. [3] The couple must have found this ebullient young woman quite startling. But, wrote Marler to Andrew MacLean, "I was delighted to meet Miss Rogers and found her most charming in addition to being greatly interested in her tour of the Far East and other parts of the world ... We will be able to place every facility at her disposal in the matters which she wishes to investigate."[4]

Isabel Marler, responding to Ethel's enthusiasm for all things Japanese, arranged for her to be presented to the emperor. Ethel

Ethel (holding life saver) and fellow passengers on the way to China from Japan, 1933. Pioneer Museum, Mindemoya, Manitoulin.

was always quick to admit that her meeting with Emperor Hirohito and Empress Kojun was a very informal affair that took place in the palace garden. As proof, she showed Denis the photo of her in her ever-suitable embroidered white blouse and skirt in front of the main gate (*Kenreimon*) of the Kyoto Imperial Palace (*Gosho*). The meeting with King Prajadhipok of Siam, however, would be much more formal. Isabel Marler had made sure Ethel would be appropriately attired by lending her one of her own gowns.

While in Japan Ethel had made a point of visiting Kyoto to see the arts and crafts and the university of that city, but the stories she relished sharing with Denis and anyone willing to listen were of her meeting with Emperor Hirohito, her visit with Mikimoto, the pearl king in Gifu, touring Peking and the Great Wall of China, and her escapades in Shanghai.

There could have been any number of occasions throughout the telling of this tale when Denis might have thought Ethel was having him on. Not least of all he must have wondered why this woman, who

Ethel Rogers and
Denis Mulvany
discussing their
future, 1933.
Mulvany Private
Papers.

was meeting with the *crème de la crème* of society, was travelling tourist class. Ethel had an answer for everything. Before stepping aboard the *Empress of Japan* she had insisted on exchanging her first-class ticket supplied by her employer. That way, she explained, she would have more money to buy arts and crafts to illustrate her lectures back home. She might not have let on that, in any case, she did not have the upscale wardrobe to travel in first class.

Ethel's stories, the way she told them, charmed Denis. He wished to capture this firefly. After Hong Kong came Singapore—and time was running out. The day after they arrived in Singapore, she was scheduled to leave for Siam. On their last evening together he asked her to go into Singapore city with him. She accepted his invitation and all through the decades held fast the details of that night, one that would add yet another twist in the course of her ever-changing life.

Denis called for a rickshaw which, only having room for two, meant that their dear chaperone, Auntie Rose, was unable to accompany them. On the way to their destination, the Singapore Swimming Club, they passed under a sign arched over the road saying, "Kiss your girl here!" As they slowly approached it, Ethel nervously wondered what Denis would do. She was torn in half, she wanted that kiss, but she also wanted him to be a model of restraint. He was, leaving her wanting that kiss all the more. At the club they found a seat on the terrace overlooking the pool, a lovely one, the first to be built in Malaya. They ordered drinks while enjoying the breeze coming off the Straits of Malacca. She had her usual Orangeade and he ordered a *chota peg*, a strange concoction with a slender layer of dark liquid topped with soda. "Whiskey," she guessed, but didn't think more of it. The distractions were many: the little *chichak* lizards dancing up and down the walls behind them were mesmerizing, the clothes on the club guests were striking, and of course, there was Dr. Mulvany, with his effort at a Clark Gable moustache, a head of tight dark curls, and that English accent.

They returned to the ship by midnight, and Denis asked if Ethel would take a few turns on the deck with him; he had something on his mind. Soon enough he was ready to let her know what it was. "Miss Rogers," he pronounced in a quiet but very certain way, "I would like to marry you."

Ethel was astounded. "My goodness, I don't even know you!"

"Well, I'm telling you what I think after these past days."

Ethel's long silence was filled with considerations about her future. Finally she thought to ask some fundamental questions. "What is your full name?"

"Denis Paul Francis Mulvany."

"Well, I am Ethel Wilhemine Rogers. And where do you live?" She then learned about where he was stationed in Lucknow, India, and the details of his life that they had not managed to cover in their short time together so far. What was it like being born in India and sent off to boarding school in England at a tender age? Where was his real home, where he belonged most? How did he feel, following in the footsteps of his father to become a military doctor?

She was quiet for a time thinking about what was left for her at home, and how lonely it would be without her father who had died the year before. Gradually she began thinking that this proposal was a wonderful thing. They did, after all, admire each other greatly. So she said, "I think *I* would like to marry *you*!" It was all so new, exciting, perfectly unanticipated, and absolutely wonderful. Before long however, Denis made known another of his desires. It was about her work. "I wish you wouldn't go to Siam." He wanted her to put an end to her job and carry on with him to India to be married right away. He persistently argued his case, reasoning that she didn't like all that formal living anyway. It was true, but on the other hand she had found on her travels that, apart from caviar, she had developed an appreciation for the work she was doing and the life she was leading. She equivocated, but honestly. "Well, I don't know that I do and I don't know that I don't." Eventually she agreed not to carry on to Siam.

Ethel did not flout the rules of convention of her day, she merely shaped them to her own interests, as required. She'd had no qualms about setting off as a single young woman on her own to travel around the world, but she had asked Miss Rose to act as her chaperone. When it came to the strictures of marriage, however, Ethel seemed less willing to push against common practice. She knew it was expected that she give up her job, and she complied with apparent ease.

In time she and Denis went to their respective cabins for what little remained of the night. But sleep was impossible for Ethel. She got out of bed, unpacked all her clothes that were folded and ready for Siam, and began compulsively ironing everything. By the time each dress and blouse was pressed and hung up she had changed her mind. It was that *chota peg*, she concluded. He must have been drunk when he proposed. She repacked her clothes, put her suitcases in the hall to be taken off the ship, and left. By then it was early morning and she wandered the city streets. When the shops opened and she had pondered her fate for longer than she could bear, she made two purchases she would never forget. In a tone laced with guilt the elderly Ethel told her tape recorder the exorbitant amount she paid— one hundred and fifty dollars for one dress and one hundred and seventy-five for another, more than five thousand dollars for both of them in today's dollars. Where all this money had come from, she never revealed. Was it the stash she had tucked away after cashing in her first-class ticket, the money she had intended on using to buy arts and crafts?

At that moment her mind must have been buzzing with questions about her future. Should she carry on to Siam? Was Denis's proposal sincere? What would he think of these purchases? Maybe there was a part of her that wanted to test him, push him as she had been pushed. Who was he to tell her to set aside her work and her pleasures, especially if he had been drunk! She returned to the ship to tell Denis she was calling off the engagement.

Meanwhile, after Denis had got up he went to her cabin and had seen that both she and her luggage were gone. He was on the deck looking for her when she walked up the gangplank.

He blurted out, "And so you changed your mind."

She blurted right back, "And so you were drunk!"

He laughed, relieved if that were the only reason she had to call off the marriage. "No one could get drunk on the amount of whiskey in a *chota peg*!" He convinced her his feelings for her were true and she, in the end, changed her mind again. Having made up, they went to the ship's dining room for breakfast. Denis, not wanting to take any more chances of losing his firefly, proudly announced to everyone within earshot that he and Ethel were engaged.

Before the ship left port she packed up Isabel Marler's gown and sent it off with a letter saying that she would not be needing it. Next, she cabled home to share the news. If anyone had been disappointed in Ethel that she so readily abandoned her work, no record was

Ethel and Denis Mulvany just married, Lucknow, India, October 10, 1933. Mulvany Private Papers.

kept of those sentiments and she never spoke of it. Her act fulfilled expectations of the day regarding women's place and responsibilities in the work force. It was commonly assumed that the main job of a young middle-class woman like Ethel was to find a suitable husband whose duty it was to support her financially. This was especially true during the lean years of the Great Depression when women in the workforce were viewed as stealing jobs from deserving men. Certainly once married, a woman was to give up any thought of work outside the home. Ethel accepted these conventions, and when Denis told her that he had already cancelled her flight to Siam without consulting her, she was astonished but did not object.

Some weeks later, however, when they were in India a month or so before their October tenth wedding date, the couple hit a similar bump on the pre-marital road. Because Ethel had had experience with the Red Cross in Canada, she was asked by some new friends, nurses at the hospital in Lucknow, to help bathe and feed local infants during a particularly busy time. She thoroughly enjoyed being with the babies and was shocked when Denis ordered her to stop, stating flatly, "It is beneath you as the future wife of a doctor, to do this work."

Ethel was furious. "Well, let me tell you, I'm not going to put up with this. I'm not going to be under anybody's orders. I'm going to go straight to Bombay and take a ship home."

By now Denis knew just how determined Ethel could be and, on top of that, there was that telegram Ethel had received from James Wilder in Montreal. Although Denis may have laughed at Wilder's attempt to dissuade Ethel from marrying him, he may have been a little rattled by the wording.

LETTER RECD BEWARE OF MILITARY POMP AND POLISHED USELESS ARISTOCRACY USE HORSE SENSE HALT CONSIDER CAREFULLY AVOID FUTURE REGRETS STRONGLY ADVISE RETURN CANADA.[5]

Although Ethel had no romantic interest in the Montreal millionaire she might have let on that Wilder had proposed to her when she'd worked with the much older man in his real estate business. In the end Denis backed down, and he and Ethel went on to find a sense of balance in their marriage. They also found a place for that telegram in their album of "Honeymoon Snaps!" She continued to do the volunteer work she wanted and was confident enough in her own worth to disregard his efforts to remake her.

Palace Chocolate Cake

2¾ cups self-raising flour (sifted)

½ tspn salt

2 tspns cinnamon

4 squares unsweetened chocolate

Or ½ cup cocoa

1 cup butter

1 cup brown sugar

3 eggs

¼ cup cold water

1 tspn vanilla

Sift flour, salt, and cinnamon. Melt chocolate in sufficient boiling water to make stiff. Add rest of ingredients. Bake in 3 x 8 inch greased cake tins. Spread with white frosting. Decorate with knots of crystallized angelica.

White Frosting

3 egg whites (unbeaten)

2 cups of castor sugar

7 tbspns hot water

vanilla

Put altogether in upper part of double boiler. Beat with a rotary eggbeater. Then place over rapidly boiling water and beat constantly until it stands up in peaks. Remove from fire, but allow to remain over hot water for 2 minutes longer. Place over cold water and beat for 3 minutes longer.

Changi POW Cook Book

CHAPTER TWO
THE TIGER WOMAN

After they were married in October 1933 the Mulvanys moved into 50 A Havelock Rd in Cawnpore, India. Their life there was not like anything Ethel could have imagined back home. They had a staff of eighteen, "twenty-two if you count the four who took care of the *two* horses." She took photos to send to the family back home, colouring in the black and white pictures with descriptions on the back.

"One corner of our home. Blue curtains and rugs, upholstery blue and salmon, rust on deep sand. It is so pretty."

"Me in our dining room. What do you know about those eyes? Always dressed for dinner even if just Denis and I. Note the wee pepper and salt dishes which Aunt Esther gave me years ago. Everyone admires them."

"'Ram Kali' one of the elephants I loved in our compound."

"Me on my horse 'Ginger.'"

Ethel was not blind to the work that went into maintaining their high life. She explained on the back of one enlarged photo, "This is a *dhobi ghat*—a place where the *dhobis* (washer men) wash our clothes.

They don't use soap but pound whey out of everything on stones. This one is at work and his brother is starching in the great tub. Clothes are not long lived in India. They get 12 Rupees (about $4) for a family of two per month." Years later she told a reporter, "The British had it pretty well-to-do in India in those days … Colonialism! Don't ask me about that. They were just as bad as the Russians, that bunch."[1] Still, the inequality she saw at the time and remembered through her life didn't prevent her from enjoying her years in India.

Soon after her volunteering job at the hospital was over she was faced with another, much bigger, challenge and one that Denis fully supported. Ethel was pregnant. She was sure it was going to be a boy so she decided to name him Paul. She was thrilled.

"Each day was a wonderful light to wake up to. I shopped for tiny, baby things. I made tiny garments, with such precious little stitches. Each of these stitches was a sort of Morse code between Paul and me."

But the messages stopped on March 22, 1934, when Ethel miscarried. She decided not to call Denis home from the hospital but coped with the pain of heart and body on her own. Before he returned that evening she had wrapped the tiny fetus in silk and then in a waterproof raincoat and buried him in the dry, white earth under the healing powers of a neem tree. The servants did not intrude but were aware of what had happened, as they were of all heartbreaks and pleasures within the walls of the house. Ethel waited until after dinner to tell Denis, believing that emotional news should not be delivered until "the nervous system has been placated with food." Then she took him to the little mound in the garden which watchful hands had by then covered in marigold blossoms.

Denis tried to console her and himself with talk of future babies, but in the meantime, the only thing that helped was a different focus. If there was no child of her own to love, she would look to the needs of other children and families. Over the next year and a half, Ethel brought to fruition a grand scheme combining interests in business, art, and education. Working with the government of the United Provinces of Agra and Oudh, now Uttar Pradesh, she put together an exhibit worth

£10,000 of arts and crafts (the equivalent of over a million Canadian dollars today) made by the artisans of the region. It was to come to Canada in the summer of 1935 and be shown at Toronto's Canadian National Exhibition and Ottawa's Central Canadian Exhibition. Along with the crafts, exotic animals were sent as a gift to the children of Canada: tiger cubs, leopards, mongooses, and lions.

Toronto and Ottawa newspapers announced the show with fanfare: "Wild Beasts of India Due at C.N.E. This Year," "Directs Striking Exhibit from India: Mrs. Ethel Rogers Mulvany."[2] Far away from the action in Singapore, headlines explained the intent: "India Exhibits in Canada: Efforts to Foster Reciprocal Trade."[3] Ethel threw herself into the work to the point where she became popularly known as "The Tiger Woman."[4] The show went on to great success, making good money for the Indian artisans.

However, success came at a price for Ethel. The stress from all the travel and the responsibility for the animals and thousands of dollars worth of goods, took its toll. It was obvious just looking at her. Her once round cheeks had lost their fullness. Accounts were never her forte, but after the exhibit her nerves were stretched so tight she couldn't cope with all the bookkeeping, invoicing, and tidying up. Luckily her adoring and unemployed nineteen-year-old cousin, Keith Greenaway, was living in Toronto and able to pick up the pieces. Ethel escaped back to India, vibrating with fatigue and anxiety and looking like a skeleton. But along with the exhaustion she had a souvenir that would give her pride throughout her life. Sir Harry Haig, the governor of the United Provinces of Agra and Oudh, awarded Ethel a King George V Silver Jubilee Medal for representing the interests of the United Provinces in Canada.

Over the next four years, spent mainly in India, she did not take on a project of that size again, but her appreciation of arts and crafts continued. Her favourite was the *manchadi* seed, long revered for bringing good fortune. Following traditional ways, craftsmen hollow out these pea-sized reddish brown seeds and fill them with a paper-thin carved elephant initially of ivory and later of bone with a tiny cap fitted to the top. She first came across them in the hands of a farmer who was selling them to raise money to send his son to school. From the India exhibit onwards the tiny seeds seemed to follow her wherever she went, symbols of the luck she would soon need.

Bon Voyage Cake

2 cups self-raising flour

½ tspn salt

1 tspn mace

¾ cup milk

½ cup butter

1 cup sugar

2 eggs

1½ cups chopped cooked prunes

½ cup chopped walnuts

Beat butter, sugar, and egg yolks until light. Sift dry ingredients and add alternately with milk. Fold in stiffly beaten egg whites. Mix prunes and walnuts in separate dish. Pour half batter in cake tin. Then add layer of fruit and nut mixture then layer of batter. When cool ice with 1½ cups icing sugar, pinch salt, 2 tbspns butter, 1 tbspn prune juice, 1 tbspn lemon juice.

Changi POW Cook Book

CHAPTER THREE

BON VOYAGE PHOTOS

E thel loved everything about India except the summer heat. On a couple of occasions she and Denis escaped north to Srinagar, the summer capital of the fabled Vale of Kashmir. There was nothing like the glorious Himalayan mountains, the elegantly carved houseboat accommodations of the city, and the floating gardens of Dal Lake. Oddly, though, just about everything else there made Ethel think of Manitoulin. The stately chinar trees that turn red and gold in the fall were stand-ins for maples. The waters of the Sind Valley River had the same icy touch as any river at home, swollen with spring run-off. Closing her eyes, she could see the houseboats of Dal Lake fitting in perfectly at old Art Kitchen's camp on McGregor Bay. She loved where she was, yet yearned for her island home and its people. To appease her homesickness, she and Denis made the long journey to Manitoulin in July 1937. They stopped off en route in England to see Denis's family. How often are family photos framed by a door as someone is heading off on a trip? In a picture taken in front of Denis's brother's house, Rosecroft, in West Sussex, the fullness of Ethel's cheeks has returned and she is handsomely

Ethel, Denis, nephew David, sister-in-law Mira Mulvany, and Denis's mother, outside Rosecroft, Haywards Heath, Sussex, England, July 31, 1937. Pioneer Museum, Mindemoya, Manitoulin.

done up with a jaunty hat, polka-dot scarf, white suit and gloves and a smile wide enough to show the perfect teeth of which she was so proud. The next time Ethel was photographed on the same doorstep two years later, neither she nor the world would be so carefree.

In the spring of 1939 Isabella Mackenzie Rogers, Ethel's adoptive mother, was gravely ill and Ethel wanted to spend time with her remaining parent before it was too late, both for her mother and for travel. She might have rightly suspected that it could be a long while before she would see her family again. Talk of war in Europe was making everyone jittery. The last time the world had tumbled into war in August of 1914, Ethel had only been nine years old, but it is an impressionable age. She and her family had had some protection against the effects of that four-year conflagration. Her older brother, Harvey, then of fighting age, remained at home on the farm. Producing food was a national service, at least until April 1918 when Prime Minister Borden, desperate for recruits, broke his promise of exemption for farm workers. Even with Harvey safe at home, young

Ethel would have noticed the loss and heartbreak suffered by the families around her throughout the Great War. For many, the shadow of war in 1939 brought on a sickening feeling of sliding into the same morass the country had crawled out of in 1918. Here they were, soon to face the same enemy.

The plan was for Denis to accompany Ethel as far as England where they would spend some time before she headed off to Canada and he returned to India. They were both suffering health problems, coincidentally both losing blood, she through extremely heavy menstrual periods caused by uterine fibroids and he through a debilitating bout of hematemesis—vomiting of blood. His case was so severe he required multiple transfusions and all the while he was still recovering from a recent appendectomy.[1] Ethel's gynecologist decided that the best remedy for her was to induce artificial menopause with a dose of intra-uterine radium. Confident that all would be well, the doctor performed the treatment and sent Ethel on her way. Unfortunately by the time she arrived in Canada, she was anemic from continuing blood loss, light-headed from low blood pressure, and, thanks to the radium treatment, suffering from hot flashes and heightened anxiety. In addition to these physical symptoms, she, at age 34, was now faced with the depressing fact that she might never have a child.

In April, not long after her arrival, Ethel buried her mother. She stayed on in Canada to recoup her strength for as long as she could. By August, she could wait no longer. It was the so-called danger period, when London, Berlin, and Rome were on high alert. Her route across the Atlantic was becoming more dangerous by the day. Submarine sightings off the east coast had been in the Canadian news for months.[2] When she stepped aboard the SS *Ascania* in Montreal, Ethel's personal grief at losing her last parent was being coloured with the fear of war, moving it onto a far grander scale. During those long days at sea she had much time to worry about all the unknowns that lay beneath the sea and in her life ahead. She couldn't count on having Denis be in India when she arrived. His orders now were to head out to Singapore where he had been reposted. Their life together in India was quickly evaporating, only to be replaced by questions flying like harpies around her brain. Would she see Denis again? When? Where would she live? Were there Germans on board ship? Were there submarines with bombs, hidden under the waves?[3]

On September 2, 1939, when the SS *Ascania* dropped its gangplank on the Liverpool docks, Ethel, already tightly wrapped in her own anxiety, disembarked into a world of broiling tension. Placards accosted her from every street corner, blasting out the latest news— Germany had invaded Poland. If Britain stood by her ally, as leaders had promised, war would follow. The next morning, the inevitable was announced on the wireless at 11:15 am by Prime Minister Neville Chamberlain. "This country," he informed Britons in a pinched voice, "is at war with Germany." King George VI's evening broadcast at 6 pm acknowledged the horror: "For the second time in the lives of most of us, we are at war."[4]

That same day, at 7:40 pm, the passenger liner, the SS *Athenia* heading for Montreal, was torpedoed by a German U-boat, two hundred and fifty miles off the coast of Ireland. When news of the tragedy reached the British public, the reality of war truly hit home. Of the 1,418 people aboard, 117 were killed.[5] Ethel, having just crossed those waters, must have felt the closeness of death, especially since she knew the *Athenia*, having taken her first trip overseas on the ship in 1931. Images of the cabins, the lounge, the dining room were all in her memory, as was the sway of the ship when she had held her camera steady to take a nighttime photo of the water over the deck's railing. "'Twas moonlight on the water and not a streetcar was in sight," she had written on the back, a line from the song "Ain't We Crazy." Now, with the *Athenia* at the bottom of the Atlantic, the world really was upside-down "crazy."

Headlines and opinion pieces made it clear that this war was expected to be as horrifying as the last one, only this time people feared bombing and gas attacks on their doorstep. Everywhere Ethel turned, there were signs of war. Thirty-eight million gas masks had already been distributed to adults and children in Britain, and now their square, cardboard containers, the latest in unfashionable accessories, were banging around on everyone's arms.[6] The swarms of uniformed men on the streets and docks were an inescapable reminder that conscription had been in force since May. Hundreds of thousands of labelled children, with luggage but no parents in hand, were filling up train stations to be evacuated to the countryside away from the anticipated bombings of cities. Black-out regulations were in effect, a practical measure and yet oddly creating the look of a country already in mourning for its future casualties.

All the fear and disorder mixed with the unknown were too much for Ethel. Within days of her arrival she was admitted to a nursing home in Worthing on the south coast, not far from her brother and sister-in-law's house in West Sussex. She was, according to medical opinion, suffering from a case of "acute mania," exacerbated some said, by the poor treatment she received from the ship's doctor aboard the *Ascania*.[7] However, within a few weeks she was settled enough to be released into the care of Auntie Rose, her old chaperone, who happened to be in London for a visit. For a short time things were looking up, but then Ethel had an accident, slipping down a flight of stairs and dislocating her shoulder. The physical pain was miserable but worse was the anguishing realization that she couldn't carry on to Singapore to be with Denis until her shoulder was travel-worthy. Already in a delicate frame of mind, Ethel spun out into a high pitch of excitability. Lila Rose was about to head home and could no longer mother Ethel as she wanted, so Ethel was sent back into the Worthing nursing home, where her shoulder and her mood could be treated. She spent much longer in care this time and, if her father-in-law had had his wishes, she might not have come out of it for a good long while more.

John Mulvany, a military doctor like his son Denis, had no patience for the woman he now regarded as "dangerously and certi-fiably insane." This was the same deeply religious man who had been delighted to welcome Ethel into the family and to have her convert to his faith of Roman Catholicism. Now he was willing to do his professional and personal best to have Ethel restrained, anything to protect his son Denis and others from the "evil consequences" which might ensue should she be set free.[8] That Ethel had not preformed her family duty and born a child and that the mental illness she suffered from was a social embarrassment, possibly considered a stain on the Mulvany name, might have played into the position John chose to take. Withdrawing into the comfort of old prejudices, especially when it concerned a mentally ill, childless woman would not have been uncommon. Happily for Ethel, though, John's other son, Daniel, completely disagreed with his father. He believed Ethel needed loving care not incarceration.

With Denis all but unreachable in the distant east, John and Daniel took up arms over Ethel. The relationship between the two men, already marked, according to Daniel, by two decades of sporadic animosity, was about to explode just in time for Christmas. In the lead-up the men exchanged erudite, Latin-studded, and increasingly venomous epistles and, thanks to the rapid service of His Majesty's mail, there was little time for calm reflection before another tirade was delivered. Meanwhile, the object of their disagreement was, according to Daniel, being held in an asylum "with bars on the windows, guards on the fires, high boundary walls, grounds full of palpable lunatics, constant supervision, censoring of correspondence," where, countered John, she was perfectly happy.[9] However, when Daniel offered Ethel the chance to recuperate at his house, Rosecroft, she jumped at the opportunity. A clear indication, insisted John, not of her unhappiness in the asylum, but of her insanity.

On December 8, Ethel was released into Daniel and his wife Mira's care. She stayed with them and their two boys over Christmas and on into the New Year. It appears that the sympathy and attention that Daniel assumed Ethel needed and that he and Mira did their best to provide did give her the strength she needed to set forth on what would be a harrowing journey. On February 23, 1940, when Ethel was finally travel-ready, she was once again photographed

Ethel and nephews Jon and David Mulvany, outside Rosecroft, Haywards Heath, Sussex, England, February 23, 1940. Pioneer Museum, Mindemoya, Manitoulin.

on the doorstep of Rosecroft before leaving, destined, she hoped, for Singapore. She stands with her arms draped over the shoulders of her two squirming young nephews. Dressed in a wrinkled tweedy plaid skirt and a mismatched blouse and cardigan, Ethel looks the very image of wartime dowdiness. Although smiling, she looks tired and her tucked-in chin adds a wariness to her gaze. Not only was her mental health barely on the mend, in all other ways she was in a state of limbo. The house she and Denis had rented in India was no longer theirs and a new home in Singapore had not yet been found. In her travels ahead she would weave through lands and waters on the edge of war. As a civilian, she had to cede travel priority to servicemen and women at any point in her journey. Even under the best of conditions the trip she faced would be challenging.

Her plan was to cross the English Channel and get a southbound train heading to the Italian coast. She would then sail across the Mediterranean and through the Suez Canal. Unable to book her passage through to Singapore, she aimed first for Bombay. From there she would find a way to cross the nearly two thousand kilometres overland to Calcutta and then sail to Singapore. Just two months before the invasion of France, Ethel completed the first step of the journey to Paris where she caught a train to Trieste—"Amidst bombs," she later exclaimed to an enthusiastic reporter.[10] Was this an embellishment? Maybe Ethel's imagination was egged on by the reporter's eagerness.

"The last four [train] cars were wrecked," claimed Ethel. "They tumbled down the mountains with all passengers lost."

Who knows what bangs, bumps, and explosions may have occurred, but in these early months of the war, in what came to be known as "the phoney war," Germans were not bombing southern France. However, no one knew how long the quiet of these months would last. Anticipating the destruction of war may not be as horrifying as being under actual attack, but waiting plays powerfully on the nerves. Whatever it was that felt to Ethel like a bomb on her trip through France and Italy did not prevent her from arriving in Trieste. To her great relief she made her connections and in early March stepped aboard the SS *Conte Verde*.

Ethel took no photos of the ocean liner, but for her and many others, it was not a ship to be forgotten. Since 1932 the elegant steam ship had travelled the twenty-four-day route from Trieste to Shanghai via the Suez Canal with stops in Bombay, Colombo, and Singapore. Built in 1923 at a time when shipping companies competed to produce the most luxurious floating palaces possible, the *Conte Verde* and its fellow ships were luxuriously decorated with the sleek bold curves and angles of Art Deco fixtures and furnishings. But since 1938 few of the *Conte Verde*'s passengers had been interested in such finery. A new class of traveller filled the cabins on board—refugees. Thousands of German and Austrian Jews left Italy aboard this ship bound for Shanghai. The Jewish ghetto of approximately 17,000 in the Chinese city was overcrowded, poverty stricken, and plagued with disease, but safer than what Europe had to offer.[11]

Ethel never mentioned the other passengers. Maybe their stories were too agonizing for her to listen to when she was doing her best to stay calm, or maybe her ability to talk non-stop was too exhausting for people who needed time to take stock of the terror they had left and the uncertainty they faced. With no friends or job to occupy her mind and an unknown future ahead, only one interest held her focus throughout the voyage: food. Menus on ocean liners were famously grand for all aboard and with Italy not yet in the war there were platefuls of delights still to be had. Ethel adored the Italian cuisine, taking particular pleasure in all the cream and butter that had been rationed in England since January. Overeating, a time-honoured shipboard indulgence, was a compelling way to fill the days and to keep dark thoughts at bay. Ethel consumed her meals with such fervour that she gained nineteen pounds in as many days on board.

When the *Conte Verde* docked in Bombay, Ethel was prepared to disembark and take on the daunting task of cobbling together land and sea transportation for the rest of her journey. However, just as she was on her way off the ship one of the stewards caught up to her with the news that her passage to Singapore had been secured. No explanation was given. It was only later that Ethel heard from Denis that her luck had been due to a thankful patient, Brigadier Alec Wildey. The fifty-year-old, who would go on to command the Artillery Brigade during the battle for Singapore, was so grateful for the emergency appendectomy performed on him by Denis, he saw to it personally that Ethel would have her ticket extended to Singapore.

After leaving Singapore the *Conte Verde* sailed on to Shanghai, delivering its refugee passengers to relative safety. Three months later, on June 10, 1942, Italy entered the war, and that escape route closed.

Vanities

1½ cups self-raising flour

½ tspn salt

½ cup butter

½ cup nut meats (coarsely broken)

½ cup milk

¾ cup chopped raisins

¾ cup sugar

2 eggs

3 squares unsweetened chocolate

½ tspn vanilla

Cream butter and sugar. Add eggs. Beat. Add chocolate (melted), nuts, and raisins. Beat. Add sifted flour alternately with milk. Add vanilla. Beat until smooth. Drop from teaspoon on greased pan. Bake in moderate oven for 15 minutes.

Changi POW Cook Book

CHAPTER FOUR

STEPPING OUT IN SINGAPORE

March 23, 1940. When the ship docked in Singapore, Ethel was leaning over the railing eagerly looking for Denis in the crowd on shore. She could tell as he peered up through his round wire-rimmed glasses that he didn't recognize her in her plumped-up state. Her blue dress with the flared skirt was the only thing she had that was big enough to accommodate her added girth. Denis, on the other hand, was naturally slight and, if anything, had likely shrunk a little in the intervening months. He had been working at the hospital and living alone in a hotel in Singapore, waiting anxiously for his wife.

Once Ethel stepped on land she left her concerns behind. After over half a year apart she was finally reunited with Denis, in Singapore of all places, where she had accepted his marriage proposal seven years before. Love was essential to Ethel, but so too was having a purpose in life to direct her energies. Now she had that, too: within a day she set out to search the neighbourhoods of the overcrowded city to find a home for Denis and herself. She began by knocking on doors west of Chinatown in the city's centre looking in the vicinity of Denis's workplace, the Alexandra Hospital. Two years later the hospital would be the site of a horrendous massacre, but in 1940 it was a gleaming new building in an attractive neighbourhood. But this and the military pouring into the city meant procuring accommodation there, or anywhere at all, was difficult.[1] Ethel ended up searching in an area of imposing two-storey houses overlooking the water on a street aptly named Pasir Panjang, Malay for "long sand." The tale of what happened on the morning she stood under the portico of number 112 and knocked on the door is where she began recounting her history to Sidney Katz in the spring of 1961. Her words on the first of the old recordings are garbled in the beginning but eventually transform and, like bubbles, rise to the surface and pop open.

> ... tried my best French, which was terrible, so I tried my Malay, which was even worse. Two or three words of Malay and two or three of French and in the muddle I said, 'Mon Mari Medicine Militaire.' This was to be my recommendation and then I wanted to tell her that we just wanted to take a few rooms and that I'd be willing to fit into the family picture in any way. She was French married to a Dutchman. Mrs.... *Madame* Roos-Boule.

After Madame and Ethel exchanged a few shared words and a lot of sign language, Madame gave Ethel a tour of the house. As they walked, Ethel chatted away in her unique lingo, pointing out the rooms she wanted to rent. Assuming that Madame understood and was amenable to the plan, Ethel took her leave and marched over to the Alexandra Hospital to tell Denis the good news. She was quite rightly chuffed, given the extraordinarily tight market. "I got a house! What do you think of that?"

It was lunch hour by then and generally the noon meal was followed by a quiet time during which the inhabitants of the city tucked themselves into cool spots for an hour or so to wait out the day's heat. But Ethel, never adept at putting her feet up in the first place, was not about to rest until the deal was done. She and Denis returned to the house where they were met by two large madly barking dogs

Mulvany house in Singapore, 1940. Pioneer Museum, Mindemoya, Manitoulin.

who roared out past the frangipani tree and around the canna lilies. Having been raised on a farm, Ethel knew better than to be scared off by this tumble of dogs. A much bigger shock was to greet her when the door opened. There was Madame Roos-Boule teary-eyed and garbed in a dusty housedress surrounded by half-filled packing boxes.

"I'm getting out," she exclaimed. "The house is yours."

Denis was confused; this was not how Ethel had explained things to him. He queried Madame in French, "Well I thought we were going to live with you here, you were going to have your cook here and we were going to cook upstairs."

At these words, tears of relief gushed out of Madame, and in no time the tears were replaced by gales of laughter. Ethel soon realized what a terrible misunderstanding had occurred. The problem as she saw it was that she had used the word *"rumah"* when asking to rent a few rooms, not realizing that *"rumah"* means "house" in Malay. Although likely a common enough mistake, Madame had been expecting she would soon have to move. The British military had already taken her sea-house at the end of the pier, they'd put barbed wire around her beautiful home, and now she thought they were coming to take it over completely.

Denis apologized to Madame by way of explaining that the confusion was due to Ethel's behaviour.

"She's Canadian. Sometimes she does things first and thinks about them after."

Ethel was not in the least surprised by his comment. His belief that colonials suffered terribly from unbridled behaviour was common enough among the English at the time. Having been married for seven years they each knew what to expect from the other. Their differences had been clear from the moment they'd met. As far as Ethel was concerned, the housing mix-up she fell into with Madame Roos-Boule was based both on linguistic confusion and the British military's habit of sailing in and taking over any property they needed without so much as a "by-your-leave or an offer of compensation."

In the end, with Madame's blessing, they moved into the upstairs of the four-bedroom house. Despite the pall of war hanging over Singapore, Ethel and Denis were eager to start life there. They moved all the trappings of their colonial life into 112 Pasir Panjang: the chintz-covered furniture, Persian rugs, silver tea set, and lamps from Kashmir that had filled their house in Cawnpore. Ethel's seal, muskrat, and ermine fur coats, which would at best provide a happy breeding ground for tropical mould, filled up cupboard space beside her evening gowns. Her dressing table was home to jewellery studded with pearls, amethysts, diamonds, and rubies. They had one servant, Bharose, who had come with Denis from India. When Kuki, Madame's Chinese cook, wasn't relaxing with her opium pipe she provided meals for all of them three evenings a week. On the remaining days Ethel and Denis managed with the help of their very own refrigerator.

Thinking back to the summer of 1939 when she had last been back to Manitoulin, where the electrical supply was spotty at best and fridges a luxury, Ethel had been so impressed with Singapore. "You could flick on your electric stove, turn the tap and know that you would get clear water and in some parts use the flush in the bathrooms." She knew that night soil buckets were more common and was quite prepared to use them if she had to. Within a few years, however, she would see those very same buckets being carted into Changi Jail, filled with the prisoners' dinner.

The social life for many Europeans in Malaya and Singapore before the war was infamously good. After the fall of Singapore, and when she was safely back in England, Lady Brooke-Popham, whose husband had been relieved of his position as commander-in-chief of the British Far East Command, confidently summed up her explanation for the capitulation of the city. She proclaimed that the "white population" of Singapore suffered from a "deadly inertia." The expatriates "continued their parties and dancing to the end. The long years in Singapore's climate, the luxurious living and the fact that they had everything done for them by natives was perhaps largely responsible."[2] Lord Brooke-Popham refrained from commenting.

Compared with England, salaries were high and clubs for cricket, golf, and sailing made for pleasant distractions. The military was endured, barely, and business ruled. This was not surprising, for trade had been essential to the people of this land from even before the settlement was first named *Singa pura*—lion city—in the fourteenth century. The tradition was carried on by British statesman, Sir Thomas Stamford Raffles, who arrived in 1819 and claimed the town for the British Empire to protect and channel its commerce with India, Burma, and Malaya. He put his plan quite bluntly in a letter to a friend. "Our object is not territory but trade, a great commercial emporium, and a fulcrum, whence we may extend our influence politically."[3] With its policy of free trade, the port was an immediate success with traders and immigrants from surrounding lands, swelling the city's population from a few hundred in 1819 to 97,100 by 1871 and 755,000 when Ethel arrived in 1940.[4]

War in Europe meant that the port was busier than ever shipping raw materials. Rubber from three million acres of Malaya plantations and tin from mines that produced half of the world's supply were constantly flowing in and out of the city. But the balance of power between the money-makers and the military began to shift as the faraway European war inched closer. Not only was there barbed wire around Ethel and Denis's new home, but it stretched for twenty miles along the coast. From their neighbourhood right around to the village of Changi in the north-east, concrete pillboxes stood at six-hundred-yard intervals, beach lights invaded the night sky, and 18-pounder guns sat ready to get their point across. All this security made Mme. Roos-Boule nervous and finally she decided to join her son in Sumatra. This left Ethel and Denis with the whole house, two barking dogs, and three staff. They could do all the large entertaining they wanted, but that was not their style. Contrary to the trappings of their life they were not big socializers. Ethel, the more voluble of the two, enjoyed company and loved her beautiful gowns and sparkling jewels, but she didn't fit with the cocktail set. On club evenings, when their attendance was expected, she would mill through the sophisticated crowd with her champagne glass filled with Orangeade, hoping she could at least look the part.

For both Ethel and Denis, the best part of Singapore lay off shore. Almost as soon as they moved into number 112 they began dreaming about the islands they could see from their upper balcony. Denis loved boats, so one of their first decisions was to have a cruiser made. For Ethel, the dream was to reproduce the pleasures of her Manitoulin home in Georgian Bay, by finding her own island in the Singapore Straits. She was soon to discover that those little islands scattered off the coast of Singapore had all been claimed, just like all the other pink bits on the globe, by the British Empire. Asking for the rights to one of the islands was deemed to be as audacious an act as asking for a hunk of the crown itself. Yet Ethel was unflagging in her efforts to get her crown jewel. After a string of bureaucratic noes in response to her pleas she decided to go right to the top. Finally after writing directly to King George VI to request one of his "tiny, wee islands" the Crown Lands Office sent her the reply she wanted. For just one dollar she could have habitation rights for ninety-nine years on an island, **provided**—and **provided** was in very black letters, "that no Malay was interested in said Island."

Meanwhile, Denis, when not at the hospital, had practically moved into the dock yards. From there he watched closely as the boat builder they had hired brought their craft to life. He and Ethel had assumed the man was Chinese but weren't sure since he didn't speak. Working with him was tricky, but with the help of detailed plans and many hand gestures, a boat was created that, Ethel claimed, was finer than the *Queen Mary*. They named it the *Honora*, after Ethel's Manitoulin birthplace. She was desperately proud of their thirty-eight-foot cruiser, with its sleek lines and purring Rolls Royce engine.

When the boat was seaworthy, Ethel and Denis began their search for an island that no Malay would want, and they quickly found it. The tiny, perfect, but suspiciously named, Pulau Hantu, Ghost Island, was situated just off the coast. Vague stories of cruelty and murder committed there told of spirits rising from their graves to roam the island.[5] This was enough to ensure that while Malays from the area would gather fruit from Pulau Hantu, they would never stay long. Ethel didn't scoff at the idea of the devil and his work and acknowledged that he had previously given her "a bit of trouble." She was confident however, that as in the past, she could get rid of him if she set her mind to it. Just to make sure that the devil knew the island was no longer his domain, the couple renamed it Pulau Shorga—Heavenly Island. It was about two hundred yards in diameter and almost perfectly round. Coconut and mango trees served up fruits for anyone willing to skirt the ghosts and reach up to pick them. The Mulvanys had a one-hundred-and-fifty-foot pier built so the boat could dock no matter the tide. When the sea was ebbing, Denis spent contented hours chipping away at the barnacles on the bottom of his prized possession. Ethel, while delighted and amused at his min-istrations to the boat, pursued her own quiet pleasure at the end of

Ethel on the verandah of the Mulvany cottage on Pulau Shorga, Singapore, 1941. Pioneer Museum, Mindemoya, Manitoulin.

the pier feeding the multitudes of fish in the water below. The red ones, *ikan mera*, glowed like swimming sunsets below the surface, while the green fish, *ikan hijau*, had a magnificent peacock beauty and, Ethel thought, an impressive intelligence. For companionship, though, Minnie the stingray was the most attentive, especially at feeding time.

Far out beyond the pier were the sharks. Ethel only got close to them once, a bit too close, when she fell overboard while sailing. Along with the *Honora*, she and Denis each had their own little sailboats, hers the *Api Shorga*, Fire of Heaven, had white sails and hull while his, the *Api Neraka*, Fire of Hell, had a red hull and sails. They hired crews from surrounding islands and raced on Sunday mornings. The stakes were more treasured than money: pounds of rice and yards of intricately designed batik fabrics went to the winners.

They chose a spot nestled under the palm trees to build a tiny cottage on stilts, calling it Rumah Manis, Sweet House. Ethel learned the technique for making the *attap* roof and walls from the Malays who crewed her boat. They collected coconut palm fronds, soaked them, stripped them, and folded the pieces over in a weaving pattern. It was a skill she would later put to good use in Changi. The only building materials for the cottage that they needed from Singapore were planks for the flooring. These Ethel ferried over on the *Honora*. She bought locally woven cloths as colourful as the fish off the pier to drape over the bamboo furniture and folding cots that were pressed into use when friends came to stay.

Once the cabin was finished in 1941, the first visitors Ethel and Denis entertained were their sailing crews, some of whom had helped build the place. After serving them dinner on the beach they pulled out Denis's portable wind-up record player and danced on the sun-warmed sand. At first the two crews from different islands sat apart from one another, but when the feasting began so did the conversations. Ethel took it as proof of what Stephen Leacock had taught her in economics class at McGill: "The League of Nations would've never have come down if only they could've got them eating together and listening to good music!"[6]

Although Ethel never mentions the amount of labour that went into the upkeep of their simple cottage, a photo from her collection gives some indication. Ethel stands on the island's sandy beach behind four adults and two children. On the back she wrote, "Our staff on Pulau Shorga." As in India, although she may have been aware of how much her lifestyle depended upon the toil of others, it did not prevent her from savouring her time on the island. For her, this corner of the world, full of play and outdoor living, furnished with tables and chairs made from what grew just beyond the front step, was a tropical version of Manitoulin.

It was a place where people fell asleep surrounded by reflected moonlight and the languid "clunk-clump-clump" of water knocking against the posts under the verandah. The Mulvanys spent as many as three-quarters of what would turn out to be their remaining days of freedom, on the island. There, just a twenty-minute boat ride from Singapore city, they were secluded from many but not all signs

Ethel and staff on Pulau Shorga, Singapore, 1941. Pioneer Museum, Mindemoya, Manitoulin.

of the encroaching war. Just half a mile across the water from them was an island which had for centuries carried the sinister name of Blakang Mati, Behind the Dead. Local stories, embellished over time, told of victims who had succumbed either to the greed of pirates or mysterious fevers.[7] Ethel thought it was "an awful sight," not because of its legendary past, but because modern day instruments of death, the guns of the Royal Artillery, were emplaced there. The island was so close there was no avoiding the reality of it when she sat on her veranda. She hated all that it stood for but was uncomfortably aware that without Blakang Mati and the military's communications systems, she and Denis could not have spent nearly as many days on their island. Denis was on call at the hospital much of the time and the closest telephone to Pulau Shorga was on Blakang Mati. He arranged for the hospital to phone there when he was needed in surgery. When the calls came through a soldier would beat a great Malay gong seven times, summoning Denis from across the water. The gong was an old one, leftover from the days when it was needed to keep the lingering demons at bay. Now, the gently curved island off the south coast of Singapore had three British forts each armed with guns pointing over the ocean to fend off the modern demons that the British authorities were certain would attack by ship, a miscalculation that helped change the course of the war, and explode Ethel and Denis's life together.

Inner Secrets

3½ cups self-raising flour

½ tspn salt

½ cup butter

½ cup brown sugar

1 egg

1 tspn vanilla

1/3 cup milk

3 cups dates

½ cup sugar

1 tbspn lemon juice

1 tbspn butter

½ cup hot water

Make dough of flour, salt, butter, sugar, egg, vanilla, and milk. Roll 1/8 inch thick. Cut in 2½ inch circle. Press edges together with floured fork. Filling—Cook dates, sugar, and water for 8 minutes. Remove, add lemon juice and butter. Cool.

Changi POW Cook Book

CHAPTER FIVE

GUNS, BICYCLES, AND SPIES

When France fell to the Germans in June of 1940, the crash reverberated all the way round to the distant cities and jungles of its Southeast Asian colonies, cracking them open to the next wave of invaders. By summer of the next year, the Japanese had moved in and set up camp in Vietnam and Cambodia, the southern part of French Indochina. From there they gazed with a calculating desire across the Gulf of Siam at northern Malaya.[1]

Ethel was frustrated not to have the ear of the higher-ups in the military command, but she was not shy to voice her opinion, to anyone she could corner, about the precarious nature of Singapore's defences, particularly about the south-facing armaments. "The guns don't swing more than forty-five degrees. What are you going to do when you want to swing them to the north?"[2] She wasn't the only one to wonder about this state of affairs. But she knew, "If you brought this up as an unhealthy situation to a British Army Officer, invariably the answer would be, 'those bloody little Nips[3] wouldn't dare attack us—the strongest bastion in the British Empire.'" Ethel was painfully accurate in her description of British racism and underestimation of the Japanese army, but the well-worn theory that Singapore fell largely because all the guns defending the city were permanently pointed in the wrong direction, southward over the sea, has since been modified.

The diamond-shaped island of Singapore lies just over a kilometre off the southern tip of Malaysia (formerly Malaya), threaded to the mainland by a causeway. Except for the city on the south shore, the island was covered in mangrove forests and farms. At its widest it measures forty-three kilometres from east to west and twenty-one kilometres north to south. It was studded with guns, more, said one Australian correspondent, "than a Christmas pudding has plums."[4] The guns were placed on the coastline to the south and east, and on islands to the south, including an 18-pounder that would be added to Ethel and Denis's Pulau Shorga after they left for the last time on December 7, 1941.[5] Of the seaward-facing guns, some were able to swing around and fire over land, but much of the ammunition they had was armour piercing, designed first to drill through a ship's hull and then to explode inside, causing as much destruction as possible. When fired over land, however, the tip of the shell burrowed down through the earth, giving soldiers nearby time to run before the secondary explosion went off deep underground. What the defenders were short of was high explosive ammunition which was intended to destroy what is euphemistically called "soft targets," meaning young men in uniforms. Such shells were designed to wound the soldiers terribly, so the enemy would be forced to use valuable resources to support them with medical aid. As well, if Singapore had truly been a fortress, by definition it would have had strong battlements all around the island. Unfortunately for the British, the back door, facing the Malay peninsula, was open. Arthur Percival, general officer commanding Malaya, had been warned about this and will forever be remembered as refusing to build more fortifications during the war because "building defensive works would harm morale."[6]

Colonel Tsuji Masanobu, one of the Japanese commanders who was planning the invasion of Singapore, knew even his German allies did not think it possible for an army to manoeuvre southward from a landing in Siam and make it through the intense heat of the Malayan jungles to attack Singapore. At least not in anything less than a year. The Japanese were carefully preparing to prove them wrong. The plan was to speed down the peninsula with the aid of a mode of transportation never before used to such success in warfare. It was to be a "blitzkrieg on bicycles." Tsuji later described how it worked. The two infantry divisions were each equipped with "roughly five hundred motor vehicles and six thousand bicycles." As expected, the retreating British blew up all their bridges but the Japanese infantry continued their pursuit by "wading across the rivers carrying their bicycles on their shoulders, or crossing on log bridges held up on the shoulders of engineers standing in the stream."[7] The repair squads attached to every company were constantly dealing with bicycle tires that were blowing out from the heat of the asphalt roads. Finally it was decided to just remove the tires and ride on the rims. In a description that would have made the British military wince, Tsuji wrote,

> Numbers of bicycles, some with tyres and some without, when passing along the road, made a noise resembling that of tanks. At night when such bicycle units advanced the enemy frequently retreated hurriedly, saying, "Here come the tanks!"... Even the long-legged Englishmen could not escape our troops on bicycles ... Thanks to Britain's dear money spent on the excellent paved roads, and to the cheap Japanese bicycles, the assault on Malaya was easy.[8]

Well, it wasn't that easy and bicycles weren't the only technological means the Japanese had to pummel the British forces. Tanks, ships, and planes staffed by trained and dedicated soldiers played their part, as did the highly refined Japanese intelligence service. "Espionage in Japan," said the author Chin Kee Onn, who was teaching in Singapore when the Japanese invaded, "had always been an elaborate science, perfected into a national art." He claimed, "It was well-known that every Japanese photographer, fisherman, planter, farmer, taxidermist, trader, barber and dentist abroad, was a potential fifth columnist."[9] General shops throughout Malaya selling cigarettes, candy, and groceries were often run by Japanese. The shop owners were mindful that these were just the sort of items the British soldiers would be interested in buying. Photography shops were known for offering good rates to develop the films of soldiers who had been on leave. How useful to be able to see through the eyes of the British soldiers!

After the British surrendered, many Europeans in Singapore discovered that one of the well-known photographers in town was a colonel in the Japanese military police, the Kempetai. A Japanese tank commander killed in the battle was found to have been a bicycle repairer before the war.[10] The skilful boat builder who had made Ethel and Denis's boat the *Honora* turned out, claimed Ethel, to be neither Chinese nor mute, but quite capable of speaking Chinese, Japanese, English, and Malay. He was, she declared, none other than General Arimura Tsunemichi, who would become head of POW camps in Changi, December 1, 1942. Before receiving that appointment, Arimura had retired, and from late 1940 until August 1941, when he was recalled into service, he was technically a private citizen. If he was in Singapore during this time, as Ethel said, he must have become quite familiar with the workings of the military harbour at the dockyard. When reminiscing in her old age, Ethel approached his deception with a certain equanimity. She believed that in the scheme of things a certain balance had been struck. The last she had heard, the *Honora* had carried seventeen Allied soldiers to safety.

The imminence of war surrounded Ethel when they were at their house on Pasir Panjang—beaches wrapped in barbed wire and uniformed men everywhere you looked. Yet these obvious signs of what was to come were not what hit home. Instead, it was a conversation she overheard between Denis and Bharose, their Indian servant, which shook her. War was never mentioned in this conversation between the two men, but its presence hovered beneath their words.

In a tone half-ordering, half-requesting, Denis said, "I wish you'd go home for a holiday to India."

Bharose, who had worked for Denis for years and who would never say "no" directly, replied that he would return to India when the Sahib went home. Denis tried to make light of the situation. He handed him a ticket, insisting that it was just for a holiday. The fact that it was a military ticket made Bharose doubly suspicious. He was fully aware that he was being offered an honourable release from service so as to escape the oncoming conflagration, but he stayed.

With war poised on the horizon, Ethel knew she had to get involved. She threw herself into fundraising for the Malayan Churchill Tank Fund. Throughout the autumn of 1941, with the war raging elsewhere, money was raised to build new tanks desperately needed by the British. Black-out dances, mah-jong drives, garden parties, and even a Battle of Britain ball at the famous Raffles hotel all contributed to the fund. In her search for financing, Ethel went beyond European expatriates and approached members of the Chinese community, many of whom were very supportive. Later, during her time as a prisoner, the friendships she made among Chinese donors would help keep her alive.

Ethel was not content to just be involved in fundraising. She wanted to be a part of the city's safety preparations, starting with the Red Cross, an organization she had served with since she was a girl on Manitoulin. But there was no British Red Cross and although the St John Ambulance had a presence in Singapore, she did not believe it had the same international standing. To remedy the situation she made an appointment with Singapore's governor, British High Commissioner to Malaya, Sir Shenton Thomas. The fact that Ethel, a civilian woman and a colonial no less, was able to secure an interview with a very busy governor in a dangerous time may have been due to a combination of astute string-pulling and the compelling aura of her confident manner. Likely never having met the woman before, Shenton Thomas would not have had any opinions about her. She, on the other hand, had her doubts about him and his mental capacities.

Nevertheless, she had a mission and had no qualms about starting at the top.

From Ethel's point of view the meeting began poorly and went downhill from there. Like so many others in authority at the time, Shenton Thomas insisted that there would be no war. As for aid services, he was sure St John's Ambulance would do just fine. Ethel was furious with this attitude and insisted that he get in touch with the International Red Cross in Geneva and set up a British Red Cross in the British colony. Thomas returned Ethel's fury, declaring it wasn't her place to decide these matters and, with that, the petitioner was excused. Ethel felt her doubts had been fully confirmed. Shenton Thomas "may have been descended from a mighty race in Wales, but he wasn't worthy of the name."

Ethel was not the only person to be frustrated with the governor who, for years after, was blamed for incompetent leadership during the battle for Singapore. Half a century later however, when secret British government documents were released, it was made public that the governor knew full well how vulnerable Singapore was and had made a request for increased air defence from the Colonial Office which was ignored.[11]

Ethel had time to cool her heels and consider her options. The Australians had brought their Red Cross with them to Singapore. Since she didn't know a thing about the country she concluded she had better join the Australian Red Cross and seize the chance to learn something about a place she'd never seen. To that end she headed to the office of the assistant commissioner of the Australian Red Cross, Basil Burdett. A rather shy, long-faced First World War veteran, Burdett had worked as a journalist and art critic during the interwar years. He joined the Australian Red Cross field force in Melbourne in January 1941 and was sent straightaway to Singapore where, in September, he was assigned the role of assistant commissioner. Ethel presented herself to him: "Here I am!" Her style may have been off-putting, but Burdett would soon have need of her skills and services.

She was appointed at the rank of superintendent and attached to the No. 1 Malayan General Hospital (MGH).

As a superintendent Ethel might have overseen a multitude of necessary but detailed jobs undertaken by the Red Cross, but that was not for her. She sought out intensity, wanting to be where the need was most dire. Ethel knew she could drive the rugged roads of Manitoulin and had no doubt she could do the same in Singapore. She also knew a thing or two about engines and, being strong and tall, was quite capable of lifting up her end of a stretcher. It was obvious to her that she belonged behind the steering wheel of an ambulance.

In the midst of all their many obligations it was hard for Ethel and Denis to find time to slip away to their south sea island of calm, but Sunday, December 7, 1941, had been one of those perfect, gentle days. They took the *Honora* back to the city that evening at sunset, leisurely slipping through the silken-flat ocean flashing with orange. The tranquility of the trip was only broken when Denis ominously said, "This is too beautiful." On the edge of war it is impossible to know what is coming, but apprehension invested that particular sunset with a potent aura.

Hours later the Japanese began their attacks.

* * *

"Wake up Ethel," Denis shouted from the upstairs veranda, "the Japs are blitzing us." She tumbled out of bed, pulled on her Viyella housecoat and joined him outside. Ethel figured that everyone with a head on knew war was coming, but as she stood peering at the sky she couldn't take it in. With her hands plunged into her pockets her fingers came across a stray manchadi seed. She turned it over and over, pressing the sharp plug into her thumb, trying to prove to herself that she was awake. The pea-sized symbol of good luck from India was a leftover from what was now a past life. With the dogs in tow, she and Denis went downstairs to the garden for a wider view of the sky. There they were joined by the rest of the household—Bharose, the bearer who had refused to leave Singapore; Kuki, the Chinese cook; and Kebun, the Malay gardener. At 4:15 a.m. sunrise was still two hours away but the sky was shimmering with moonlight, street lights, which had never been turned off, and anti-aircraft fire. Ethel could see the defensive flak was falling well short of the bombers who appeared to be "just sailing along as though it was an afternoon in June and they were out for their health." From beyond Raffles Square eight kilometres away she heard the crunching sound of the bombs being dropped and saw what looked like fireworks in the form of flowers. Some were garlands of sparkles, others cascaded like Niagara Falls in bloom. Red lights were interspersed with blue flashes in the shape of forget-me-nots. Not that anyone was in danger of forgetting that night. It all made perfect sense to her in that moment. "Of all the things in the world the Malay love, it is flowers—children and flowers." That, she assumed, was why they used fireworks, "To be remembered. And wasn't that smart? You aren't being remembered in fear, you will be remembered for being the dropper of flowers."

Ethel's poignant memory of fiery blossoms that night is unique yet fully in keeping with the Japanese desire to politically win over the hearts of all Malays and other Asian Singaporeans. From where she stood, Chinatown, one of the hardest hit areas, lay between her and downtown. Inside the myriad of shops lining the narrow streets of the Chinese neighbourhood, pyrotechnics were being collected in preparation for the upcoming New Year's festival on February 15. As she looked towards the heart of the city, the flowers she witnessed in the sky may have been explosions of Chinese fireworks sparked by falling bombs.

Messages tumbled from the sky as well. They came in English, Chinese, Malay, and Tamil, warning that this war was being waged only against the Europeans. Cartoons of fat European planters sank down through the air, white men lounging with cool beers in hand while Tamils laboured all around them in the burning sun. Malays were advised to "Burn all the white devils in the sacred flame of victory."[12] Asia was to be for the Asiatics in what would be a grand new "Greater East Asian Co-prosperity Sphere."[13]

Ethel had no idea how well coordinated the Japanese were, initiating bombing strikes on Hong Kong the same day as Singapore and just hours after the attack on Pearl Harbour. But even from her vantage point on the ground, she was impressed with her enemy's level of organization. Not only were leaflets being dropped from the air, but they were also hand delivered. Although Major Mulvany didn't get one, to his great discomfort, Kebun, their Malay gardener, did. Kebun had no desire to get caught in the middle between the Japanese and his employers. He advised Ethel and Denis he was leaving right away.

By Ethel's reckoning, the Japanese sent about twenty planes that first night. She was surprisingly accurate in her details even though her view was limited. Although sixty-five Japanese naval aircraft had been scheduled to attack Singapore early December 8, only seventeen G3M bombers, nicknamed Nells by the Allies, made it to their destination that night due to poor weather conditions. Along with Raffles Square, two airfields had been bombed. In total 63 people were killed and 133 injured.[14] The next raid came on the night of sixteenth to seventeenth of December, followed by another on the twenty-ninth to thirtieth in which Ethel and Denis's house was destroyed.

For a time on that night of the first bombardment, everyone on the lawn at 112 Pasir Panjang was mesmerized by the sights and sounds of war. Then suddenly the picture show shattered into reality. It might have been the smell of flaming destruction carried on the morning breeze or the resonating boom of a particularly close attack. Whatever it was at that juncture, they all stopped gazing at the sky and charged into action. Ethel and Denis rushed upstairs to dress. There wasn't an extra moment to even glance at the bed and wish they could crawl back in time between the sheets. That phase of life was over for good. Denis flung on his uniform, Ethel pulled on her clothes, yanked her Red Cross arm band over her shirt sleeve. Bharose already had a quick breakfast prepared for them by the time they came down. After their last bite, the couple sped off to the

Alexandra Hospital where Denis worked in emergency and where Ethel made herself useful at Red Cross headquarters.

The air raids were horrifying and deadly for those in the city, but a game-changing destruction occurred two days later on December 10, in the waters beyond the island. The British battleship HMS *Prince of Wales* and battle cruiser HMS *Repulse* were hit by Japanese bombers off the eastern coast of Malaya and sank within hours, killing 840 sailors.[15] These two ships made up the core of the Royal Navy's offensive power in the region and the significance of their loss was clear. Singapore was on her own as far as any naval assistance was concerned.

The Mulvanys would never again visit their island paradise nor would they take another pleasure ride in the *Honora*. Realizing their boat could be put to good use, Ethel made time to go down to the docks where the *Honora* was moored and stocked it with food, filled the tanks, and stashed extra gas-filled containers in the bow. With the sails loaded on board and the red ensign flying, she made one final trip, taking the *Honora* round through the channel, and handed it over to the navy. The last time Ethel saw the cruiser, the blue ensign of the Royal Navy was flying atop her.

When this was exactly, Ethel never says. She wasn't too particular about affixing her memories to calendar dates. Sometimes she would just remember the day of the week, "it was a Tuesday." From then on Tuesdays were responsible for carrying the weight of some long past event, like the death of a friend. Other times she would attempt to pin down the temporal whereabouts of some occurrence through a process of triangulation. Trying to remember when she saw the *Honora* for the last time, she recalled it was the same day she had seen the pulsing lights of shell fire for the first time, and the day Bowby, their dog, had died while gazing at the same acid brightness of war. She and Denis had gone to their house for what would be the last time to pack up a few essentials before moving into billets closer to No. 1 MGH, which had been forced to move quarters. She described the scene:

On this particular day a fierce Battle was raging across the Straits. "Our" house was on a hill where the view of the battle was a deadly looking business. We were standing watching it, awed by the horror of the deadly, gruesome beast—war—that was backing us to a dead end. The dogs were with us. They were watching the crossfire very intently. I'd had enough, so I called to the dogs and started towards my truck. Brutus came running ahead of me, but when I looked back there was Bowby standing facing the Battle. I went back and my husband came over to him. "He is dead," he said. It was true—dead, but still facing the enemy. His feet were braced in show fashion. I left. I never saw Bowby laid down.

At Ethel's request Kuki, the Chinese cook, took Brutus; Ethel suggested they try to escape back across the causeway and into the Malayan jungle. Many of the pets in Singapore did not survive. Their owners, not knowing what lay ahead for themselves, feared their pets would be wounded or starve to death, and so took them to vets to be put down.

With their few possessions, the Mulvanys, along with other colleagues, moved into their temporary home, the Grand Palace of the Sultan of Johor. Ethel was awed by the gleaming elegance of the Anglo–Malay architecture and rueful that the one chance she had to sleep in a palace she barely had time to put her head on the pillow. The move had been necessary because the No.1 MGH had changed locations and was now situated on the mainland at the Johor General Hospital, too far from their home to commute. In the days that followed, hospitals further north in Malaya were evacuated, leaving only No. 1 MGH to serve the peninsula. It took over the top floors of the newly built government hospital, supplying five hundred beds for surgical and medical cases.[16]

A few days after Christmas, Bharose came to visit Ethel and Denis in their palatial billets. He arrived with bad news: their home at 112 Pasir Panjang had received a direct hit. Except for the few things he had been able to salvage, all that was left of their home was a crater of rubble. Ethel had little energy to dwell on what was gone, but over time and the inevitable mental circuits she made of the house, small losses pricked at her. She thought of the teddy bear that she had dragged around the world with her, and what about Aunt Esther's robin-shaped pitcher? There was that high-school athletic medal that she had been so proud of. She knew these things were insignificant and yet they were part of a series of markers outlining the shape of her life that were now gone.

Medical Hint:
For Rheumatism

Mix 1 teaspoon of flowers of sulphur
with ½ wine glass gin and take three
times per day.

Changi POW Cook Book

CHAPTER SIX

LOADED TO THE HILT ON BENZEDRINE

Being attached to No. 1 MGH, it was Ethel's job to pick up the wounded being brought in by train from farther north in Malaya. The days poured into each other, as did her descriptions of events. The details, though, whether from one trip or many, coalesced into one, and became glued together with a powerful hatred of war. Of one thing she was sure: "There's no train that pulls so heavy as one that's full of boys that are wounded."

The locomotives arrived under cover of darkness wearing Red Crosses on top and on their fronts, where, as far as Ethel was concerned, cattle catchers should rightly be if all were well with the world. Eerie blue lights replaced bright headlamps and the normally ubiquitous train whistles were silent, for fear of alerting the Japanese. The enemy bombers were not bound by the rules of the 1929 Geneva Convention banning attacks on Red Cross vehicles, so those working on the ground had to move quickly.[1] When the doors were thrown open the smell of shredded men cooped up in the stifling tropical heat must have been nauseating, but for Ethel it was the sight that shocked her most. Oozing bodies were all over the floor of the train lit by a deathly blue glow from the lights. She was warned time and again to watch her step. For some it no longer mattered, but others were grimly hanging on to life. None of it made sense to Ethel. These were such young boys, many of them calling out in agony for their mothers. How could war have come upon them so swiftly?

With the enemy overhead, Ethel was in a hurry to unload this mess of bodies. It wasn't until after she got her first casualty onto a stretcher and was lifting him off the train that she noticed that the towel wrapped around his skull had slipped off and the insides of his head were oozing out. The horror for her was that this man, a major, was still alive. Then there was the boy whose jaw was broken. He desperately wanted to tell her something but the bones no longer matched up and his teeth just lamely clicked out a message, something about his mother.

In this twisted world someone had placed a badly wounded Japanese prisoner beside an equally horribly injured but armed Nepalese Gurkha, a member of the force famed for their martial skills. Ethel knew when a soldier is wounded and taken into care his gun and ammunition are removed, but this young man was left with his *kukri*, the traditional curved knife used by Gurkhas. She understood why an exception had been made: "If you take a *kukri* away from a Gurkha, he just dies en route he's in such a panic." Furthermore, she could see that so much of his right side was gone, whoever had placed him there must have assumed him incapable of reaching for his knife, let alone being able to use it. But in the time it took Ethel to retrieve another wounded soldier and bring him to the ambulance, the Gurkha had bent himself around to reach the knife at the foot of his stretcher.

Ethel grabbed it from him. Reacting as if she had just stabbed him, he shouted at her in Hindi, "What did you do that to me for?"

Ethel pointed to her sleeve and to the train and said, "It's Red Cross. We're for mercy, you can't kill this boy."

* * *

Driving the ambulance during battle, Ethel described herself as working "under compulsion, like a person works on the battlefield, like a mad person ... and you were." The bipolar illness she suffered from is likely to have intensified her experience of war, increasing its vividness and confusion. On top of that, she had been "loaded to the hilt with Benzedrine." These uppers, which came into common use by combatants during the Second World War, kept them awake and in a heightened state of awareness.[2] Ethel and those she worked with on the medical teams were each issued nine of the small yellow pills at a time. These kept Ethel and the other staff going for hours until finally each in turn would sink into sleep where they stood, if they were not able to make it back to their quarters.

These quarters, soon enough, were to change when the hospital was forced to move once again. The current location, right across the water from Singapore's naval base, had become a daily target for the Japanese and was now just too dangerous. On January 25, 1942, the staff received orders to evacuate and move to the Gordon Barracks, at the Changi military station on the north-east tip of Singapore Island. The station was named after the sleepy little village there. In time the name would become synonymous with imprisonment. Ethel filled up her ambulance with patients and hospital gear and joined the stream of traffic driving over the Straits of Johor on the causeway, the umbilical cord joining Singapore to the mainland. Going in the opposite direction, a steady throng of people was heading north to villages on the mainland. Thick black smoke from the burning oil and coal stores blanketed all travellers, filling their eyes and nostrils with heavy dust and sticking to their sweat-soaked clothing. Ships were sailing out of the harbour attempting to flee the inevitable. Ethel couldn't get over the preposterous contrast between the confusion in front of her and the headlines from the daily press stating, as she put it, that this was merely a case of "retirement to a pre-arranged position."[3]

The hospital stayed at Changi until February 10. During that time, the staff were out of radio contact and had no newspapers but were uncomfortably aware that the hospital stood between two front lines. The Japanese were set up on Pulau Ubin, an island at most a mile off shore to the north, and behind No.1 MGH were the British guns. The borders of safety surrounding the hospital gradually tightened. On February 8, 1942, the medical officers' quarters were hit. The next day, the nurses quarters were bombed. The Japanese had been aiming just beyond at the British guns. One of those guns—a mobile howitzer affectionately called "Big Nancy"—was worked past her limit and eventually blew up, wounding her crew. Ethel was called out in the ambulance to take in the surviving casualties.

The raw details of that trip never left her. In an instant she could be back there, ordering actions step by step, not allowing any peripheral detail to distract her from the life and death decisions she faced. On one loose-leaf page, set apart from all her other writings, she recorded her memories just as they streamed out.

> 10:43 pm convoy leaves at once to evacuate crew of Big Nancy. The ambulance crew was loaded with Benzedrine—robots going and going and going like a hen with its head cut off and didn't know enough to fall down done.
>
> We went with blue parking lights on Lorries only. I had what used to be a pig lorry. It had been converted and now had a Red Cross fore and aft and on top. Our flashlights had blue lights too and from the glow of that blue light was revealed a scene of suffering men torn to ribbons. Lord help us. Tourniquet and pack a few. We had to [move] mighty quick too because low-flying strafes may be over any second.
>
> You picked up the ones whose pulses told you "Take me, I'll live." One of these was Putland. Oh! He was ripped to bits but I lifted his shoulders and dragged him over to the lorry. Whether I'd get help to get him into the lorry was another matter—"Well I hope I'll get help!" I think. No one here. Well haul out your two poles then. Tie your soldier on. Hoist up the two poles. You put

the head of the man pointing up—unless he has had a leg shot away—which you had tourniqueted (you hoped to heaven) and then the blood wouldn't start spurting again and if it has, put him in a feet up position. The poles would come to rest on the end of the truck platform. Then you'd rush around to the other end of your two-poles-with-soldiers-tied-to-it-contraption, and "Hoist!" Hoist hard he's heavy. Now he's up level with platform. "Shove!" Into the pig lorry!

This boy was talking all the time from the time you took his pulse. "Take Leggett, take Leggett. Leave me but take my pal. That's Leggett!"

After he's in the truck I go out. Leggett is very, very low. He's going I think. But who am I but a Benzedrine-loaded ambulance driver?

Yes. I'll take him. "Here give me a hand! You over there!"—to one of the other drivers.

It's Leggett. And we put him on the shelf above Putland. And tell Putland he's there. Someone else grabs the hem of my uniform as I stepped over him he mimed a message. We could hear the tanks coming in the distance. You couldn't let yourself ask, how long will they live? Or how will they die—being eaten by Kringahs (big strong mandibled ants)? Or will those tanks squash them—squash them as you have seen where others have been squashed just flat, with old bits of khaki over some of them. The stench of all this is beyond man to lay words to.

And so it goes you're loaded to bulging. Throw in bull low. Groan out and away from those dying lads. No place for even one more.[4]

Far above in the chain of command and on the other side of the world, Winston Churchill was being apprised of the dire situation in

Singapore. He cabled General Archibald Wavell, Commander of the Allied forces in South East Asia.[5] His words carried a poisonous weight.

> February 10th: There must at this stage be no thoughts of saving the troops or sparing the population. The battle must be fought to the bitter end at all costs ... Commanders and senior officers should die with their troops. The honour of the British Empire and the British Army is at stake ... With the Russians fighting as they are and the Americans so stubborn in Luzon, the whole reputation of our country and our race is involved.[6]

Before leaving Singapore that day, Wavell relayed Churchill's message to his commanding officers. The orders Denis and others received further emphasized British honour. Chinese troops, closer to the fighting at hand than either the Americans or Russians, had, Wavell emphasized, "with almost a complete lack of modern equipment ... held the Japanese for four and a half years. It would be disgraceful if we yielded our boasted fortress to inferior forces."[7] This was to be a fight to the death.

Given the chance, Denis would have searched for Ethel in the melee of that day, pulled her aside and read her his copy of the orders so they could share at least a glance of acknowledgement of how close death was hovering. Under the circumstances though, Denis and Ethel and all the other medical workers at Changi were too busy to consider how the leaders were deciding their fate. Far more immediate was the pressure being applied by the Japanese army. In the early hours of February 10, the day staff at the hospital, who had just gone off duty, were called in to pack up the ward equipment and patients. Every wounded soldier, his bedding, and belongings had to be gathered together using only moonlight. Storm lanterns and torches were forbidden. The evacuations began that morning.

Their destination was the core of the city's colonial district. After a quick stint at the Singapore Cricket Club, the hospital was eventually pushed to the water's edge, making its final home in the largest structure of the city, the one which ironically above all, had emphasized the power of the empire. The Fullerton Building, an edifice of Aberdeen granite, was home to the General Post Office housing up-to-the-minute technology to speed communications to all points of the empire and beyond. On the upper floors, where the patients were taken, was the elite Singapore Club, replete with rooms for dining, gaming, and sleeping. For many of the patients their wounds were the only ticket they would ever have allowing them entrance into this club. For in-pouring refugees it was an otherworldly scene in which they were led on a winding path through injured bodies up to the bar where, in proper colonial style, fresh lime drinks were still being served.

When the decision had been made to move the hospital into town, Ethel had loaded up her slapped-together ambulance and prepared for what would be her last trip. In all of her time driving, sometimes unwittingly crossing back and forth over enemy lines, this was the only time she got hurt. Her ambulance was at the head of a convoy of trucks with a dispatch rider leading the way on a motorcycle. The Japanese had a quietly efficient way of killing these riders that required no guns or ammunition, only a wire, strung across the road at neck level. Ethel never saw the wire, only its effect. In an instant the rider in front of her was headless but the bike carried on. It drove for another eighty feet or so, gradually slowing and finally, weaving drunkenly, it toppled into the ditch.

Ethel was so stunned, she ground the gears down, coming to a standstill without realizing what she was doing. At that point the shrapnel began to fly. Two wounded soldiers were squeezed in on the seat beside her. The sergeant next to her had been wounded in the arm and was leaning heavily over Ethel. As the ambulance came under fire he caught a tiny piece of metal in his jugular. The blood spurted from his neck with the force of a water main landing warm and sticky over Ethel's left side. The mere sliver that had fatally sliced his vein had broken off a much larger hunk which continued on its flight between his neck and Ethel's and became embedded in the leather seat behind her. In the instant before, Ethel had felt a sting on her calf and had leaned forward to grab her leg. She didn't realize at the time that it was a sniper's bullet that had grazed her flesh. Had the bullet come a moment later, she would not have been leaning forward when the shrapnel flew in the window and she, too, would have been hit at neck level. It wasn't much of a wound, but it was enough to have saved Ethel's life and spring her into action. She gripped the wheel, pulling herself away from the hot shrapnel embedded in the seat, and stepped on the gas, leaving the headless body of the dispatch rider behind.

Changi Macaroons

Grate one coconut. One egg or custard powder. One dessertspoon condensed milk. Two dessertspoons sugar. One pint stoned dates. Mix coconut, egg, sugar, and milk, mould gently but firmly into cones with a date in the centre. Place on a greased tin and cook in a hot oven until brown and cool.

Miss Barbara Walker, British Nursing Sister (b. 1914)

Walker also helped stitch a square for the Australian Changi Quilt.

Changi POW Recipe Log Book

CHAPTER SEVEN

SILENCE OF THE GUNS

W hile Ethel had been concentrating intently on getting wounded bodies to safety, the city of Singapore on the southern part of the island was consumed by chaos. More than half a million refugees competed with army deserters and civilians for food, medicine, and a dangerously short supply of water. There was no place to hide from the constant bombardment and no place to bury the quickly rotting corpses. Under these conditions, the spectre of a cholera outbreak was closing in as fast as the Japanese. On the thirteenth of February, 1942, the Allied forces were barely holding onto a protective perimeter around the city. Fearing that angry, drunken, and jubilant Japanese soldiers might commit atrocities as they had done in Hong Kong, Sir Shenton Thomas ordered all stocks of alcohol be destroyed.[1] At noon on the thirteenth, what amounted to a million gallons of liquor began running through the streets, creating a cloying stench as it mixed with blood and blackened rain filled with flecks of oil from the thick smoke billowing out of burning storage tanks. The soldiers, whether it was seasoned veterans or the thousands of Australians who had only just arrived weeks before, were sagging and demoralized. Their opponents had blazed over the island, but what the Allies didn't know was that the Japanese commander, the stocky 56-year-old General Yamashita Tomoyuki, was desperate for his troops to move faster. His army was critically short of fuel and ammunition, and he knew his men could not survive a siege of the city. He later wrote in his diary:

> My attack on Singapore was a bluff, a bluff that worked. I had 30,000 men and was outnumbered by more than three to one. I knew that if I had to fight long for Singapore I would be beaten. That is why the surrender had to be at once. I was very frightened all the time that the British would discover our numerical weakness and lack of supplies and force me into disastrous street fighting.[2]

It never came to that. Faced with civilian casualties of around two thousand a day and a complete breakdown of the water supply on the fourteenth, Lt General Arthur Percival, General Officer Commanding Malaya, did not believe he had a choice.[3] On February 15, 1942, he surrendered Singapore to the Japanese. At 5:15 that evening the 55-year-old general stepped out of his car in front of the Ford factory, the meeting place chosen by the Japanese high up on Bukit Timah hill. Although wrung out from exhaustion, the tall, spare man strode with flag in hand up to the factory to face the soberly triumphant General Yamashita. These two enemies, both veterans of the Great War, had fought on the same side during that conflagration but now different political interests ruled their actions and alliances. In front of the excited clicking of Japanese cameras, Percival bent his boney shoulders over the table and signed the demand for unconditional surrender.

His nickname, "the Rabbit," although a jibe about his buck teeth, seemed an apt description of his leadership style, which had lacked the charisma and drive of his opponent's.[4] After the Japanese general's near miraculous success, Yamashita was hailed the "Tiger of Malaya." But, both in spite of his military prowess and because of it,

Yamashita would soon be banished to Manchuria. Japanese prime minister, Tojo Hediki, felt too threatened by his colleague's triumph to allow him the opportunity for any such future successes.[5]

Singapore was renamed Syonan, "light of the south," and just months after its conquest, Indochina, the Dutch East Indies, and the Philippines also fell into Japanese hands. With these territories came access to much needed raw materials and, unexpectedly, a weighty responsibility. To their surprise, the Japanese were now saddled with hundreds of thousands of prisoners. In total the Imperial Army captured more than 130,000 Western civilians (50,000 men, 40,000 women, and an astonishing 40,000 children) and 140,000 Allied military personnel, spread out over Southeast Asia and the Pacific areas.[6] They had assumed that at least the women and children would have been evacuated. Civilian internees were so low on the list of priorities that the Japanese had almost no policy to govern their treatment.[7] As for the military personnel, they could not understand how these soldiers could surrender and bring such dishonour on themselves, their families, and their countries. For the Japanese it would have been unthinkable. On the tiny island of Singapore alone, more than 37,000 British and nearly 15,000 Australian forces were immediately imprisoned by the Imperial Japanese Army after capitulation.[8]

The Japanese were not the only ones who considered this situation unthinkable. The fall of Singapore, said Churchill, was "the worst disaster and the largest capitulation in British history."[9] The British were now under the heel of those they had dismissed as weak and inept, and their empire began its passage into history.

* * *

At the moment of ceasefire on February 15, a chillingly macabre silence descended on the city, invisible as poison gas. "The horrors of capitulation," Ethel later noted, "were just too stark in their hollow monotone. What was there to hope for?" She remembered exactly where she was when the silence fell. "I was coming through a ward in the [Fullerton] Post Office Building where we had extended our hospital. I stopped at the foot of a badly wounded soldier. I seemed to be rooted there until he said, 'Is this what we fought for?'" That question would haunt her.

For nurses and female volunteers who remained at the hospital the immediate concern was not philosophical. News had spread quickly of the rapes and murders that had happened when Hong Kong had fallen less than two months before on Christmas day.[10] The women assumed it was only a matter of hours before they would be facing drunken, vengeful Japanese soldiers. With little else they could do, they waited. After night fall, the first Japanese soldier entered the makeshift hospital. To Ethel's surprise, the young sergeant, neither angry nor drunk, looked straight ahead as he walked through the ward. His only mission was to be seen.

The next Japanese soldiers she saw were massed outside. Having just taken out a body to the verandah that was being used as a temporary morgue, she looked down to see a mob. They presented like "a picture of Hades ... violent, gross, more animal than animals." Separating this mob from the hospital doors was a line of Japanese soldiers with their backs to the building blocking their angry fellows from entering. Someone working at the hospital had picked up a leaflet explaining the situation. A general—Ethel thought it was Arimura, the man who had built her boat—had issued a proclamation that "on pain of death" no woman was to be molested. Malayan author Chin Kee Onn contends that there were cases of strict Japanese military punishment for soldiers who committed rape, but he also makes the point that "War without rape is as impossible as fire without smoke."[11] In this new world that the Japanese claimed would create an "Asia for the Asiatics," rumour had it that, despite Arimura's proclamation, Chinese women were being attacked. Swirling stories from the outside told of women being subjected to all the inevitable and foul acts that enemy soldiers can visit upon women in wartime. During the Sino-Japanese wars of the 1930s, Japanese soldiers who had survived the guerrilla tactics of the Chinese had learned a special hatred for Chinese fighters who blurred the line between soldier and civilian.[12]

Early the next morning, Ethel had her third encounter with Japanese soldiers. She wrote in her notebooks about this bizarre mix of human-heartedness and murder.

Two Japanese soldiers brought in a wounded British soldier on a crude platform that had been tarred and salted at the bottom to discourage "warrior ants." They placed the stretcher down on the floor at my feet. They bowed to the soldier that they had brought in and then they turned and walked out of the Ward.

The British soldier whose name was Burns smiled at me and said "don't ever ask me to fight the Japanese again—I never, never will." I lifted his dressing on his back and I knew that he would never fight anyone, not anymore. There was this horrible hole in his back. I felt his forehead, and looked at his glassy eyes. "It was a sniper," he said, "one night one of those lads got me." "And do you know," he said, "they came and dressed my wounds and brought me rations and water each night after that?" I was just held with the spell of the horror of war as I listened to this dying boy.

Ethel saw war from the filthy underbelly of the conflict. She was well aware of the differences in the uniforms worn by friend and foe but at times saw good in the foe and evil in the friend. In the end, the guts spilled out of the beautiful young bodies of both just the same.

Part Two
Getting to Hunger

Oliver Twist Cake

1½ cups self-raising flour

½ cup brown sugar

½ cup butter

2 eggs

½ cup milk

1 cup blackcurrant jam

½ cup chopped nuts

½ cup raisins

1 tspn nutmeg

Blend butter, sugar, and eggs. Add jam, nuts, and raisins. Sift dry ingredients. Add alternately with milk. Pour into well-buttered tube pan. Bake in moderate oven for 40 minutes. Ice with—

Jelly Foam Frosting

2 egg whites

2 tbspns cold water

1¼ cups sugar

Pinch salt

½ cup redcurrant jelly

Mix jelly, sugar, and water. Cook until it forms ball in cold water. Pour slowly over stiffly beaten salted egg whites. Beat until proper consistency.

Changi POW Cook Book

CHAPTER EIGHT

THE ROAD TO JAIL

Over the next few weeks Ethel worked at the Fullerton's temporary hospital doing what she could for the wounded men before finally packing them up to be transported into prison hospitals. Then it was the turn of the medical staff. She and Denis would be going in separate directions, but before boarding their trucks Ethel handed Denis a quick note. "My Own Dear Boy, This is a dark cloudy day but behind the clouds this morning there was the brightest star." She had faith they would be together again and moreover wanted him to know, "My darling I am so proud of you and your work."[1] He tucked the note away and kept it for the rest of his life.

In the humid afternoon heat of March 2, 1942, Ethel watched as Denis and other male officers and soldiers were loaded into vehicles to be taken to the military barracks at the tip of the island. "His truck left just about the same time as my truck ... We were sitting in the back, and he went on one angle of the road and we women went on the other ... He never turned around." Ethel watched as the back of his head grew smaller in the distance. The tight black curls on the man she had once fallen for now belonged to a prisoner of war.

The truck Ethel and the other women were in drove along the south shore of the island heading east, a route which at any other time would be noted for its paradise-like vistas of sand and sea. They were told they would be taken to the city suburb of Katong and should pack enough food and clothing for ten days. It wasn't far, less than eight kilometres. Their truck ground to a halt in front of the Roxy Theatre. The white stuccoed cinema was steps away from the swimming beach and in the past had never failed to please its patrons. When the ceiling fans broke down in the intense heat the doors would be opened, and the audience could be assured of a refreshing sea breeze. It had reminded Ethel of the Palace, a 1920s era Toronto movie house that had a certain elegance about it. Not now. In its present state, the Roxy was more like a gigantic ant nest, swarming with over four hundred women and children, refugees who had fled from all over Malaya and distant parts of the British and Dutch colonies. They had been searching for security within the so-called "Fortress Singapore." There were so many they were spilling out of their theatrical shelter into surrounding bungalows and outbuildings.

This was an in-between world, a land where all the rules of an empire and a marriage that had governed Ethel's life had been burned away and their replacements were not yet even imagined. As she stepped off the truck and tried to take in her surroundings, she had the sense of being wheeled into an operating theatre where someone else was in control and there was no turning back. More than weak, she felt her knees were aerated and her whole being enveloped in aloneness. But Ethel wasn't one to wallow in any single sensation for long. She needed to find a spot to lay down her few belongings. Amid the maze of people at the Roxy, she met up with a familiar face, the very beautiful dark-haired Freddy (Elfrieden) Bloom, an American journalist. Freddy and Ethel had first become acquainted through their husbands. Freddy's first husband, a young medical officer in the Royal Army Medical Corps, had been good friends with Denis.

Tragically he had died of pleurisy, just twenty-eight years old. Two years later and only nine days before the fall of Singapore Freddy, in an act of hope and love, married another British military doctor, Philip Bloom. The letters she wrote to him while in captivity, which he never received because of the separation between the men and women, became her diary. She wrote with a droll honesty about her situation, and had much to say about Ethel.

Ethel and Freddy, along with Kate Clarke, a thirty-year-old public health nurse, and Katherine de Moubray, a forty-three-year-old mother of two, set up house in two empty rooms in a former groom's quarters above an old garage. Katherine, a slender, fine-featured woman, was married to an official in the Malaysian Civil Service. He was imprisoned with the other civilian men, but their two children were in England at boarding school. Bereft of family, Katherine had brought a small four-legged companion with her. The terrier had befriended her when she was sitting on the steps outside the Fullerton Building waiting for transport out to the Roxy. After sharing an army ration biscuit with the little dog, Katherine admitted to anyone listening, that she "loathed leaving her." Even among all the mess of anxious discussions going on, Ethel overheard her and, with a take-charge manner that Katherine would come to detest, but was glad for at the time, announced that "it was all arranged the dog was coming too."[2]

The garage roof leaked, and missing floorboards meant everyone had to step with care, but they soon discovered that these minor discomforts were more than compensated by the bit of privacy their quarters provided. That evening, away from the crowds in the theatre and surrounding houses, the four women indulged in a cup of Nescafé after lights out while they quietly discussed what the future might hold. Early the next morning, though, Ethel found the charm of their accommodations greatly diminished when she woke up to see what she thought were moving walls and realized with disgust that their rooms were home to many fellow creatures. She never really got used to the sight, much less the irritation, of bedbugs.

In these early days at the Roxy, Freddy and Ethel were fast friends in spite of having little in common, other than being lumped together, as "flamboyant" North Americans, in a very class-conscious expatriate British society.[3] Freddy was no farm girl from the backwaters of Manitoulin. She was a cool wit who had grown up in New York City, the only child of indulgent and doting parents who loved people and included their daughter in their travel and social life. Katherine de Moubray summed her up as one "bred to modern arts, graces, luxuries and pastimes."[4] But Freddy was not an extrovert like her parents. She saw herself more as an observer. She was impressed by Ethel's practical skills and energy. The four of them living in the garage were tasked with supplying fuel for the stoves. "Ethel," she commented, "turned out to be a natural woodchopper (her strength is astounding) but the rest of us were rather clumsy."[5]

Katherine was the least adept. Exhausted from the unaccustomed work, she gashed her leg with the axe. Fortunately the wound was not too deep, but it meant that she became exempt from this chore. Ethel, on the other hand, had learned how to wield an axe on Manitoulin Island and was more than willing to apply her knowledge to felling and cleaning coconut trees around the Roxy. It was gruelling work made all the more onerous by the tropical humidity and pestering mosquitos, but she had her system. On one occasion, however, as she was clearing round the tree readying it for chopping, she tripped over a long wire. Tired and angry, she took out her frustration on the tangled cable that had felled her. A Japanese guard standing nearby saw her pulling with all her might and screamed. With gestures that needed no translations, he commanded her to stop. It was a land mine, possibly a dud, but to be respected nonetheless.

No matter how skilled Ethel was with an axe, the wood was so green it barely warmed the water to cook the rice rations they were given. Still, the food arrived at the appointed times thanks to Constance Medwyn, who was in charge of cooking for their group. By Freddy's rather ungracious description, she was an "ex-chorus girl" who had lost her figure somewhere along the way and was by then a "fat sixty-five"-year-old.[6]

The food was not enough to satisfy anyone. Fortunately, noted Freddy, a few of the women brought with them their own "little private stores." There was an English sensibility to what they had grabbed from their own cupboards or scrounged from the ruins of Singapore: tinned asparagus tips, canned sardines, powdered milk, chocolate, and biscuits. Those who had some were happy to eat, but "Every time we had a bite," said Freddy, "we'd look at each other and the bites would stick."[7]

For their six days at the Roxy, Ethel dug latrine holes, chopped wood, and organized her life and anyone else's who would let her. She scrounged the neighbourhood for bits of wood, scraps of fabric, nails—things that might improve their standard of living in what Freddy satirically referred to as their "beloved Woodchopper's cottage."[8] But before they got too settled the women were told to pack up their things and be ready to march to Changi Jail, where the civilian men were already interned. The new, British-built maximum security institution at Changi was located outside the city centre and had been intended to house the worst criminals culled from the surrounding regions of the empire.

It was not likely many of the women would have seen the inside of it, or any other prison for that matter. They might not all have belonged to private clubs, but most of these women had not had to cope with the harshness of poverty that can lead to confrontations with the law. The benefits of middle or upper class life had surrounded them with the luxuries of education, medicine, entertainments, security, privacy, and freedom. In the East, if not always back in Britain and Europe, they'd had servants to help with the cooking and cleaning. They might have occasionally questioned the quality of their food but never before had they seriously doubted they would have enough to survive. They had no inkling of what they were walking into and no experience to help them prepare mentally or physically for this trip of unknown duration.

The distance to Changi, fourteen kilometres, multiplied in Ethel's memory over the years, but what really irked her at the time was having to get up unnecessarily early. To make Japan the symbolic centre of Asia, the Japanese commanders had turned the clocks ahead an hour and a half, putting Singapore on Tokyo time. It meant that the women and children were ordered to rise in the moonlit hours of March 8, 1942. It didn't help tempers that they were then forced to stand and wait. Shifting from foot to foot for three hours gave each one plenty of time to second guess every decision they had made about what to bring. Who knew how important those choices might be? A family photo album weighed about the same as a selection of tinned foods, each sustaining in its own way. Shorts might be more sensible on the march, but a cotton dress with pockets was useful, if one could only decide what to put in the pockets. The Japanese told them they could load some belongings in a truck going out to the jail, but no one knew if they could trust their new captors. It was safest to wear or carry whatever was most precious. One oversized woman began the journey with an equally oversized Turkish-style Axminster rug rolled up and balanced on her hip. Ethel imagined that the carpet must have had pride of place on her living room floor and had meant the world to her. But the woman could only support the weight for so long. When her treasure fell by the wayside, so too did the exhausted rug lady. She was picked up and driven the rest of the way in the back of a truck, squished in with the very old, the sick, and those with legs too tiny to make the trek. As for the rug, likely it quickly found a new home.

Others chose to carry smaller, lighter treasures. One British woman brought a spool of thread that she guarded for as long as it lasted. Nora Morris cleverly brought both needles and thread with her that day as she walked into camp with her ten-year-old daughter, Olga. Rather than pack her clothing, Nora Morris wore her seven dresses, a feat of determination in 30 °C heat. She filled her pockets and bags with jars of Marmite, tins of condensed milk, and packets of aspirin.[9] The wisdom of her choices would soon be clear.

Trotting along with the crowd at ankle level was Katherine de Moubray's little four-legged friend, now named Judy. Like Toto on the road to Oz, she had good survival instincts. The night before, a dire order had come down: all dogs whose owners had managed to protect them through the battle and during the days at the Roxy were to be destroyed. Some of the women used a few of their precious stores of *Veronal* sleeping pills so they could hold their pets while they fell asleep for the last time. Others caged up their dogs and left them hoping their end would be swift. Judy, however, didn't officially belong to anyone. With no one responsible for her, she made herself scarce that night, reappearing in the morning in time to march with the women.

At first glance, some of the outfits worn by the women seemed eccentric in the extreme. Like clowns in a travelling circus, they were done up with hats made of lampshades, upturned flower pots, bits of cardboard, and draping towels. Ethel thought the elegant cream coloured hat with a rose on the side perched on Rose Reid Donnell's head looked better suited for a garden party than a prison entrance. She knew, though, that the Australian woman's fair skin burned in an instant and her head covering, like all the other millinery concoctions, was shrewdly worn for protection against the intense tropical sun. Practical yes, but Rose might also have been hoping to catch a glimpse of her husband, the lyrically named Robert Buchannan Bell Donnell, who was imprisoned on the men's side of the jail. It wouldn't hurt to look her best.

Then there were the fashionable dressers, some of whom Ethel thought appeared ready for a gala event at Government House. Like Rose, they were Brits married to men of business now imprisoned on the other side of the jail: Anne Courtenay, eleven years Ethel's senior, Angela Bateman, a sixty-year-old artist, and Eileen Pearson. They were all soon to become Ethel's friends, unlike another notably well-dressed woman, the formidable Eleanor Hopkins. Although right from the beginning there was no love lost between Ethel and Eleanor, Ethel had to admit, the slight, good-looking, forty-two-year-old

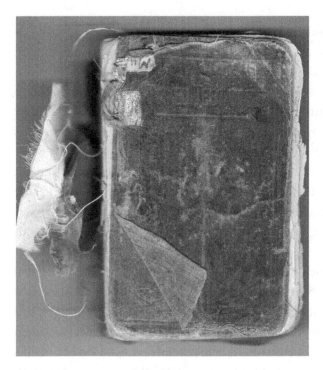

Ethel carried this bible into Changi Jail (1942) and home to Canada (1946). While in Changi she chewed the spine off for the protein in the glue. Pioneer Museum, Mindemoya, Manitoulin.

medical doctor dressed with flair. She walked into Changi Katharine Hepburn style, in an elegantly tailored linen slack-suit, one of many in a rainbow of colours that she brought with her.

Ethel's own outfit, a white skirt and blouse, was just like the one she had worn that day in the spring of 1933 when she had met the Emperor and Empress of Japan. However, this time she marched off to become a "guest" of the emperor in a pair of tennis shoes instead of elegant pumps and stockings. If she had given any thought at all to the colour symbolism of her all-white outfit it would have signified mourning in the Asian tradition, definitely not surrender to the enemy. She was one of fifty or sixty who had made a pact that morning. They would crawl if need be, but never drop.

Finally the march got going at 10 a.m. Ethel was ready with her camera case slung over her shoulder, packed with mementoes and a few treasured books that their head servant, the bearer Ram Bharose, had rescued from behind enemy lines among the ruins of their bombed-out house. Stuffed in there were two photo albums; her father's small red New Testament bible and a hymn book from Ned Pratt; the children's book *Dutchy Van Deal*, a 1914 gift from her grade-four teacher; and, finally, her 1932 Canadian cookbook, *A Guide to Good Cooking*. Around the edges she squeezed in the lipstick Denis had found in the glove-compartment before they had abandoned their car, a jar of cold cream, and a tin of heal-all Mecca ointment. In her small brown leather suitcase, which she must have traded off from one sweating hand to the other as she walked, she carried the mainstay of what would be her wardrobe for the next three and a half years—a blue dress, a red and white sun suit she had worn at their island cottage, two sets of underclothes, and, that most versatile of garments, a sarong. Lastly, too precious to trust to the transport truck, she draped the quilt her mother had sent from home over her arm.

The Japanese guards made sure that the straggle of women only went as fast as the slowest walker, so there was plenty of opportunity to socialize and meet new people for those with the energy and the desire to do so. Ethel fell in with some of the many nurses who had either chosen not to leave Singapore or had missed the last boat out before the city fell, but it was "that crazy American, Gene Bales" who really grabbed her attention. Gene, a film actress, was married to Dale Dernier Bales, a saloonkeeper and former vaudevillian in the US. When business faded in the 1930s he and Gene ended up in Singapore. There they ran the well-known Coconut Grove club, and Dale famously plied his trade under the name of Bill Bailey.

Even though Ethel didn't use much makeup, she loved that this outrageous American woman did. She was certain that Gene Bales had all the "paint and powder" in Singapore. As for clothing, Gene ambled comfortably along the road to Changi in a pair of white shorts and a shirt with the tails hanging out. Ethel had never seen such a marvellously carefree fashion statement. But what topped it off for Ethel, in spite of her strong Christian views, was that Gene Bales could swear at the Japanese in the most beautiful, flowing language. "It was like the best Tennyson you've ever heard!"

Photograph of Keith Greenaway, RCAF, that Ethel kept in her bible throughout the war. Pioneer Museum, Mindemoya, Manitoulin.

To help them along their journey the women pilfered the dump outside the Roxy, gathering up bottles and filling them with drinking water. Garbage, transformed into treasure, provided Ethel with an old tomato tin she would use for her meals in Changi. One woman rehabilitated a tumbledown old pram, inspiring others who dragged into commission an array of wheeled vehicles they had found on the beach. Iris Parfitt, previously an artist and teacher in Penang, north of Singapore, documented with cartoon-like pictures and words the straggling line of exhausted women winding their way into Changi Jail. "Perambulators and push-carts loaded with pails and pots, bedding and food for the children, were steered on their towering, toppling crazy course through the throng."[10]

The slowness of their procession meant there was plenty of time for them to be seen by the local inhabitants, a vivid display of the dramatic change in fortunes for all involved. This enforced parade would be the prisoners' introduction to deliberate acts of humiliation by the Japanese that would haunt them throughout their imprisonment. More than an outgrowth of their policy of Asia for the Asiatics, the treatment of Allied civilians by the Japanese was studded with a desire for retribution for the way their own captured citizens had been treated by the British.[11] Japanese from all over Malaya had been seized as soon as their countrymen's bombs had begun falling on British-held territory. They were initially transferred to Changi, the same jail Ethel was heading towards, before they were sent to India. Ethel had seen some of those prisoners just a few months before, huddled together on the docks waiting to be transported to Delhi, where they would be installed in lethal conditions within the crumbling walls of Purana Qila, the Old Fort.[12] Seeing their obvious discomfort, she had approached a British soldier guarding them and, showing her Red Cross badge, asked if she could bring them some food and drink. For no good reason she could fathom her request was refused.

In spite of the hostility between the women and their captors, the guards allowed the prisoners to rest a few times throughout the seven-hour march, a gift for which Ethel was very grateful. It wasn't long into the ordeal before she began looking out for a neem tree by the roadside. She wasn't interested in its delicate white flowers, only the multi-purposed leaves of the village "pharmacy" tree she had come to know of in India. At the first opportunity she collapsed into the shade and stuffed a handful of the leaves into the heels of her tennis shoes, hoping to soothe the raw blisters that had quickly grown, burst, and bled without the buffer of socks. In this climate and under these conditions a small ailment could become a big concern in a short time.

The trail of women continued to weave their way along, leaning towards whatever shade there was, but never straying far from the road. No one thought long about trying to slip out of sight and melt into the jungle. They wouldn't last long before the outline of their features would give them away to the first person they approached on what had become their island prison. They stayed on the gravel road until the coconut palms and rubber trees of the countryside gave way and they came face to face with a modern version of a medieval fortress. The insurmountable jail walls were studded with towers looming over each corner and a great steel portcullis slid ominously open as the prisoners arrived.

As they passed through the gates, the spirit of the women who had vowed not to falter on the road to Changi took over, and they slowly began to sing. The newly imprisoned men, on the other side of the jail, helpless to carry out their traditional role as protectors, cheered the women on from behind bars. Maybe Rose Donnell's husband caught a glimpse of his wife in her flower-topped hat and witnessed her dignity as she and all the other women sang out, "There'll always be an England, and England shall be free, as long as England means to you, what England means to me." At the time the Vera Lyn song, already a classic, carried with it a grim undertone of worry. Some wondered if England really was going to survive the horrors of war, but Ethel wouldn't allow herself to doubt. Looking at the men's faces behind the bars, she knew she was supporting the war effort in the best way she could, with her mind.

When the first line of women, including Ethel, Freddy, and Kate, got inside, exhaustion took over and they slid onto the floor of the entrance corridor. As the gates clanged shut behind the last woman Ethel felt a pressing suffocation. She knew well the sensation of claustrophobia. This time she recovered from it quickly, but on each subsequent occasion that she felt her mental state in free-fall, it took longer and longer to recover her balance. Many may have suspected Ethel had a mental health problem, but Freddy knew for sure. She made a point of adding an editorial comment to that effect when she published her diary in 1980, thirty-five years after it was written. "[Ethel] was a handsome, vibrant Canadian whose past history of nervous disorder was known to me but to nobody else in captivity."[13] Maybe this addition was a way of explaining the cutting remarks she would make about Ethel later in her diary. But it would turn out that Freddy wasn't quite so close-lipped about Ethel's mental health as she made out.

Toad in the Hole

1 lb sausages

batter as for Yorkshire pudding

Prick and place sausages in Pyrex
dish with a tablespoonful of fat.
Place in hot oven for quarter of an
hour till thoroughly hot. Take out,
pour over prepared batter, cook for
half an hour. Serve at once.

Kate Hunter (McQuillan) Greig,
Scottish nurse

Greig married marine engineer
John Hamilton Greig in Singapore in
1936.

Changi POW Cook Book

CHAPTER NINE
ON THE INSIDE

Ethel's first impression of the inside of Changi was of bugs, hundreds of them crawling along the corridor wall where the women first sat down. As her world closed in around her she became fixated on what she thought was a dark mass of insects flowing in patterns like a flock of birds. She got up, picked one off the wall and squished it between her fingers. From the sharp, turpentiney smell she was sure it was a bedbug, and the mass of them seemed to be creating deliberate forms on the wall. Gradually letters, then words seemed to come into focus. Ethel had heard that members of the Royal Norfolk regiment had been stationed near the village of Changi in early February. She feared that in the heat of battle some of them must have retreated to the jail where they became trapped, and expecting the worst, wrote with their own blood what they thought might be their final epistles:

"Give my love to my wife and daughters."

"Tell Anne Peroux that it isn't as bad as she thought it was. Jim."

Bedbugs eat fluid rather than dried human blood,[1] but whatever was crawling through Ethel's imagination just then appeared to her as a real and vile horror living off the words of dying men.

Beyond the designs of blood-engorged bedbugs, the jail appeared to Ethel as a jumble of isolated locations imprinted with fear. Concrete walls, porous and flaky enough in parts to pick holes through, were topped with shiny broken glass. Towers that loomed overhead seemed built for hangings and below them were "courtyards within courtyards within courtyards leading into cell blocks." Her sense of Changi was like Alice's first impressions of Wonderland after falling down the rabbit hole. Ethel too saw warrens of doorways and passages always leading in on themselves, never to freedom, and never to the men on the other side with the exception of the sewage drains that linked the two parts of the jail.

Mary Thomas, a fellow internee, had a less haunting impression of the jail. The thirty-six-year-old Englishwoman examined her new home with the eyes of a no-nonsense school teacher, which she was. "Aesthetically," she admitted, "it was a very fine building even when seen from within the compounds, being beautifully designed and proportioned."[2] Obviously her compatriots had not skimped, nor had they gone half-measures on security. Around the perimeter were twenty foot high double-walls with watchtowers at each corner and a large front gate with turrets on either side. She sketched out a map of the women's part of the jail, showing two three-storey cell blocks—A and E—perpendicular to one another. Each had outdoor compounds that were separated by a carpenter's shop. At one corner of the shop stood the delicately named "Infirm ladies' annex," set up to house the weak and elderly. The dungeon, a storage room which would be used to secret away prisoners' treasures, was next to the hospital. The poetically labelled "Rose Garden," initially devoid of greenery, stood opposite E cell block and had the all-important rice store in one corner. Sewage drains ran around the perimeter and formed a boundary with the men's side. Whether it appeared as well-designed or as a rabbit warren, this was now home.

Sketch of Changi Jail cell on the men's side, by C. Jackson. Pioneer Museum, Mindemoya, Manitoulin.

Katherine de Moubray, who had gone ahead by truck because of the gash on her leg, was there to meet Freddy, Ethel, and Kate. While Ethel was mesmerized by the bed bugs, Freddy sank with exhaustion onto one of the mattresses from the Woodchopper's cabin that had travelled in the truck with Katherine. The other new entrants found energy they had lost en route and began racing through the jail searching for a cell to claim. Instead of joining the frenetic crowd, Ethel and Freddy listened while Katherine described the ominous state of the cell blocks. They had electricity, but the sparsely placed bulbs were hardly enough to lift the gloom on the bottom two floors, much less on the dark slippery iron staircase joining all three floors. Only on the third floor at either end of the corridors were there windows that offered something other than a view of concrete walls.

They were so high though, you had to find something to stand on before you could catch a glimpse of the sea. As for the cells, there were twenty-two of them lined up like sentries facing each other on either side of the corridor. Katherine didn't dwell on the tiny barred windows at the top of filthy ten-foot high walls, nor on the squatter toilet in the corner of each cupboard-sized room. The horror for her was the central concrete mound in each cell, "a sort of mortuary cement slab," counterfeiting as a bed.[3]

After half an hour, it was announced that a new wing of the prison was being opened up to deal with the overflow of new prisoners, and the three of them thought they had better go and find a cubbyhole for themselves. The cells, eight feet long, seven feet wide, eleven feet high, were designed for one but now had to house two to three people.[4] By Ethel's calculation, "the space allowed for each prisoner was an inch less than a grave." Staring at the cells all three women were of the same mind, but it was Ethel who gathered herself together and stomped off to find an alternative. Katherine was in awe that Ethel "somehow got in touch with some Japanese officers and persuaded them that we personally cannot stand these cells."[5] In response, the men pointed Ethel to a storage room for tools and told her she and the others could sleep there. The tool shed had room for five, so the inhabitants of the Woodchoppers cottage—Ethel, Freddy, Katherine, Kate Clark, and little dog Judy—moved in together with Ellen Moir, a forty-year-old English woman married to Brigadier Robert Gifford Moir, former communications commander during the war. Once they had all agreed on who was to be where, they made up their beds with repurposed tablecloths, canvas sheeting—whatever they had brought with them—and went about trying to make a home for themselves in the three feet of space they had between the beds. Ethel had the satisfaction of spreading out her mother's quilt that she had carried all along the march, creating a small refuge of memories to crawl under at night in this hard, new world. When the women were settled Judy claimed one of the green cushions on Freddy's bed.

the four long, well-behaved British-style queues snaking out the door. It was demeaning having to line-up like school girls under the noses of their overlords, and in front of them the women weren't about to push and squabble. Equal access to publicly available food quickly became a golden rule upon which survival depended. However, with nothing to do but wait, the queues could become perfect petri dishes for growing complaints. When Ethel was lined up with her good-natured friend Euphemia, there wasn't much point in grumbling, but when in the company of other complainers, she vented. The soup, she said, was flavoured with no more than grass, stringy buffalo grass that tasted like nettles. What made it far worse was that the slop was served out of the old night soil buckets of Singapore. The buckets had been boiled many times over before being put to this use, but as far as Ethel was concerned, "If you see something that typifies a chamber [pot], and then you're told to eat out of it, I don't care how clean it is, you're eating out of a latrine!"

It would turn out that in comparison to what the prisoners' fare would be in the last half of their internment, their food during these early days and months in Changi was almost reasonable. Still, a few hours and a few missed or meagre meals are enough to start funnelling most thoughts to food. The stomach objects noisily to the lack of fuel, patience fades, and civility withers. After just days of this shortage, light-headedness will creep in along with dizziness, headache, nausea, exhaustion, constipation, and abdominal cramps. In time the women would have felt the points of their hip bones when they lay down to sleep on the cement floor or, if they were lucky, wooden platforms and mattresses. Pulling on a shirt or doing up a bra would be a daily reminder of the deepening ridges of their ribs.

This was just the early stages. Likely even the prison doctors had little idea how a long-term semi-starvation diet would affect everyone. Even with medical experts in their midst and hunger such a prominent feature of the human condition, especially during the Great Depression, it was not something that had been scientifically examined in great depth. But from February to July of that same year, on the other side of the world, a medical study was being conducted on how the human body degrades when starved. In Poland's Warsaw ghetto, a group of twenty-eight Jewish physicians undertook the horrific task of examining and describing the effects of starvation on one hundred and fifty children and adults. They were determined that the world would know what they were experiencing. The studies were smuggled out of the ghetto, buried until after the war, and published in 1946.[10] One of the team, Dr. Julian Fliederbaum, who later killed himself, describes the steps of starvation in adults. At the beginning,

> Constant thirst and persistent increase in urinary output
> (4-5 liters) ... are the first signs of even a short period of hunger
> or of a drastic change in the diet as occurred during the war
> ... Other early complaints include dryness in the mouth, rapid
> weight loss, and a constant craving for food. [11]

The Changi POWs were suffering from this first stage of hunger disease in the early months of their internment. On a lighter note, but ominous under the circumstances, Fliederbaum continued, "Disappearance of surplus fat. This stage was reminiscent of the time before the war when people went to Marienbad, Karlsbad, or Vichy for a reducing cure and came back looking younger and feeling better."[12] Looking svelte is one thing, but hunger, even in the early stages, is uncomfortable, and like any other pain it is a constant reminder, our body's way of demanding, "Do something!" So Ethel did.

Using what weapons she had, she began her resistance by arranging a tea party. The two constant supports she had to rely on in this miserable new world were her religious faith and her belief in the value of the Red Cross. Easter was coming up just a month after they arrived at Changi, and she decided that on this, the most significant of the Christian holidays, a celebration should be had. What better accompaniment to the festivities was there than a feast? Of course there would be no banquet of roasted sacrificial lamb dripping with rosemary-flavoured fat, laid out beside cream-filled mashed potatoes and mounds of colourful vegetables. However, with a lot of work, the women could have a sit-down tea party of rations.

Ethel had been wondering what kind of projects to work on with the Red Cross. She had started a Red Cross corner where people dropped off things they didn't need, got credit for them and bought items that others had brought in. Women could also offer, for a fee, their mending or ironing skills. The long-term plan was that someone would take the money raised and shop for hard-to-come-by things in Singapore city. Having made up her mind to put on this tea, Ethel strapped on her Red Cross armband and made her way over to the jail office. There she proceeded to lecture the Japanese officers about Christianity. Wearing them down with her proselytizing might have been part of her thinking, but she was clear-headed enough to realize that most of her words fell flat around her feet. Yet she wanted to believe that "sometimes they listened as if they were listening." More likely in spite of her lecture rather than because of it, the officials granted Ethel and the Red Cross women permission to hold a tea on Saturday, April 4, and to have a sunrise service the next morning. Under Ethel's erratically guiding hand, a newly forming group of Red Cross women threw their energies into decoration and food preparations for the party and the rehearsals for the morning hymn sing.

To rally enthusiasm for the Red Cross and the upcoming festivities, Ethel gave an after-dinner talk on the organization the evening before the tea. It was one of the regular Friday night general interest lectures that the women had started. Three weeks before, Ethel had spoken about Kashmir, and the audience had been happily transported out of their concrete walls into the mountain-rimmed valley. But this time her presentation caused an uproar. It began humorously enough with self-effacing tales of her early years in the Red Cross on Manitoulin. Then the tone changed as she focused on her efforts to set up a British branch of the Red Cross in Singapore. She was not shy to name names of those she thought incompetent. Gladys Tompkins, a nursing sister from New Zealand, was thoroughly entertained by both the talk and the ensuing fireworks. Accusations flew back and forth. Katherine de Moubray was appalled at Ethel's manner, criticizing her for being tactless and sensationalizing. That night the boundary lines were inked-in on what would turn out to be two sides of a long-lasting feud between Ethel and her Red Cross supporters and Eleanor Hopkins and the women's leadership.

In spite of this brewing internecine war, the tea was a great success. The men heard of it through their inter-camp rumour mill, the "Coconut Radio" and it was written up in their camp newspaper, the *Changi Guardian*.

> [The women] had "a mighty good lunch" at tables arranged in the shape of a Cross with tablecloths—imitation and real. (There is not a bedsheet left in any of the cabins, we are told). Paper flowers and whatnot, all the frills and fancies that delight the feminine heart—or as many as could be gathered and fashioned out of odds and ends—and oh was there Easter party ... Red Cross section with Mrs. Mulvaney [sic] seemingly everywhere at the same time, was responsible for most of the organization.[13]

Of course some were less impressed with the tea for three hundred. In an Eeyore sort of way Katherine dismissed the event as "not worth the trouble." This was no feast, no high tea with hot-cross buns. As far as Katherine could tell "there was nothing but rations supper, only the buns were much bigger than usual." As for the promised luxury of a sit-down meal, she only noticed that "there was difficulty seating all. Friends didn't really get together."[14] Freddy wasn't so negative, in fact she conceded that the "the tables looked most civilized."[15] Gladys Tompkins fully agreed: "Red Cross corner beautiful. Red and white flowers made of paper, white cloths on table and seats for everyone."[16] The party food may have been no more than their daily ration but Ethel and others were able to see how they could alter their reality through hard work and the power of make-believe.

Although Ethel worked like a whirlwind to organize a sit-down meal in a place where chairs were as common as snow banks, what was most important to her was the sunrise service. Under her direction, the women chose a hymn and a choir leader, and rehearsed their positions and timing. After hearing of the upcoming event the men on the other side developed an elaborate plan so as many as possible could get a few seconds at a window overlooking the courtyard to witness the service. Just before dawn on Sunday, April 5, when the women were all in position, the men clinging to the bars at their windows and one Japanese guard looking on, they began, "Low in the grave He lay, Jesus my saviour." In Ethel's telling, by the time the sun had tipped up over the prison wall they reached the final line, "With a mighty triumph o're His foes He arose a victor from the dark domain."[17] Gladys Tompkins wasn't so sure they had the timing right, it was too early for the sunrise, and the women finished singing in the dark. Freddy thought the whole thing quite depressing and an expression of mere religious escapism, "a handful of women lifting their feeble voices to their Lord, rejoicing that He had arisen, asking for His protection, liberation and," she added, with her characteristically dry wit, "the return of their furniture, linen and clothes."[18]

Oblivious to the attitudes swirling around her, Ethel was buoyed by what happened next. After it was all over and the women were shuffling back into the jail, the unarmed guard, Ichichara, stepped over to her and quietly said, "Mrs. Mulvany, Christ did rise."[19] He reached into his pocket and took out a small orchid with its tangle of roots attached and handed it to her. For Ethel this gift was a faith-affirming miracle, never mind that these delicate-looking flowers grow with dandelion-like frequency and vigour in the warm humid climate, and who cared that it was just one of a number of flowers that the Japanese had sent in for the service? This orchid, given with those words, was a sign, and Ethel loved signs. She tended the flower with care and set about searching for a special home for it.

While Ethel was wildly busy with as many activities as she could manage, some within her orbit felt the strain of her hyperactivity. Freddy and Katherine made noises about their things going missing and ending up in the Red Cross corner. Finally they could not stand it any longer. Having no right to throw her out, they resorted to ostracizing her, or as Freddy expressed it, "Ethel sent to Coventry."[20] In May new arrangements were put in place, and Ethel folded up her mattress, packed her things, and left. She found two new roommates, Ellen MacKenzie and her two-year-old daughter Bridget, and moved into their room off the newly organized occupational therapy block. Ellen had lovely red hair that Ethel admired, knowing that with hair dyes in such short supply, it was all natural. In time that was the only feature she appreciated about the thirty-seven-year-old woman. Ellen was divorced and remarried to Hugh Campbell MacKenzie, a police officer now in Changi. Divorce was not something Ethel could accept and probably she was quite open about her prejudice. For now, though, the living arrangement would do.

Hodge Podge

1½ lbs neck of mutton

2 carrots

1 onion

2 qts cold water

½ turnip

parsley

½ parsnip

1 dessertspoon salt

pinch allspice

½ tspn pepper

½ cup rice

Cut the mutton into small pieces and put them in the saucepan with the water and salt. Boil gently for 2 hours, skim off the fat and add the vegetable dices and the rice. Boil for one hour longer. Just before taking from the fire add 1 tspn of chopped parsley.

Betty Millard, an Australian singer (b.1883)

Changi POW Cook Book

CHAPTER TEN

SHOPPING FOR FOOD AND ANSWERS

As soon as Ethel got into Changi, she was consumed with thoughts of getting out. She wanted to feel the freedom of sea breezes at her back and to breathe in something other than the acrid scent of too many women trapped in a world of damp concrete. But more than that, she needed food and so did everyone else around her. Her Red Cross corner had been slowly amassing funds, and she was determined to get to the markets in Singapore city and buy whatever food she could. To this end, day after day, sometimes morning, noon, and evening, Ethel went to the old jail office and petitioned camp commandant Lieutenant Okasaki Tetsuji for permission to buy food in Singapore city. The office loomed large to Ethel, an appearance enhanced by the sparse furnishings: one table, a swivel chair with slats at the back and a few shelves on the walls. Other than the shelves, the walls were "as bare as the back of your hand." A white circle, three feet in diameter, was painted on the floor about six feet in front of the desk. Prisoners were to stand in the middle of it and bow to the waist before speaking. Most of the time, Ethel left the commandant having gained nothing more than permission to return.

Okasaki, like the room, was scrupulously tidy. "Very dapper, very smart." As far as Ethel was concerned, he was "absolutely the bee's knees of smartness." She couldn't get over how immaculate he was. "His nails, his hands, his hair, just everything. He shaved sort of six weeks back each morning." She assumed from the fine material in his uniform that he must have been from a wealthy family. His sword was always at his side, and she could see from all the medals on his chest that he was a combat soldier. Like Ethel, he was thirty-eight years old and he too had been raised as a Presbyterian, although in Ethel's view, his Christian background didn't make him a good man. His silky smooth manners hid a nasty interior. "He hadn't a kind soul. I mean he wasn't a soul that went out to you and drew the best out of you. He was a hard man ... He could issue orders to shoot fifty and never turn a hair."[1] Hard though he was, her constant petitions gradually wore him down. Ethel finally got permission to go into Singapore using an old camouflaged five-ton army truck that had been abandoned by the British. She was careful to make sure Okasaki was not toying with her. "Is there an engine in it? May I have gas? Water? Oil? Grease? *And*, the key! And may our men service it for me?" In case she had forgotten something she asked permission to return. Ethel was proud, both that she could drive a truck and that she had finagled permission out of Okasaki. She had no idea that on the men's side of the jail Alexander Duncan-Wallace, a Singapore bank manager, and J.S. Long, an assistant police commissioner, had also managed to convince Okasaki that they needed to shop in town.[2] Likely Okasaki realized that allowing the prisoners to buy their own food was a financially astute move on his part.

Even though the truck at Ethel's disposal didn't have a Red Cross flag attached to it, as far as she was concerned she was acting in the name of the organization. She chose her friend, Anne Courtenay, to go with her. Just before climbing into the rumbling beast for the first time, she took off one of her Red Cross buttons and gave it to Anne, placing her second in command. With Anne in the passenger seat, Ethel "threw it into bull low" and stepped on the gas. After much screaming and rifle waving by a sentry who had not expected the truck to budge, a guard ran over, climbed in and sat between Ethel and Anne. He gripped his rifle between his knees, stuck his bayonet through the canvas roof, and they set off on their first shopping excursion in early May 1942, two months after their arrival in Changi.

Driving down a road leading away from the prison with the breeze blowing in their faces was a delicious taste of freedom for Ethel and Anne. War had taken its toll on the landscape but there were trees still standing, an ocean that still lapped at the shore, and the promise of food to come. It was good, for a moment. Then something caught Ethel's eye. She glanced to her right and saw a line of nine men standing in front of a pit with a firing squad behind them. "And there was such a bang in their backs that it threw them forward, and they go kick themselves into their own grave, and it's true they just go in kicking. Kicking themselves into their own grave." Too afraid to stop or catch the eye of the guard beside her, Ethel stared straight ahead and kept her foot on the gas.

* * *

For years after, she compulsively replayed the scene, trying to make sense of it. She concluded the men must have been Chinese. Their nationality is significant. China and Japan had been formally at war since 1937, but the fighting had gone on much longer. In 1931, Japan had invaded Manchuria with an eye to acquiring more land and access to the resources they needed to develop their empire. Although driven south, the Chinese resistance fought on, aided in part by money and supplies sent by Chinese Singaporeans. This Sino-Japanese war had dragged on far longer than the invaders had planned, and even Japanese civilians were living under food rationing because of the shortages it was causing.[3]

By the time Japan invaded Singapore the loathing of the Japanese soldiers for the mainland Chinese and those who had helped them was epic and fully reciprocated. Within three days of capitulation, the Japanese began screening out Chinese males for their assumed anti-Japanese activities. From February 18 until the end of March 1942 thousands of Chinese men and some women were massacred. This much is agreed upon. As for the numbers of lives lost, there is a cavernous discrepancy. Japanese sources acknowledge the deaths of 5,000 men while Chinese sources say 30,000 were killed in Singapore alone and another 20,000 on the Malay peninsula.[4] These killings became known as the *Sook Ching*—"purge through cleansing."

It is difficult to know what Ethel could truly have seen in the space of a glance as she drove by that day. Were there precisely nine men as she said in her taped conversations with Sidney Katz, or were there many rows of nine and she just didn't finish her description before jumping into another thought? There is reason to question her details here because in her unpublished memoir she said that there were over 300 awaiting execution. Possibly the rounded-off figure of 300 was an exaggeration spun out of a painful memory simply meant to signify *many*. After all, it is unlikely she could have counted 300 of anything in a mere glance and under these terrifying conditions. Sitting alone with pen and paper, Ethel's nightmarish memories may have so enveloped her that the numbers of the massacred multiplied in her mind as she wrote. And then there is the question of the date. If she remembered the day correctly, it was approximately five weeks after what is generally accepted as the end of the *Sook Ching*. She may have got her dates wrong, or possibly the killings continued and we are just not aware of it.

Other former POWs have written and told of barbarous acts for which they were the only ones who survived to bear witness and had the courage to do so either in writing, conversation, or in the courts of justice. Vivian Bullwinkel, an Australian nurse who was evacuated out of Singapore on the *Vyner Brooke*, told her war story, but long after living through the horror. When her ship was sunk on February 14, 1942, many of those who survived were captured and imprisoned, but twenty-three women and a number of men were gathered up by a patrol of Japanese soldiers on Bangka Island, east of Sumatra.[5] The men were taken to one side of the island and shot. Then the women were told to form a line and march into the sea and were similarly executed. Like all the others, Vivian Bullwinkel was hit, but her wound was not fatal. She feigned death until the Japanese had left and, with the help of locals, survived and eventually surrendered to the Japanese. Fearing reprisals for what is now known as the Bangka Island Massacre, she waited until after the war to speak publicly of her experiences.

The murderous nature of warfare continually seeps beyond the boundaries of present historical inquiry, forcing a constant re-examination of the past. In time and through continued study, the variation between the "facts" told by competing scholars about the *Sook Ching* may come closer to a meeting point. Meanwhile, the discrepancies in Ethel's versions of the killings she witnessed stand as markers generating questions about memory and truth.

* * *

Ethel had to keep herself together as she drove the truck the rest of the way into Singapore city. There were women and children back at the jail who needed her to succeed on this shopping trip. The murderous images had to be pushed to the back of her mind and attention paid to the world in front of her. Shopping was a lot more complicated in Singapore's market areas of Little India and Chinatown since Ethel had last been there. The Japanese had put into effect a rationing system covering most of the foods people wanted and required: rice, flour, bread—the starches needed to fill the corners of the belly; eggs, fish, and meat for protein; vegetables for vitamins; salt, essential in a hot climate; oil, a necessity for cooking; and sugar, to add grains of sweetness to an arduous life.[6] The distribution and trade of the rationed foods was controlled by monopolistic firms which unofficially decided how much rice went to the black market for their own profits, how much went to official traders, and what amount would be left over to fill ration cards. Singaporeans came to suffer from the same starvation-related diseases as the prisoners. During the occupation, however, the Japanese military were so careful to conserve stocks of rice for their own consumption that government warehouses were found full of it at the end of the war.[7]

Many of the shops in the market area now stood unnervingly empty. Anxious owners without the right connections never knew when or if they could get supplies to restock the shelves. The twisting streets of Little India were full of black marketeers selling food and cigarettes that had been hoarded or looted. These were the "mushroom millionaires" who had achieved overnight financial successes.[8] Queues that rivalled those Ethel was familiar with back at the jail were so long here that people, mainly women, earned a few cents by selling their spots in them.[9] Singaporean women who had lost husbands and homes in the war were forced to sell whatever they could—old shoes, bottles, chipped basins, and gramophone needles—to feed their children. As Ethel, Anne, and their gun-toting Japanese minder searched for what to buy through Chinatown alleyways, hawkers advertised their wares with hungry intensity. Crouched in the middle of lanes behind flimsy baskets and tin bowls they bargained over bananas, coconuts, garden greens, ginger roots, chillies, and, on that first shopping day, dried fish.

Ethel zeroed in on the *ikan puteh*, dried white fish. The little fat-bellied creatures were gutted and spread out to bake in the sun on the street, filling the air with their ripening scent. Ethel could take the stench of rotting fish guts but when she saw dogs walking over the drying fish on the side of the road and occasionally urinating on them she wavered about her choice. Still, they were cheap and available so she bought them by the shovelful. She realized that she and Anne made quite a sight pitching the smelly little fish into the truck. "Anne Courtenay you know, one of the belles of Singapore, I mean, well she'd be invited round to any house ... She was a club woman and so was I. Which means, why we never even picked up our own handkerchiefs, and there we were shovel by shovel of dried fish."

The drive back to the jail was likely a quiet one, without a word being spoken about the executions as they passed the spot where it had happened. Ethel had done what she had set out to do. The fish would give the prisoners protein and flavour, but for her it would be a flavour tainted with dog urine and horror. Whatever happened that day, Ethel had the courage to carry on with what became weekly shopping trips, each time with a different helper. Sugarcane, yams, and rotting bananas were added to the prison menu. Despite the blackened state, the bananas were eaten with gusto, skin and all. Another big hit with the women were Spratts puppy biscuits. With fewer dogs left alive on the island, Ethel was able to buy up the dog food at a reasonable price. Touted by the London-based company as an energy food to give dogs the strength to chase their own tails, it was the perfect snack for prisoners with nowhere to go.

Not only did Ethel buy food, she also sold goods on her excursions and bought toiletries and other necessities for the women. Her fellow prisoners gave her brooches, wedding bands, or little odds and ends to sell so they could afford to buy extra food or luxury items such as soap. While Ethel's shopping expeditions continued, not all was calm back at the jail. Even before her shopping trips began, Ethel presented a problem. Lucia Bach, a matter-of-fact music teacher originally from Wales, thoroughly appreciated Ethel's endless energy and forceful character, but was sure her friend didn't have a drop of common sense. It amazed her how Ethel managed to juggle all the special requests that the women thrust upon her. Mary Thomas also had doubts about Ethel. She didn't question Ethel's sincerity and personal generosity but realized that, "as a business woman she had one great weakness, which was that she could not keep accounts." Her "harum-scarum system ... caused much criticism in the camp."[10]

Ethel was barely managing, in much the same way as she had done when bringing the India exhibit to a close in Toronto during the summer of 1935. She'd had a mental breakdown then but was able to escape home to Denis in Cawnpore to recover, while her cousin Keith made sure all the columns in the account books added up. This time however, she was trapped in her haphazard world and soon became a lightning rod for criticism in the camp. Already within a month after arriving at Changi, Katherine de Moubray and Freddy had agreed that they could not trust her. Now they were sure that evidence was mounting up that in her overly exuberant enthusiasm Ethel was "shamelessly bagg[ing]" their belongings to sell for the Red Cross. Katherine noted in her diary some of the damning second and third-hand rumours she had heard about Ethel stealing.

> We hear that Margaret Webb had sold two diamond bracelets through her, and accidentally stumbled on the fact that there was a colossal discrepancy between what Ethel got for them and what she gave Margaret. Something in the region of $1,000. Also through Kate [Clark], very hush, hush we hear that the nips[11] consider she swindled them over something (possibly the Margaret Webb deal also) and now think that she is feigning madness to avoid them.[12]

Ethel was quickly becoming a polarizing character in the camp. Lucia Bach explains,

> Now she was strongly disliked by our camp commandant who is Dr. Hopkins ... She was a Mrs. and very elegant, rather beautiful and extremely clever. She was head of the committee and had a lot of power over us all. Personally I didn't like her very much. There was sort of always a feud between her and Mrs. Mulvaney [sic] because Mrs. Mulvaney [sic] was sort of favoured by the Japanese, was allowed to go out of the camp with certain members of the men's camp to do shopping for us ... She, as I say, was rather friendly with the Japanese. She spoke a little Japanese. And they preferred to communicate with our camp through her rather than our elected Commandant. We could say the camp was divided into two digs—those pro-Mulvaney [sic] and those anti ... They always thought she was lining her own nests.[13]

Ethel admitted that of all the rivalries in the camp, the worst was the one between herself and Eleanor Hopkins. Disgusted by the battles, Freddy claimed to be doing her best to steer a course between the two adversaries, yet she was not above cattily suggesting why the Japanese might have favoured Ethel—"She literally drooled over every Japanese sentry"—and Freddy's diary entries throughout May 1942 were studded with cutting remarks about Ethel, even accusing her of being a stool pigeon.[14] Weakened from a bout of dengue fever, a mosquito-borne virus well-described by its sobriquet, break-bone fever, Freddy had no patience to spare.

As would be expected, Freddy was more solicitous of Ethel in public. In the *Pow Wow*, the women's camp newspaper that she edited, she wrote a few words that take on a sly tone when set beside her diary entries.[15] "Something went 'Poof' and our human dynamo Mrs. Mulvany finally had to give in. Camp has not been the same since 'Mul' went into hospital and all are wishing her a speedy recovery."[16] Ethel was obviously running herself ragged. Clusters of painful boils—carbuncles—forced her into the camp hospital where she received some of the prisoners' limited supply of morphine to quell the pain. Considering Ethel's condition, Freddy softened for a moment in her diary. "Feel rather sorry for Ethel"—but her good will ended abruptly—"otherwise despise her lying, sneaking, selfish ways." She tried to raise her criticism up a notch from the personal by saying that she was not critical of Ethel herself, "but because she has made such a farce of the Red Cross." But personal criticism was rarely far from the surface. "[Ethel] smeared her personality over everything, pasting it down with more lies. But she did not do a darn thing to get Red Cross comforts into the camp."[17]

Katherine agreed. The two friends' diaries were in sync on this, mirroring the conversations they must have had about Ethel. Although exasperated no end with their now former roommate, talking about Ethel must have helped fill their days, relieve the boredom of prison life and, not insignificantly, provide a focus for their frustration at finding themselves trapped in a concrete hell. More than that, when two or three heads are bowed together to whisper about others, bonds of friendship are formed, boundaries defined, and the reputations of others are built up or torn down. This can happen at any time, but when the whispers occur within the echoing walls of a crowded jail where the resources required to sustain life are shrinking daily, the power of gossipers looms large.

Dorothy Nixon, a British librarian, became an object of interest by the anti-Mulvany contingent for the mere fact that she told one of the camp leaders, Cicely Williams, that she respected Ethel. Under these conditions that was enough to cause Cicely, an otherwise open-minded physician, to develop a withering opinion of Dorothy, at least according to Katherine, who wrote approvingly of this view while adding a dollop of her own condescension. "Cicely likes Dorothy Nixon, only find [sic] her so frightfully partisan. She appeared to have a brain, but she can hear no wrong against Ethel Mulvany and no good about anyone who's anti-Ethel Mulvany—pathetic."[18]

Like Freddy, Katherine was rather piously and repeatedly "prepared to feel sorry," "darn sorry," "naturally sorry" for Ethel. Still, she could not figure out what in all of Ethel's "wild activity" was actually legitimate Red Cross work—"any other name could have covered their activities."[19] It seems that in their exasperation she and Freddy were determined to run down anything Ethel called her Red Cross work. Ethel was well aware of this criticism in the camp and understood what her opponents were seeking from the Red Cross. "They wanted the Red Cross to come in in parcels and when it wasn't coming in in parcels, they didn't accept the idea that you could be Red Cross in other ways than just the ordinary formal way of serving." Because the parcels were not getting into camp, although through no fault of her own, the challenge for Ethel was in imagining new ways of fulfilling the mandate of the organization. To her the Red Cross meant the alleviation of human suffering wherever it's found, in whatever way it can be done. She lay awake at night wondering what could be done. There must be more to do.

Ethel had been faced with questions of how she was going to serve as a Red Cross representative as soon as the British were defeated in Singapore. After capitulation she had been approached by a Japanese commander who made her an offer he assumed she would not refuse. He told her that since she was affiliated with the Red Cross she would not have to be imprisoned but could live in the city with Hans Schweizer, the Swiss delegate of the International Red Cross in Singapore, who was a manager at the Swiss furniture manufacturer, Diethelm and Company. Ethel would have been quite happy to avoid jail, but before she accepted she asked the officer, "How many visits may I pay to our Allied prisoners of war, here on the Malayan peninsula?" He flatly stated there would be no visits. "Well Sir," she replied, "you are imprisoning me. Under Red Cross you may not accept what you cannot give, and I can stay out as long as I can give them relief and the alleviation of human suffering. But I cannot sit here and save my own self." Those were Ethel's rules and she stood by them knowing what the consequences might be.

* * *

Life outside the prison camps was pleasanter than inside, but it was not easy. Schweizer said that he and other neutral Europeans were forced to depend on the good will of "un-named market women, stall-holders and shop-keepers who supplied us with food and other necessities, often at reduced prices, although we could offer no reward."[20] The Japanese stuck to their word. They never allowed an outside Red Cross representative to visit the internees, but Schweizer did manage to get some comforts into the camps such as cigarettes, sweets, soap, and talcum powder. The items were welcomed but, except for the sweets, disappointingly inedible. Some women were even game to try eating the talcum powder which reportedly "had a sweetish queer taste and unless mixed with kanji [rice porridge], it set rather like cement, but it was something to eat for a change."[21]

Schweizer was able to arrange a shipment of food and medication in 1943, delivered in the Diethelm and Company van, which the military prisoners dubbed the Blue Angel. At that time the civilian prisoners received one Red Cross package to be divided among seven people. The next and only other package to arrive was in April 1945.

When these much anticipated British parcels arrived, the prisoners found the food furry with mould and crawling with weevils, understandable considering they were dated May 1942. Regardless of these additives, the contents would have gleamed like hope at the bottom of Pandora's Box. Tins of meat, bacon, salmon, syrup, sweet pudding, and cheese were enough to bring tears to the eyes and drench the tongue with saliva. Digging a little deeper they would have found dried milk, sugar, and tea—all the makings for the drink that characterized the British Empire.

The reason so pitifully few food packages arrived in the prison camps had nothing to do with Ethel on the inside or Schweizer on the outside. Although a signatory to the 1929 Convention Relative to the Treatment of Prisoners of War, otherwise known as the Geneva Convention, Japan did not ratify the agreement in 1931 as Germany and Italy had. This meant the Japanese were not bound by international agreement to consider the protection and rights of prisoners of war. The Red Cross did send parcels to the East but few shipments were accepted and of those that were, many of the supplies never made it to the intended recipients. After the war, warehouses in Singapore were found full of Red Cross parcels that the Japanese had chosen not to give to the prisoners.[22]

Pumpkin Scones

2/3 cup mashed pumpkin (cooked)

pinch of salt

fat

2 cups self-raising flour

milk

egg (optional)

Mix with knife. Bake in oven for
10 minutes.

Audrey Katherine Goodridge
(b. 1920)

Goodridge was married to Capt. R
Goodridge and gave birth in Changi
to daughter, Penelope (April 1,
1942). All three survived the war.

Changi POW Cook Book

CHAPTER ELEVEN

SHOP FOR SOME PUMPKINS IN STALL 38

Many within the Chinese community who survived the slaughter of the *Sook Ching* became part of an underground movement. They were sympathetic to the plight of the prisoners and helped them in ways they could, providing money, food, radio parts, and that most valuable of commodities, news.[1] Like many prisoners, Ethel had a network of friends outside the prison walls with whom she connected in ingenious ways. She rarely missed an opportunity for contact, even if it appeared morbid. When a prisoner died, she, Euphemia Redfearn, and Lucia Bach would gather together to roll leaves into little bundles they then fashioned into funeral wreaths. Sure that the dead would be delighted to help out their fellows one last time, the women inserted messages in the leaves, as many as they could without risking detection. Outwitting the Japanese was a joy at any time, and in this case it was doubled because the three of them managed to get extra food in the process. Early on in their wreath-making activities, Lucia had slyly convinced the ghost-fearing guards that the women must have begonias for decoration, insisting the flowers were needed to calm the spirits of the dead. The women used most of the bitter tasting blossoms, chock full of vitamin C, to quiet their own demons of hunger.

When the gravedigger, also part of the underground network, came to the jail to retrieve the dead bodies, he picked up the decorative wreaths. During the night the Chinese involved in the resistance movement took the wreaths from the fresh graves in the cemetery and replaced them with similar ones. The cemetery had been used as a place for secret communications, even before the occupation, when Chinese communists had hidden a transmitting device there.[2] The wreaths with notes went to a tiny coffin shop where caskets, some empty and some filled with the dead, were piled high. While hired mourners outside the shop moaned and cried for departed souls, the coffin shop owner would slip down the street to Mr. Fong, the cobbler in the stall on the corner, and hand over the notes. Return messages for the prisoners were placed in a hole dug out from the sole of shoes brought in for repair by Ethel or someone from the men's side of Changi. Serving as a leather envelope, the sole would be nailed back in place with the note inside.

Seong, a wealthy Chinese merchant who had made his fortune in foods and spices before the war, sent war news to the prisoners through intricate systems like this one. Ethel knew that Seong, whom she had met while canvassing for the Malayan Churchill Tank Fund, had been trying to get in touch with her. Her shopping days allowed for chance encounters with old friends, so she might have expected to run into him, but not in the way that occurred on one particular shopping day in mid-June, 1942.

The Japanese had begun tightening the rules around her excursions into town. They insisted that before the shoppers left the prisoners had to decide what food they wanted and request permission from the officials to purchase that alone. There had been an intense debate on the morning of that day's outing of whether to buy sugarcane or pumpkins, two foods that were likely to be in the market that time of year. Cane won out, mainly for reasons of irresistible sweetness and coveted calories. Also, being long and thin, it was easier to fit more in the truck than rounded pumpkins, which, everyone agreed, had far too much empty space in their middles.

The shopping began in the regular way, with Ethel and the woman she had chosen to be her companion that week winding their way through hot crowded streets bordered by wooden stalls and filled with hawkers squatting on the ground beside their produce. Their guard was just two steps ahead of them when suddenly a beggar stepped directly into Ethel's path. He was covered in black shaggy rags but it was his bare feet that caught her eye. Nearly two decades later, while talking to Sidney Katz, she clearly recalled how, "His feet were all splayed out. I remember the big toe, how it kind of went apart from the others." When she finally looked up she realized with shock that it was Seong in front of her disguised as a beggar. Not wanting to let on that she knew who he was, she made a point of angrily shoving him aside, admonishing him to get out of her way. He leaned into her and with a voice Ethel likened to a low moan he slurred out, "Shopforsomepumpkinsinstall38." As he spoke she felt him push something—she didn't know what—into her pocket.

"Talk about Houdini. He did it just as well as Houdini ever could've done it." As she headed towards stall 38 in the market, she didn't dare look at the mysterious lump in her pocket. Trying her best to appear calm, she checked over the sugarcane and fruit and took time to "chew the rag" with the sellers, hoping her guard would not sense her nervousness and grow suspicious. What was she going to say to the Japanese officials back at Changi when she returned with pumpkins rather than the sugarcane she was supposed to buy? No one could ever be sure what the price of a small infraction might be. She went ahead anyway and bought the pumpkins from the Chinese stall owner, telling him how many she wanted and letting him choose which ones. Her fellow shopper must have wondered what was going on, and no doubt Ethel won her cooperation with some "trust me" glances. The two of them loaded up the pumpkins and Ethel drove the truck to Changi as if it were her "prize filly," agonizing all the way that some of these mysteriously special pumpkins might bounce out as she drove over the bumpy road.

When she got back to the jail she had to peel herself out of the truck. Her nervous sweat had soaked right through her dress and stained the seat with the shape of her body. There was no choice now but to tightly grip her panic and keep going. On this occasion, as happened every so often, a selection of men had been escorted in by armed Sikh guards to help unload the produce and hand it over to the women. The job was a coveted one. Messages had been secreted to the men's side beforehand to tell them which women would be on that day's work detail so that they could organize who of their number would be sent over. It was a chance for husbands and wives to lay eyes on each other, exchange a few words, maybe touch hands, and it made all the difference in the world to those involved.[3]

To Ethel's amazement, as the pumpkins were passed out of the truck from man to woman, the Japanese never asked why there was no sugarcane and she remained tight-lipped. The last woman in line carried the produce down into the cool dungeon, which Ethel used as a storeroom for the Red Cross. The path from the unloading yard through the prison and down to the dungeon was guarded by both the Japanese and about fifty women who made sure none of the pumpkins were spirited into the cell blocks. Ethel waited at the dungeon with her key. The only other key was kept by the Japanese, so whatever contraband was discovered in that room was on her. She unlocked the door and pointed out where the pumpkins were to be put. By this time not only was she soaked in sweat, she had a searing headache. Too anxious to search the pumpkins to find out why Seong had told her to buy them, she locked the door and shut herself in the latrine, the only private spot in the entire prison. She sat still for a time, checking to see if anyone was spying on her. "It was," she explained, "a thin latrine. In a prison everything is thin." When the coast was clear, she slowly slid her hand into her pocket and carefully pulled out the bundle. It was money, "blinking great wads of money.

Thirty-eight thousand dollars ... about twenty thousand Canadian" carefully tied together with black string.[4]

The next morning, after finishing an almost imaginary breakfast, she went back to the dungeon, terrified about being caught with some forbidden substance. Feeling all around each of the pumpkins, she discovered that a wire had been used to cut through the top of fifty of them. The insides, far from being empty, were filled with money. Somehow the stems had been glued back in place. Ethel figured only God knew what kind of glue could cause two moist substances to adhere; certainly she had no idea what it could be. She quickly pulled all the money out and put it in a woolsack she had found in the dungeon, then tucked it right behind the door, hoping that would be the last place anyone would think of looking. She had been too scared to count properly and wasn't sure how much there was. They were Straits dollars, that she knew, but the figure that stuck in her head blurred over the vast expanse between three and five million. Either one would have been a shocking amount of money for anyone to have, but Ethel could hardly believe that she, a Manitoulin Islander, had her hands on that much. It was a dangerous blessing and she didn't want that kind of responsibility. She wanted to get out of there and pretend, forget, lose track, not say anything. By her reasoning it would be a good thing to consciously mix up her own thinking. If the whole thing wasn't straight in her own head she couldn't possibly tell the Japanese anything resembling the truth if they found the money and started questioning her.

Ethel wasn't the only one to be in possession of great sums of money. Prisoners often received smuggled cash from secret supporters in town. Mary Thomas estimated that most of the money the prisoners used to buy extra food was smuggled into the camp by Chinese sympathizers at great risk to themselves.[5] However much Ethel may have insisted that her confusion was part of a plan, she knew well enough that she was spinning out of control. The anxiety she felt, the profuse sweating, headache, confusion, and panic, although understandable under the circumstances, were part of a growing mania which, according to those close to her, had been ramping up over the months. Freddy wrote in her diary, "Ethel ... is energetically unwinding the Red Cross ... Some are suggesting a hanging." A few months later there was less humour in her words: "Ethel making a darned fool of herself. Unfortunately there have been signs of her old trouble."[6]

As she was putting the money in the woolsack, Ethel wondered if she should seek out the help of a doctor, someone to counsel her, but she quickly scolded herself. "No Sir, you're not going to be *chicken* like that." She tied up the sack with twine and locked the door to the dungeon behind her and, instead of going to a doctor, went to see Georgina White, better known as Knobbsie. Ethel had a deep respect for this wise British woman, believing she was the only person in the camp who never spoke ill of others, no matter what side they fought on or where they came from. Knobbsie, "so thin you could see every knob on her backbone," and her husband, Graham White, an Anglican archdeacon interned on the other side of the jail, were much appreciated at Changi for their kindness and were greatly mourned when both died in prison in 1945.

Ethel knew that Knobbsie would be able to give her guidance through their shared faith. What she needed at that moment was a limit to her fear. She needed to have an answer to the question that clawed at the back of everyone's mind: "Where is this going to end?" Knobbsie's reply helped steady Ethel. With her signature smile she gently reminded Ethel of the Bible story from Matthew 18:12. "If a man have an hundred sheep, and one of them be gone astray, doth he not leave the ninety and nine, and goeth into the mountains, and seeketh that which is gone astray?"

Ethel believed in a divine protector. In a quiet moment she later pulled out her little red-covered New Testament bible she had brought with her, found the passage and underlined it. The words calmed her, bolstering her faith that somehow her God would keep her safe. Ethel's faith didn't need proof, but it would have been easy enough to view all the money she had received as just that. Now she could buy so much more food and so many other necessities for the prisoners.

* * *

Although rattled to the core, Ethel kept on with her shopping trips. She bought rice polishings, the brown husks covering the grains of rice that were removed to produce the expensive white rice. The polishings, often swept up off granary floors, were mixed with broken and rotting grains of rice, sand, and maggots. The additions to the polishings may have been close to inedible but Ethel knew that at least the brown husks were healthy. They were like the wheat bran back home on Manitoulin farms that was fed to the pigs. The same thing happened in Malaya; livestock were often the recipients of the minerals and fibres in the rice polishings. During the war however, both prisoners and the local inhabitants of Singapore ate the polishings which, in addition to being nutritious, were also cheap.

Ethel bought gooey, orange-coloured raw palm oil, peanuts, and soy beans. When she found big Chinese radishes the prisoners ate both the long white root and the tops, cooked or raw. In fact they ate everything but the dirt and, she admitted, no one was too particular about that. The shopping list went on: *gula malaca*, a richly flavoured palm sugar; *blachang*, a paste made of dried shrimp mixed with chilli. The paste smelled to high heaven, but she knew, not only "did it spice up food ... it's absolutely jam banged full of vitamins."

When eating, it became a point of pride for many of the women to behave as if they were attending a dinner party. They pulled out their best manners and used them to imagine away their wretched surroundings. This was particularly true for Ethel when she ate *blachang*. Each serving was treated with the regard paid to precious threads of golden saffron. She put her ration on a leaf, then, using a sliver of bamboo, delicately dipped into it adding this morsel of hot fishy zest to the edge of her container of *bayam* soup. After sipping through the seasoned portion she repeated the process until all was gone. There was an understanding among the women that the edifice of their lives was supported by decorum, or as Ethel put it, "You have to be nice about yourself." Sticking to social graces prevented them from devolving into the sub-human creatures that some of their jailors took them for. That, and sharing food with precise equality, helped maintain at least a working veneer of respect between them as they coped with constantly diminishing resources.

The mechanics of sharing equally were challenging. They included counting the number of grains of sugar in a teaspoon or, as Ethel found out, deciding how to ration sardines among prisoners who were packed in as tightly as the fish. She came by a tin of North American sardines at the market. One of her Chinese friends had found it and, knowing she was Canadian, had made sure it was available for her to buy. Ethel gathered together her group of friends, her *konsi*, of about five or six, and then invited a few more so they could have a sardine party. Each received a bite of fish and a sip of the salty fish oil. To make everything fair, names were checked off a list ensuring no one tried to sneak seconds. While Ethel walked around offering her fat-rich treat like a fancy hors d'oeuvre she nattered on about the glories of Canada. She knew no one was listening, but for a few minutes her stories, scented with fish oil, carried her all the way back to Manitoulin. She spoke of what she would do, how she would go to church, the dress that she would wear, what it would feel like to sit in her pew, but mainly about what she would eat. She made a pact with herself—"When I get home I'll always have a tin of Pedikodiak sardines in the cupboard." Relating this story to Sid in 1961, she told him to look in her cupboard: "there's three tins right there. I don't eat them often, but I have them, just in case."

Many of the women were deeply grateful for all of Ethel's shopping efforts. Iris Parfitt used her artistic skills to paint a Christmas card of thanks in 1942. On the front was written, "Christmas Greetings to Mrs. Mulvaney [sic] from the many who have benefited by the unstinted trouble she has taken to supply our needs."[7] Under the words, two hands are pictured gripping the corners of a brown shopping bag out of which pour all the valuables

Christmas card to Ethel Mulvany from thankful fellow prisoners, 1942. Pioneer Museum, Mindemoya, Manitoulin.

that made such a difference to prison life: paint brushes, ink, soap, pineapple, Malaysian cigarettes, underwear, coffee, thread, playing cards, and the tins of food that had an almost magical power to relieve anxiety about the future. Below, a pair of hands reach eagerly towards the tumbling treasures. Inside the card are the signatures of many appreciative women. Those "shopping days," said Mary Thomas, "gave us one of the greatest privileges we ever enjoyed."[8] Ethel cherished her card. When things got bad it was always there to remind her that no matter what she had gone through on those shopping days, she had been able to diminish some of the suffering in the camp.

Some however, were not so impressed with Ethel's shopping days. Just after New Year's, Gladys Tompkins, who had grown to

139

respect Ethel over their months in prison, was shocked when she
heard the news—

> terrific bombshell when Mulvany walked in and showed a
> printed notice which had been handed to her and signed by
> Dr. Johns to say he had been to the Japs complaining that she
> interfered with the camp fatigues etc ... It just seemed incredible
> that one British person would go to our enemy and tell tales. Not
> to mention a man to tell tales on a woman. [9]

The women within earshot of this announcement either knew
who Brian Maurice Johns was and were aware of his reputation
or quickly found out from those who did. The New Zealand-born
surgeon had been head commandant on the men's side since
July. He likely came up against Ethel in his efforts to get the men
needed supplies from outside the prison. Everything about her, her
haphazard accounting, her intuitive shopping style and her, at times,
abrasively confident manner, would have grated on him. As a man, a
successful surgeon, and an elected leader with a forceful nature, he
was accustomed to getting his way, to the point that he was known
as "The Man Who Played God."[10] Powerful though he was, Johns may
not have fully realized the nature of the woman he was deriding nor
the amount of support she had, even among the men. Tompkins
noted in her diary that after news of Johns's complaint against Ethel
came out, one thousand of the men asked him to resign and that the
whole of the men's executive quit en masse.[11] In the end the fuss was
smoothed over. Johns remained in his position as commandant until
he was ousted by the Japanese in April 1943, and Ethel carried on
shopping with the aid of her gifted fortune, bringing all manner of
goods back to the jail.

Posy Pudding

4 oz self-raising flour

4 oz fine soft breadcrumbs

3 oz shredded suet

½ tspn salt

1 egg

½ cup raisins

2 tbspns marmalade

2 tbspns sugar

milk to moisten

Decorate well-greased basin by pressing raisins firmly against sides and bottom. Sift flour, salt, and sugar. Mix in breadcrumbs and suet. Add marmalade to egg and add to dry ingredients with sufficient milk to make stiff batter. Place in basin. Cover with greased paper. Steam 2½ hours.

Marmalade Sauce

1 large tbspn marmalade

1 tspn cornflour (blended with little cold water)

juice and rind of ½ lemon

1 cup water

1 tbspn sugar

Simmer water, lemon rind, and marmalade for five minutes. Mix sugar and cornflour with a little cold water and stir in. Add lemon juice and boil for 5 minutes. Strain. Serve.

Changi POW Cook Book

CHAPTER TWELVE

THE LOGIC OF A DREAM

Even while Ethel was still able to go shopping in Singapore city—an activity which would come to an abrupt end in October of 1943—it didn't matter how many pumpkins, pieces of sugarcane, shovelfuls of dried fish, or extra eggs she brought in, it was never enough to satisfy her hunger. She felt the power that the aching emptiness in the belly could exert over a person: "of all the pains you have ever had in your life there is nothing like that debilitating, that going-down-the-valley-one-by-one pain of hunger. There's nothing stronger. There is nothing where the body is more vulnerable to absolute capitulation, to any vice." There were young women Ethel knew of in the prison whose youth and beauty could be used as a commodity to gain food. Ethel was sad for the consequences such an exchange was likely to have on them, but not for a moment did she look down upon them for having sex with the Japanese guards to survive. She knew circumstances had cornered them, and she was fully prepared to admit she would have done the same but for the fact that "I was old. I was thirty-eight, forty and didn't have the opportunity they did."

No one was short on hunger in Changi, but Ethel may have felt its pain more acutely than some others for the simple reason she was burning through precious calories at an extreme rate with her constant whirlwind of activities. If she was experiencing a manic phase of her illness, and it certainly appears that way, not only would she have been whirring about all day, but many of her nights would have been caught up in busy wakefulness, as was the case on one particularly long night. She had been lying on her mattress with a roiling, empty stomach and, in the relative quiet of darkness, she recalled a poem about food. Lyrical couplets conjured up delicious images of roasted meats and simmering stews. She prodded her memory for more and rhyming words began popping out, one pulling on the other, each offering their own platter brimming with delectables, ranging from savoury to sweet. Not long after, she thought of the poem again while in the midst of one of the habitual afternoon conversations the women had about food as they gathered in the courtyard. With their chores done in the morning, they changed their clothes after lunch and came to these gatherings dressed in the best they had for what became their own version of the Mad Hatter's tea party. In their foreplay to illusory feasting some decorated their prison clothes with imaginary corsages while others brought descriptions of flowers for a centrepiece. "I would have wayside daisies with sprigs of fern," said Ethel's friend Euphemia Redfearn. Engaged with their collective dream, others smoothed an invisible cloth over a pretend table and marked each place with a plate, carefully laying the fork by the napkin, the knife and spoon just so on the other side of the plate, with a cup and saucer for the tea. Ethel imagined little salt and pepper dishes on the table like the ones her Aunt Esther had given her years before. Of course, no table would be complete without the luxury of sugar and cream for the tea and a butter plate with its own soft-edged knife.

The poem hovering beneath all of Ethel's imaginings was "The Depression Ends" by Ned Pratt from his collection, *Many Moods*. Not one to hold back, she told anyone who would listen about how

Ned had set his poetic table during the hungriest years of the Great Depression. In his fantasy he imagined what he would do if only he had the magic "rod of Prospero for an hour:"

Having no reason for my scheme
Beyond the logic of a dream
To change a world predestinate
From the eternal loom of fate
I'd realize my mad chimera
By smashing distaff and the spinner,
And usher in the golden era
With an apocalyptic dinner.
I'd place a table in the skies
No earthly mind could visualize

The table he places under a canopy of stars is laden with sumptuous dishes reserved exclusively for the world's destitute. The invitees—"The most unkempt and motley throng / Ever described in tale or song ... all the gaunt, the cavern-cheeked, / The waifs whose tightened belts declare / The thinness of their daily fare"—looked much like the women of Changi, more so than the women's vanity would have appreciated. Ethel might not have recited that part, but she recalled Pratt's mention of "the dust of flour-bins" on offer to those waiting in the breadlines of the Great Depression, like the scraps served to those who waited in prison camp queues. What inspired Ethel, though, were the rich, delicious flavours that were conjured up by the menu on offer, especially the barbecued meats, fish, and fowl that formed the centre of the feast and the soufflés, syllabubs, dumplings, and trifles that graced the end of the meal.

If, as the saying goes, hunger is the best sauce, the pleasure Ethel got from reciting Ned Pratt's delicious concoctions must have been shared by the women of Changi as they listened to her. But not everyone liked discussing food all the time. In a *Pow Wow* article, the women's camp newspaper, from June 17, 1942, entitled "Food—What is it?" Freddy Bloom alluded to all the food talk going on in camp. "Some of us supplement our present meager fare by discussing delicious concoctions of former days, and exchanging special recipes of favourite dishes—while others turn away from such conversations with a hungry groan, to distract our thoughts on higher planes."[1] Likely Freddy included herself with the latter group, but by the time she wrote her editorial on December 9, she and others had found their own, P.G. Wodehouse version of these make-believe get togethers.

> Our favorite game in Changi is going to dinner parties when we get out. We have been to stacks of them especially during quiet hour in the afternoon. The dinners are usually given in the Ancestral Home of Influential Friends. There is usually a charming hostess and the man on our left is invariably a Handsome Intelligent Man of Means.[2]

In Freddy's account the emphasis is more on witty repartee and the usual attire—"a simple little black Alexis model and sable"— than what is found on the plate. Nevertheless, these fabricated dinner parties were obviously satisfying. Freddy's more utilitarian side regarding hunger is reflected in the "Changi Cookery hints" section of the women's newspaper. Readers were advised not to throw out any prune stones "without first cracking them for the kernels. These are good alone or make a very palatable addition to fried savory rice."[3] The list continued: pineapple skin can be boiled to make juice, papaya seeds add a mustardy flavour to rice, save all your cheese rinds and spinach stems. Weekly detailed analysis of such necessities as calcium, phosphorus, iodine, and iron amino acids graced the newspaper. If the readers ignored this information they did so at their own peril.

Those who were moved to rely on the delights of fiction, as well as the science of nutrition to survive, gathered in small groups with Ethel and her companions around an empty space in a bare yard to talk about foods they had no hope of tasting. The conversations always began with the question, "What would *you* serve?" and the ideas flowed from there. Repeatedly, the would-be cooks started their fantasy meals with the same fundamental essence of their own edible culture, bread and butter. This hankered-after staple with its creamy yellow topping evoked all kinds of memories. For Mary Thomas, the deep cravings she had for the crusty wholemeal bread of her home in the Cotswold hills of Gloucestershire turned her thoughts all the way back to the wheat that was ground at the local mill to make the flour her mother used. She remembered flour bins like the ones Pratt wrote of standing in the kitchen of their six-hundred-year-old house. In her mind's eye she saw the two scores in the crust of each loaf through which steam would escape from the fluffy innards, filling the air with the beckoning smell of fresh warm bread.[4]

Ethel's thoughts often lingered on butter and how her mother made it in the old churn in the kitchen of their Manitoulin home. Other cooks delved into memories of their sideboards pulling out just the right platters on which to serve their offerings. Some took care to garnish the food they dreamt of, attentive to colour and arrangement. When the American Jean Hogg spoke of the rice casserole she would cook, she added that it was best turned out on a large serving dish. That way guests would be treated to the contrast of orange carrots and black raisins with the juicy, simmered meat crowning the whole affair. Others got right down to the business of producing the most rib-sticking dish they could think of. For one woman that was a pork pie enriched with a cup of lard.

As the women talked, their mouths began to water and soon they started having to swallow their saliva. After these sessions it dawned on Ethel that she was left with the odd but very pleasant sensation of having actually eaten. She was sure it was all the saliva she was swallowing and it reminded her of the childhood spitting contests she used to have with her younger sister Margaret. The two of them would lie about in the branches of the old apple tree in the yard swirling spit around in their mouths, trying their best to build up a nice fat glob of it, one that would be sure to fly the farthest. She and Margaret may not have been swallowing their spit but they certainly could make a lot of it and so could the hungry prisoners. All they had to do was talk about food. She insisted that all that talking and swallowing felt good. "Many of us slept with a feeling of having had a meal."

Ethel's hypothesis was unusually put but not far off the mark. Science writer Sharman Apt Russell describes a similar theory in her book *Hunger: An Unnatural History* of how the process of digestion can begin with the mere thought of food. Chemical messages flow through the cerebral cortex to nerve cells that in turn send messages to the stomach and pancreas that then produce digestive acids and mucus. Salivary glands are stimulated, the mouth waters, and the body is primed. Ethel articulated what many other prisoners of war experienced in their gut. Thinking and talking about food and the production of meals made the prisoners feel markedly better and more alive.

As the imprisoned women added more and more details to their mouth-watering fabrications, they became more disciplined in their food talk. Descriptions of table-ready dishes gradually backed up to include lists of ingredients, measurements, and cooking instructions. Ethel thought it was all well and good to enjoy these discussions, but she wanted more. She insisted the cooks must write down their recipes "because when you don't put something down, you reckon it's only going into the air, so you want to think it, and then you want to commit it to paper." Paper was scarce, but with some luck she discovered a pile of old *Strait's Times* of Singapore in one corner of the prison's humid dungeon.

The women carefully ripped off the blank margins surrounding each page of damp newsprint. With pencil stubs gathered from here and there they recorded their recipes, perhaps using their knee for a writing surface if they were squatting, or having a friend turn around and using her back to write on the long tails of paper. Ethel gathered the strips and when she had quite a bundle she realized she needed a better way to organize the recipes. So she went to the Japanese authorities, explained her idea for a cookbook and asked for more paper. They supplied her with two unused ledger books, one red and one blue, into which the recipes could be transcribed. Intentional or not, their generosity had an exquisite edge to it. The hard-covered books had been designed by the former British jailors to keep track of their prisoners' food at a time when the world was ordered differently, and Britain was still calling the shots.

Each sturdy page of the large blue accounts book was printed with bureaucratically precise red ink columns separating date, quantity received, quantity issued, balance, and balance brought forward. Labelled tabs running down the side tell of a culinary mix of British and Eastern foods that were offered in the prison: tamarind, ghee, white sugar, Chinese soi, hops, condensed milk, tea, coconut oil, flour. While the women would have sold their grandmother's jewels (and eventually did) to have had any of these items in their daily diet, these were not their dream foods. Some hungry soul, running her finger down the tabs, crossed them all out and replaced them with: biscuits, breads, buns, puddings and sweets, meat dishes, cocktails, and savouries.

Winifred Zelie Barr had the honour of being the first to write a recipe in this ledger book. With lacey scrolls and even letters that had been moulded over her career as a school teacher, the sixty-six-year-old set down her instructions for June Biscuits. Next in line was Ethel's first shopping partner, Anne Courtenay. She was all business, dashing off her paragraph with minimal reference to amounts, times, or temperatures, just a quick mention of what the soda bread dough should feel like when the mixture is right. Audrey Goodridge wrote pages and pages in clear, small letters that uniformly leaned to the left. Then came the plump messy script of twenty-five-year-old Betty Smalley. The book was passed around from one cook to another so they could transcribe their dream foods into a more permanent form. As a healthy treat, the job of copying some of the recipes was given to women who were hospitalized but still able and needing a task and a purpose to occupy themselves. Death was so closely linked with a lack of food that Ethel believed even an imaginary feast was medicinal. To that end she was convinced that recipe writing should

Handwritten recipes in log book, Changi Jail, 1942. Pioneer Museum, Mindemoya, Manitoulin.

be indulged any time the pain of hunger became acute. Even when hunger went beyond pain, Ethel was sure that culinary dreams could "galvanize people by presenting them with a table in the skies."

The women prisoners were not the only ones being galvanized by food talk. On the men's side of Changi Jail, Campbell Newington, who had been an inquisitive consumer of local fare during his time as a planter in Malaya, was motivated to write down each recipe he could remember. Later, when all the prisoners were moved to Sime Road camp in May 1944, he solicited contributions to his collection. He appealed to the women, still segregated from the men, via the inter-camp postal service. The Japanese had loosened their grip just a little by then and allowed the exchange of mail between the two sides. It was censored, but no one seemed to fuss about the exchange of a few cookery tips for flower and vegetable seeds and, most importantly, for tasty new recipes.

Even with all these new flavours and food descriptions to add to his collection, Newington wanted more, so he started up a Gourmet's

Club. For an hour a week, he and some of his fellow male prisoners gathered around a box on which they balanced a tired sheet of asbestos—little did they know or maybe even care what that might do to them—and, dressed in no more than their thread-bare loin cloths, they created formal dinners with complete menus served on tables elegantly set with words.

Another POW, in faraway Dresden, Germany, was similarly dreaming of his favourite dishes and would one day include them in a short story called "Guns Before Butter." Kurt Vonnegut spent the last half year of the European war as a prisoner, much of it working in an underground slaughter house. He wrote the hunger he saw, felt, and would never forget. His character Kniptash lovingly described what his first meal back in the States would be:

> "First," said Kniptash fiercely, "I'm going to order me a dozen pancakes. That's what I said, Lady," he said, addressing an imaginary waitress, "twelve! Then I'm going to have 'em stack 'em up with a fried egg between each one. Then you know what I'm going to do?"

> "Pour honey over 'em" said Coleman. He shared Kniptash's brutish appetite.[5]

Just over two hundred kilometres from Dresden, Ruth Kluger was also deeply engaged in abundantly rich food talk with her companions in Poland's Christianstadt labour camp. "A favourite game was to surpass each other with the recital of generous amounts of butter, eggs, and sugar in fantasy baking contests."[6] For Susan E. Cernyak-Spatz, a survivor of the concentration camps of both Terezin and Auschwitz, Poland, this activity was all about practicality. "We called it cooking with the mouth." [7]

American Colonel Chick Fowler, imprisoned in Bilibid Jail, Manila, cooked with his pen as well as his mouth. He carefully copied the treasured recipes his fellow prisoners were eager to share with him. The contributors were from all parts of Asia, Britain, and Australia.

Some wrote simply, some with lyrical detail, but none as poetically as the Welsh sailor who contributed "Brandy Pottage—Welsh":

> A good chicken, a noble piece of ham, and a little shoulder of lamb,
> Small to have the least of grease.
> And then a paste of the roe of trout with cream,
> A bit of butter and the yolk of an egg, whipped light and poured in
> When the chicken, proud with a stuffing of sage and thyme
> Has been elbowing the lamb and ham in an earthenware pot
> Till all three are as tender as the heart of a mother
> Then ...

Then in went the vegetables and after a time, "noggins" of brandy and home-brewed ale. When it was done he advised the cook, "Drink the liquor, praise God, and start upon the chicken."[8]

In 1946, Fowler's aunt Dorothy Wagner published her nephew's collection of recipes, written on flattened out envelopes, testing each one and adding her own commentary. The "English translation" of brandy pottage advised readers, "This dish must not be hurried or trifled with and it should only be prepared for people you love and whose palates you esteem, for an occasion worthy of remembrance." In doing so "you will understand how the unknown Welsh sailor could feed his spirit on the memory of Brandy Pottage."[9]

Ethel Mulvany, by organizing the collection of recipes she and the other Changi women were dreaming of, was participating in a quiet, deeply human act of resistance, just as starving prisoners throughout a world at war were doing. Surrounded, trapped, slowly being squeezed of life, she and others were fighting back with their imaginations as much to keep hold of their dignity and humanity as to keep their bodies alive for another day. Their communal food fantasies could hardly take their hunger away; what they succeeded in doing was taking the prisoners away from their hunger. For an hour or two each day the women of Changi escaped the prison while they remembered and shared their dreams. Their stories were a form of alchemy, that ancient art of transformation.

The war was not over, but some of the suffering could be held at bay, at least for a time.

Colcannon

Boil potatoes. Mash. Add pepper,
salt, and plenty of spring onions.
Add sufficient fresh milk to make
nice consistency. Serve piping hot—
making hole in centre and adding
large helping of butter.

Changi POW Cook Book

Traditional Irish Song

Did you ever eat Colcannon, made from
lovely pickled cream

With the greens and scallions mingled
like a picture in a dream?

Did you ever make a hole on top to hold
the melting flake

Or the creamy flavoured butter that your
mother used to make?

Chorus:

Yes you did, so you did, so did he and so
did I.

And the more I think about it, sure, the
nearer I'm to cry.

Oh, wasn't it the happy days when
troubles we had not,

And our mothers made Colcannon in the
little skillet pot.

CHAPTER THIRTEEN

RECIPES OF LONGING

Rivers of butter have flowed down miniature mashed potato mountains on children's dinner plates for generations. The rich layer of nostalgia and well-known song accompanying this utterly basic recipe for colcannon must have momentarily cocooned the contributor as she wrote it down. She, and all the other contributors, stepped into another world filled with the scent and images of home and food shared with family as they recalled what they could of the ingredients, times, temperatures, and quantities required for their recipes. Only occasionally did Ethel jot down personal notes beside a recipe in the ledger books. Alongside Swiss salad was an epitaph to her best friend, "W.W. Redfearn—Tough—my beloved friend. She died a POW and so did her husband. Her only son was killed in battle." Ethel thought the world of Euphemia Redfearn who, no matter the circumstances, always put on a brave face. The tiny, curly-haired Euphemia had learned resilience early on while growing up the youngest of eleven children in the ragged gold rush town of Clunes, north-west of Melbourne. Even weakened with tuberculosis and lying in the camp hospital she didn't complain but, instead, asked Ethel to serve her descriptions of delectable meals.

More than sixty women participated in the hungry dreamers' recipe collection, some providing just one recipe and others many more. Audrey Goodridge was so enthusiastic about the project she contributed nearly forty recipes to the collection. The young mother of a newborn daughter escaped her hardships and worries and travelled widely through her culinary reveries. She went to Spain for lamb cutlets a là Navarra, Italy for cauliflower a là Romana, up to Vienna for schnitzel, on to Russia for fish zrazy, and all the way back home for chocolate biscuits. Isobel Grist, who contributed fillets of sole with mushrooms, grapes, and cheese sauce, may have imagined cooking this dish in the dream home she and her husband, Donald, an agricultural economist also interned in Changi, wrote about in the secret letters they exchanged.[1] Maybe Isabel's image of that house had been inspired by the thatched cottage and garden of roses on the cover of *Gone Afield* by Cecil Roberts that someone had brought into Changi. The guide book to village life was good for more than its cover, it contained a recipe for pilgrim cottage chutney which was added to the POW collection. A spoonful of chutney would have added so much piquancy to the tasteless prison fare that it would be hard to resist the pleasure of copying down each of the ingredients and imagining the tangy scent that would bubble up from the cooking pot. Most of the recipes in the cookbook were added from memory, but there were a few like the chutney that came from printed sources. Cauliflower cheese was culled from an August 7, 1940, issue of the classic British humour magazine *Punch*. The oh–so Canadian recipe for butter tarts that Ethel contributed was from her copy of *A Guide to Good Cooking* put out by Five Roses Flour in 1932. Ethel wasn't the only woman who had thought to add a favourite cookbook to her meagre belongings when she marched into Changi. She knew of at least ten other cookbooks in the prison and carefully listed them in the back of the red ledger book. They ranged from the upscale *More Caviar and More Candy* and the fashionable *Vogue's Cookery Book* of the 1930s, to the free pamphlet *New Charm Chocolate Cookery Book* put out by Cadbury's in Claremont, Tasmania, in the 1920s.

The prisoners couldn't help but think about food. All the same, retrieving and organizing memories of quantities, times, and temperatures required stamina which was in short supply. The humidity melted away energy, drooping fatigue followed in the wake of malnutrition, jungle sores ate into the flesh, and boils attacked the skin in the most tender of spots. Malarial fevers and beriberi, brought on by a lack of vitamin B1, lurked through the camp. Lingering anxiety of not being in control of their own fate slowly siphoned off the prisoners' good humour. But if the gate to the culinary imagination could be opened, a familiar world awaited, a land of make-believe populated by brand-name favourites known throughout much of the British Empire and North America. The products of Misters Heinz, Kraft, Campbell, and Nestle were summoned up by the women for their recipes, as were Quaker Oats and the ever-popular British Bisto gravy powder. For decades the raggedy waif-like Bisto twins, Bill and Maree, were seen in advertisements lifting their noses to catch a whiff of Bisto gravy floating out of a cooking pot. For women raised on Dickens, the thought of Bisto might have tugged at memories of Oliver Twist who famously had the temerity to ask for a second helping of gruel, a bowl of which the prisoners would have relished.

Oliver Twist made it into the cookbook on his own accord, in the guise of a cake named in his honour, to be iced with the froth of jelly foam frosting. The magical call of J.M. Barrie's Never Never Land lingered around the recipe for Peter Pans. Without the fairy dust that would allow her to fly away with Peter, some humorous wit resorted to gently snubbing her captors by calling for *English* peppermint oil for mint humbugs, "Not Japanese." Perhaps the contributor of Mikado pudding hummed some of the songs from Gilbert and Sullivan's comic opera, *The Mikado*, as she wrote her recipe. The popular old opera from 1885 is set in Japan and revolves around the emperor's edict against flirting: "All who flirted, leered or winked / (Unless connubially linked), / Should forthwith be beheaded."[2] The jokes, made clearly at the expense of high-ranking Japanese officials, did in fact reflect the romantic situation at Changi.

Male and female prisoners at the jail, even those "connubially linked," were kept strictly apart, forcing them, like the fictional characters, to invent creative activities to circumvent the restrictions they faced. The drain talkers were some of those daring lovers. They would arrange to be on either end of the sewage drains connecting the men and women's sections of the jail so they could hang down over the stench of the sewage pits and call out words of love and encouragement to each other while their friends stood as look outs in case a Japanese guard should wander by. The "dustbin parade" allowed separated lovers to at least see each other.[3] On garbage days Josephine Foss, affectionately known as Fossy, a former headmistress in her mid–fifties, took on the responsibility of organizing which women would carry the garbage pails to the fence and hand them to the men who would empty and return them. By stealthy prior arrangement, women were matched up with their husbands on parade day. No speaking was allowed but the exchange was so keenly anticipated that women dressed in their best, all for a look, a glancing touch of the hand or a quick exchange of smuggled notes. Ethel could only look on with envy at these stolen moments shared between lovers. Denis was beyond her reach, likely working in a camp hospital on Havelock Road, before being sent to one of the military camps around Changi.

* * *

In her quiet times Ethel turned back to her ledger books. As the blue one circulated around the recipe writers, she wondered what to do with the second one. At first she thought it could be a copy of the first. That way it would be insurance in case anything happened to the first one and would provide employment for those who copied the recipes. The plan quickly fell apart. The red ledger never went into anyone else's hands. Ethel just kept writing her own fantasies in it, beginning with the title: "Meals we shall eat when prison days are over." Disregarding the headings at the top of each page—"Name," "Nationality," "Crime," "Sentence," "Fine," "Commitment"—she started copying recipes. She gorged on them, squeezing in twice as many per page as were in the blue book. Some were repeats, some new, and many were without a contributor's name, but all of them provided her with a calming, rule-governed structure. Ingredients and method, temperature and timing, these marked the way into another, fully absorbing world where peace and full bellies replaced moral quandaries, hatred, and racism.

The book opens with recipes for the prisoners' favourite food, bread. Ethel begins her contribution, savouring each step from the moment she asks her Malay servant to go to the market to buy five cents worth of ragi (yeast). Upon his return she takes ten of the small biscuits of yeast and crumbles each one into a waiting bowl filled with flour, salt, sugar, and water. Then comes the moment when she digs her hands deep into the mixture and begins kneading the dough until it comes alive. She did not write her recipe using lists followed by cool-headed instructions. Instead she wove ingredients and method together into a story that expands over two days as the dough rises, is kneaded, divided, and rises again. She was careful to remember that some of the leaven should be held back and stored for the next baking day, so the process could be repeated again and again as needed. In this way, in this dream, fresh bread would always be available.

Where the recipes ended in the book, the meal plans began. Each menu was wrapped around a core of protein. Lamb was first: roasted, chopped, barbequed, in a pie or a casserole. With meticulous care Ethel outlined an appropriate appetizer or soup—"if desired"— potatoes or other starch food, vegetables, a garnish or relish, salad, and to finish, a dessert. In her visions, chocolate fudge cake was best suited to complete a roast lamb dinner, whereas chocolate chiffon cream pie was just the thing to finish off a lamb casserole flavoured with mint jelly and India relish, with side dishes of buttered broccoli, French fried eggplant, and summer fruit salad.

There are empty spaces in the book where Ethel could have added more foods for thought but never did. More recipes to be culled from friends or the cookbooks in the jail. Or maybe in her whirring thoughts the next activity on her list became more attractive and important. Whatever the reason, she knew the power of purposeful activity in keeping her mind from slipping into the despair of hopelessness and boredom. That battle, however, was only becoming more difficult as the days of hunger bled on.

Part Three
Dreaming It Up

Stacked Hearts

2½ cups self-raising flour

1 tspn salt

½ cup sugar

1 tspn lemon juice

4 oz butter

1 egg

3 tbsp honey

2 tbsp warm water

Beat well together. Roll out 1/8 inch thick. Cut. Bake 7 minutes in moderate oven. Put these together with honey butter cream.

Honey Butter Cream

1½ cups sifted icing sugar, 1 tbsp butter, 1 tbsp honey, 1 dessertspoon cream, 1 tbsp lemon juice. Beat well and spread.

Changi POW Cook Book

CHAPTER FOURTEEN
STITCHING STORIES

For more than just the obvious reason, Ethel always looked forward to the moment when the judge's wife, Violet Aitken, beat the gong announcing meal time. The mere appearance of Violet made Ethel smile. "Violet, by golly but didn't she wear her hair up like a rat's nest." Not quite the description you'd expect of a nursing sister married to the chief justice of Singapore. "She had blue pants. See, she was a forerunner of these jive kids, one leg could be up and one down but did she ever say golly. She was a good one. Always was the same person ... It wasn't that she was sloppy, she was just a good-fellow-well-met, you know." Given their grooming and wardrobe limitations everyone got to know each other's look almost as well as her own. In the afternoons, most of the women made an effort to present themselves at their best. There wasn't much they could do about hair that had faded to grey over the months they had been without their Myleto hair colouring or about their sagging curls after their impermanent waves had lost their bounce. But a little sprucing up once the heat of the day had subsided became part of the routine. Betty Smalley appeared with the same regularity in her red dress in the afternoon as did Ethel in her blue one. Putting on a good face for the world made things better, whether it was for an imaginary tea party or for a very real quilting bee, yet another of Ethel's projects.

During the first six months, when she wasn't talking about or writing recipes, organizing teas, running the Red Cross corner or shopping in town, Ethel was mulling over how to arrange a meeting with the men, both the civilians on the other side of the prison and, more importantly for her, with the military POWs held elsewhere on the island. It didn't seem to matter how often she petitioned the camp commandant to be allowed to merely communicate with the men, Okasaki was firmly against it. Of course the more stubbornly he thwarted the prisoners' efforts, the more inventive they became, as was the case with Freddy Bloom. On an officially sanctioned trip into Singapore city to get an X-ray, she smuggled out letters from the wives of military men. If anyone had looked carefully, they might have noticed that her dress was nicely filled-out, rather than drooping off her undernourished frame like clothes on a hanger. She took quite a chance. One male internee who was discovered passing notes to a prisoner of war working party was beaten with knotted ropes and sticks and underwent water torture.[1] Luckily, Freddy was able to hand over the letters to someone at the hospital who passed them on to the husbands. Ten days later, Ethel received a letter in return from Denis at his military camp, and, soon after, Freddy received one from Philip, both sent by some equally secretive method. Not all couples were so lucky. Elizabeth Ennis and her husband Dr. Jack Ennis, whom she had just married in February under the deadly sparkle of exploding bombs, were only a few miles apart, but they might as well have been on different continents for all they knew of each other's welfare.

Ethel wanted some sort of communication to be permitted— on the up and up—and without risk. She was looking for a system where all the women who had husbands and lovers in the military camps would have a chance to connect with them. A free exchange of notes would be good, but face-to-face meetings were what she really wanted. She yearned to lay eyes on Denis, if not encircle him with her arms, and she knew there were other women who dreamt of being close enough to touch their loved ones. A committee was to be drawn up to work on bringing couples together, but Ethel had little patience for committees. If writing letters was a risky and uncertain business, and speaking directly was impossible, why not try stitching out a message? The women could make quilts in the name of the Red Cross, add their signatures to them and get the Japanese to send them to men in hospital. That way at least the men would know the women were alive and thinking of them.

With a touch of political savvy, Ethel came up with the idea that if the women first offered a quilt to the hospital where Japanese soldiers were recovering from their wounds, it might act as a bit of a sweetener. If that quilt was accepted there would be a better chance that the Japanese would allow other quilts to be sent out to British and Australian soldiers who were recuperating in hospitals for POWs. Once the idea hit, Ethel got going. First she started buying white cotton sheeting while out on her shopping trips in Singapore. She called on old sewing hands, who, despite being in prison, managed to have a stash of supplies. Old rice bags, snippets from the women's own clothing, and hoarded threads were found and made ready for use. To those who were interested in participating, six-inch squares of fabric were given out along with the suggestion that, as well as their names, they could sew "what was dear to their hearts" on the British and Australian quilts. The quilts were to be emotional picture albums, telling the story of the women's desires.[2]

As word spread about the quilts, excitement grew and more and more women wanted to lend a hand. Most wanted the chance to work on their own square of dreams, but there were others, cellmates or friends, who were happy to combine their efforts in groups of two, three, or more. Women who had written recipes for the cookbook were eager to get going on a new activity. Even if they didn't have family members in the military prison camps this was an opportunity to work together as well as to express individually what desires filled their heads throughout the long days. Violet Aitken was one such woman. Although her husband was just on the other side of Changi, she chose to while away the hours with other embroiderers as she stitched a square of gentle blue and yellow flowers for the Japanese quilt. When she got to work on her square for the British quilt, the assistant tea-maker, gong-ringer, and hungry prisoner gave full reign to her cravings. The words "Changi Life Saver" on her square surround a life belt which in turn encircled her dream food, a loaf of bread.[3] Eunice Austin-Hofer, a forty-year-old horse breeder from Australia, stitched on her square for the quilt honouring her countrymen a fine brown-crusted loaf resting beside a bottle of wine under a tree bough. The whole picture lies inside a dream-bubble with the words, "And thou beside me in the wilderness." Nursing sister Sheila Early imagined what would be top of mind for a British Tommy. She stitched a host of treats inside his dream-bubble, including cigarettes, a bottle of wine, and a loaf of the old favourite British brand, Hovis bread. Trudie van Roode, a Dutch schoolteacher, went far beyond this staple food and stitched her own version of a whole well-laid table in the sky.

Not all the squares were filled with delectables. Barred windows and thick prison walls reflect the cringing confinement that shrank the prisoners' lives. Ethel found the square made by Iris Parfitt and her cellmate Joan McIntosh-Whyte painfully evocative. They sewed a stick-thin figure lying crumpled in one corner of a Changi prison cell with the words "How long oh Lord how long" hovering in a shaft of light coming through the barred window.[4] Others steered clear of both reverie and reality and instead embroidered symbols of home: myths, maps, flowers, and flags. With the support of her friend Margaret Burns, a Salvation Army officer, Ethel worked two maple leaves under the word "Canada" on a square for the Australian quilt.

And then there were those who didn't participate, the naysayers who thought all the hours spent making the quilts were wasted. Katherine de Moubray was exasperated by the "queer mentality" of people she saw in the jail and was acidly cynical about the whole project:

> People seem so unbalanced. Just as these squares (cut out of good sheeting) that the women are embroidering to make patchwork bedspreads, beyond providing entertainment and occupation for the women—seem so futile. One is for the hospital here I think, so one is for the Japs at the General Hospital and one for Changi military. God knows where else and what use a patchwork quilt can be to a hospital the Lord only knows. One feels the sheeting would have been more useful as sheets.[5]

If entertainment, occupation, and the creation of something beautiful had been the only outcomes of this project, that would have made it all worthwhile for Ethel, but she was determined to push the women's traditional feminine skills to greater use. In time, even Katherine succumbed to the general enthusiasm for the project, and she and Freddy both sewed a square for the Australian quilt. Freddy went a step further and produced a flowered square for the Japanese quilt: a sly yellow daffodil, twisted cobra-like on a black stem, ready to strike. Although the message appears decidedly ill-intentioned, Ethel accepted the square, but she did reject or edit others. One woman offered up a scene of a British soldier bayoneting a Japanese. She sympathized with the thought, but Ethel said, "You can't do that. This is Red Cross and we're not going to fight."

When Ethel first approached Lt Okasaki with her proposal to present the quilts to the hospitals, he asked about the spirit with which the women had made them. Ethel assured him that each contributor had had to qualify to do a square by being willing, at least in theory, to help a wounded Japanese soldier. That stipulation prevented a number of women from participating. Ethel knew full well that for some even the thought of giving aid to the enemy was sickening. They had simply lost too much in this war already. She was also aware, from her own experience, of the preoccupying power of hatred and its ability to shrivel the mind in an already shrunken world. What made it worse were the tormenting doubts about how she could possibly call herself a Christian and feel this way. She fought back, in a way that was second nature to her, especially in a growing state of mania, by keeping very busy.

Once all sixty-six squares for each quilt were finished they were stitched together with bold red thread onto a white backing. On the reverse of each quilt was a discreet but formal message in black thread that was very important to Ethel. Except for the nationalities noted and the calendars used to mark the year, the message was the same on all of them. The Japanese quilt read:

> Presented by the women of Changi internment camp 2602 to
> the wounded Nipponese soldiers with our sympathy for their
> suffering. It is our wish that on the cessation of hostilities that
> this quilt be presented to the Japanese Red Cross Society. It is
> advisable to dry clean this quilt.[6]

The words let it be known that these works of art were to be taken seriously as diplomatic overtures, particularly the Japanese quilt, which included a hint of conciliation by using the date 2602, in place of the Gregorian calendar's 1942. The Imperial Japanese Army and Navy had adopted this calendar to equate the beginning of time with the year the first Emperor of Japan, Jimmu Tenno, had come to power in 660 BCE. Just as clocks had been put ahead so that the hours of each day in Singapore were measured by the sun rising and setting over Tokyo, so too with this calendar, the victors marked all of history with their own cultural imprint. In its own low-key way, the quilt's message directed the recipients' attention to the time when the Red Cross, not the militaries, would have control over the quilts. Only then, at the end of the war and, they fervently hoped, when the Japanese were gone, would the shops once again be open for business and able to offer their services to dry clean the quilts, as was suggested. Maybe the authors entertained the thought that with some luck it would all happen just as next year's spring cleaning got underway.

In the meantime, the finished quilts were put on display on the men's side of Changi in September 1942 as part of a craft fair. Tom Kitching, who had worked for the Survey Department before the war and was interned on the men's side of Changi, was struck by the artistry and quality of the quilts and took a moment to jot down his impressions in his diary. "There is a remarkable display of talent, industry, and patience at the camp exhibition ... Among the contributions from A—Block are three quilts worked for presenting to the Red Cross."[7] The next day the men's "in-house" newspaper, the *Changi Guardian*, reported that "each patch provided a mirror of wit and humour, tragedy and pathos and the indomitable spirit existing in the women's camp."[8]

The value of the quilts as a poignant and artful reflection of prison life was on record, and now Ethel was ready to test their usefulness as communication devices. She had it in mind that all the military wives who had participated in the project would go to the hospitals where the POWs were treated and personally present the quilts. Okasaki thought differently. He would only allow Ethel to present the quilts to their intended recipients. It stung her not to be able to get the husbands and wives a chance to see each other on this occasion. After mulling over Okasaki's restrictions, she decided she would deliver the Japanese quilt on her own but refused to present the others. It would have meant that she alone would get to see her husband.[9] The rule was firm in her mind, as the Red Cross representative she could not receive a privilege that was not granted to others. For the other two quilts she asked the lieutenant if he would deliver them in the name of the Red Cross. He agreed, and, at her insistence, he promised that on the day of the delivery, as a stand-in Red Cross representative, he would leave his sword behind.

When the quilts were distributed to the Allied prisoners, the news slowly spread throughout the hospital and the military camps. It took a long time for Jack Ennis to hear from his new wife Elizabeth, but he was thrilled when he finally saw the Australian quilt for the first time in June of 1943. Elizabeth Ennis, who even in her own mind wasn't a skilful embroiderer, had managed to stitch hope right into her square in the shape of an ocean liner sailing away from a palm-treed island with her name and the words "Homeward Bound" underneath it. When Jack received her message of optimism it cheered him up no end. He felt that he and Elizabeth, and others like them who had sent and received messages via these fabric communiqués, shared a special bond. They were "the quilt people."[10]

* * *

After the deliveries had been made, Okasaki asked Ethel why she had wanted the Imperial Japanese Army to receive their quilt first. She avoided mentioning that the Japanese quilt had been designed to soften up the jailors. Instead, with pent-up anger at not being able to arrange to have all the quilters present their work in person to the military men, she demanded, "Do you want the truth or do you want me to lie like a prisoner of war?" Naturally he asked for the truth. The version of it that she offered had nothing to do with the quilts leaving the prison, it was all about the Japanese themselves leaving the island. "You can shoot me for it then, because we're going to squeeze you out. We'll squeeze you that way like an isosceles triangle, and you the apex, will march out and go home." Okasaki warned her of the consequences of such talk but she brushed aside his words, retorting, "You asked." In her combative manner and words, Ethel was giving voice to the whispered hopes of the prisoners.

Her anger and frustration built as she talked. As proof that the Japanese would be forced out of Singapore, she began spinning a web of magical madness and soothsaying, claiming that Okasaki's men would see visions before the final days and that she had the mythical powers of the seventh son of the seventh son. "I know you're going to be squeezed. This is only 1942, but your chips are falling fast." When Okasaki questioned how she knew this she pointed to herself, "It tells me here." To convince him of her powers she said, "Did you know my mother was fay? And my own birth mother was fay, and I'm fay?" Okasaki had no idea what a fay was, and rather than stopping to define the nature of a fairy, Ethel forged ahead, comparing her own magic with the power of a particular technological device which, when in the hands of the imprisoned Allied soldiers, was bedevilling the Japanese. "We know there's a radio that has a little bit of a thing like this that man invented, that picks up out of the air, words that go far. I can pick them up from eternity."

Ethel was well known to the Japanese from her first day in Changi as someone who would speak her mind, and do so repeatedly, but this was surely playing with fire. The Japanese executed prisoners for being in possession of radios. But she didn't stop. Again she challenged Okasaki. "Now then, do you want to hang me as a witch?" The lieutenant must have been stunned by Ethel's maniacal behaviour and talk of secret radio communications from beyond the end of time, yet his answer indicated that he harboured no anger. "No we won't," he said, "because you're fay."[11] He bowed to Ethel's wild magical world and laughed with her as she turned and walked out of his office. This was the man Ethel and others described as hard-hearted. It was unlikely he would have shown this patience and humour in the face of such a confrontation unless he thought her quite insane. In his book on POWs in Hong Kong and Japan, medical historian Charles Roland comments that some Canadian prisoners of the Japanese thought that their captors had "a certain respect for mentally disturbed people."[12] True or not, Ethel's wild behaviour gave her the perfect cover to give voice to the hatred that every prisoner had on their minds.

Her wild tales indicate the extent to which her world had been unravelling, even from the time when her brainchild, the quilts that would become world famous, were being stitched together. The stories she created are the wrenching flip side of her extraordinary imagination which had the power to dream up chimerical banquets that sustained a community of hungry prisoners. The pressures both within and without were coming to a head. Yet she showed remarkable strength of character in holding herself together, at least for a little longer.

Golden Glory Pudding

1 cup self-raising flour

3 tbspns cocoa

1 tbspn sugar

1 tspn salt

5 oz butter

½ cup cold water

Sift dry ingredients. Cut in butter. Add enough water to hold ingredients together. Divide dough in four balls. Roll out into rounds about 8 inches across. Prick well over. Bake in quick oven for 10 minutes.

Cream Filling

2¼ cups milk

½ cup flour

¾ cup sugar

3 tbspn butter

¼ tspn salt

2 eggs

cold milk to make paste

Heat milk—2¼ cups. Mix dry ingredients to paste with cold milk. Mix. Cook 10 minutes. Beat egg yolks. Add. Cook 3 minutes. Beat in butter and vanilla. Fold in stiffly beaten egg whites.

Join chocolate pastry layers with filling. Spread remainder on top. Sprinkle with ½ cup toasted coconut. Chill. Serve.

Changi POW Cook Book

CHAPTER FIFTEEN

THE RED CROSS SILENCE HUT

Ethel was caught between two conflicting desires. On the one hand she was increasingly anxious to have projects to throw herself into. On the other hand she craved quiet and solitude, and in this she was not alone. The jail was bursting with inmates. There was nowhere to get away from people. When the Japanese officials had, at the request of the women, instigated an afternoon quiet hour, Ethel had so hoped that it would provide some relief from the noise. However, the children in camp were notoriously unsettled. Mothers tried to keep their little ones still by reading to them, and bigger boys were sent over to the men's camp to play games, but prisoners continued to complain about the noise. "There was," as Ethel put it, "nowhere on earth there wasn't somebody yakety yak yakking." Never mind that she could out-talk just about anyone, she was earnest. Mary Thomas was tormented by the cacophony within the prison: clattering wooden shoes, constant chattering, water splashing into clanging pans. What made it worse was that all of the tumult "reverberated off the walls which seemed to magnify the deafening row and added to the slum-like atmosphere."[1]

On the other side of the prison wall, George Peet claimed, without irony, that he was ready to scream for quiet. His cravings for solitude, he admitted, were "almost morbid." Like Mary, he knew the concrete walls were to blame. "Having no chairs to sit on, we always found a wall to lean against, and sound travelled along those walls in a remarkable way." To escape from the nerve-rattling noise the men of his cell block designated one small grey corridor as a place of silence and called it "The Sanctuary."[2]

The idea of a place of refuge was appealing to Ethel; however she wanted something more than an empty hallway. An idea came to her when she was reading a children's Sunday school book about Moses. She saw a picture of a tabernacle in it, the temporary dwelling that Moses built for God in the wilderness during the Exodus. That was what she wanted, a place to house the divine, which in this case was the perfection of silence. She envisioned the building as something along the lines of the cottage she and Denis had built on Pulau Shorga with an *attap* roof and a large interior room. A number of small cubicles around the sides would allow a few women at a time to revel in the absolute luxury of privacy.

Not only would it be wonderful to have a sanctuary, constructing it would be time well spent. Ethel thought it through carefully. To build the hut the women would first have to gather wood and palm leaves. That would give them the chance to get outside, breathe the air beyond their cement enclosure, and take in the pleasure of flowers, green grasses, and vine-covered trees. Ethel wanted to mix people up, get those who didn't normally socialize with each other out working together for more stimulation. In her mind, the whole project was going to be like the barn raisings she remembered back on Manitoulin where members of the community would all work together in a common effort.

To get started, Ethel went to the commandant and began petitioning repeatedly, just as she had done to get permission to go out shopping. Lt Okasaki had been reassigned and it seemed the new commandant, Lt Suzuki, had a little more heart. The routine was the same, though: Ethel returned again and again, bowing and explaining. She described the kind of attap hut she wanted to build, drawing a plan for him and telling him what her qualifications were and that it would be a Red Cross project. When she finally got permission she chose sixty women to go out with her to fell the coconut trees that would hold up the structure. They were allotted one axe between them and Ethel accepted full responsibility for any accidents that might happen with it.

On the first morning the women were to go out, they lined up, prepared with head scarves to keep off the sun and long sleeves and leg coverings to foil as many of the malaria-carrying mosquitoes as possible. Joan Draper, a thirty-three-year-old pharmaceutical chemist, was so excited at the prospect of getting out and possibly catching a glimpse of her husband on the other side of the jail that she got all fixed up with face powder and a dab of lipstick. Beside her was Eileen Pearson and even Knobbsie, who, delicate though she was, was eager to help. Ethel was thrilled at the women's interest but then, to her great consternation, the commandant summoned her into his office. She handed the axe over to Anne Courtenay, her second-in-command. As she walked, Ethel felt the women's gaze follow her and above them, the men's as they peered through the bars of their windows.

By this time the divisions in the camp were firmly entrenched between the Red Cross pro-Mulvany group and the anti-Mulvany crowd. Ethel felt many were just waiting for her to make a misstep. What a public failure this would be if the project were cancelled. Embarrassment crept over her as she walked into the office. But her fear was unfounded. What Suzuki wanted was to have her explain how they planned to get the very tall coconut tree trunks needed to support the hut into the courtyard of the rose garden where it was to be built. They could get the tree in through the gate all right, but then it would come to an abrupt corner too tight for the log to fit around. Relief must have spurred Ethel's creativity for she immediately came up with the idea that they could rest one end of the tree trunk up against the wall and then vault it over the high wall directly into the rose garden.

Suzuki was concerned that the roof tiles would break in the process, but Ethel had a solution for that, too. "We'll get those big planks, put them on the roof, and we'll run it over. It won't touch the tiles." He allowed that this would work, and because she was so intent on this Red Cross hut, he said they could have a fatigue of men to help with the heavy work. Ethel didn't waste a minute coming up with a list of names. She wanted to have every Canadian she knew of, including Dave Milne and Brock Jamieson, both of whom had worked for the Ford Company in Singapore. Then there were her religious choices, Bishop Wilson, Father Moran, and Colonel Lord of the Salvation Army.

The men made the most of their time outside the jail, leaving notes for their Chinese friends which would be retrieved under cover of night. The women missed out on the opportunity to spend time outside the jail walls, though at least they got to see the men, some of them husbands, as they were coming and going through the courtyard. Initially, the men hustled along with their work at quite a clip, but soon enough they slowed their efforts to stretch out the precious time they had, time where they could see the women and feel the breezes beyond the prison walls.

After they had manoeuvred in the palm trunks it was the women's turn to work with the fronds to make roofing material. To Ethel's great surprise both Lady Heath and Lady Thomas were among those who wanted to participate in the project. In her opinion, and she was not alone, the two were a pair of "namby-pambies" who thought rather too well of themselves. They had managed to reproduce in Changi the aristocratic order that had served them well on the outside. Each had her own private cell as did Sir Thomas on the men's side, his being furnished with armchair and fan. The ladies had a coterie of servants to wash their clothes, bring their food, and generally do their bidding.[3] Ethel did not expect to get a good deal of useful labour out of either of them, still they were willing.

To make the attap for the shingles the women soaked the coconut fronds to render them pliable and took the sinewy fibre from the midriff to use as lacing material. For the postholes, Ethel had it in mind that they should be three and a half feet deep. When the Japanese asked why, she really wasn't sure but had no intention of admitting as much. She just knew that up on the Manitoulin if a building didn't have a cement foundation, postholes had to be that deep. She thought it must have been to keep them steady against the wind so that's what she told the Japanese. Only after she returned home after the war and was talking to her brother Harvey did she realize that the reason was so the post wouldn't heave with the frost, which of course was not an issue in Singapore. She assumed the Japanese had a good laugh at her at the time; she certainly did later on.

At the front of the hut, the women constructed awnings out of canvas rice bags to discourage the torrential rains of the wet season. With that addition, Ethel thought it was beginning to have the look of an elegant Indian tent. As busy hands slowly formed the external structure, other women were occupied decorating the interior. Behind the central area to the front of the hut they made five private cubicles divided by walls of rice sacking. For the common room, they gathered any odd bits of dilapidated attap and made small pallets out of them.

By far Ethel's favourite piece of furniture was the high-backed throne she and Anne Courtenay made out of orange crates and canvas bag cushions. They put a smaller crate beside it, just big enough for a book and an ashtray. Ethel had never smoked and was not impressed with the habit, but in Changi she saw the immense calming pleasure that smokers got when they inhaled and then released their cares on soft clouds of smoke. Tobacco was expensive and hard to come by, but on occasion Ethel was able to buy some for her fellow prisoners on her shopping trips. She could imagine that whoever was queen for the day would find as near to contentment as possible by putting her feet up on the little stool in front of the throne and indulging in a luxurious smoke while quietly reading a book.

Ethel and others working on the project realized they needed to put some rules in place or there would be squabbles over who got to sit in the Silence Hut and for how long. They decided to have a manager who would take the bookings, either for an hour or a day. She was to make everyone comfortable and ensure that silence was maintained.[4] Giving full rein to their dreams of opulence—prison camp style—each woman would be exempt from chores and could arrange to have a friend bring rations to the cubicle. Regulations for the common area would be different. Shorter amounts of time could be spent in there, and it could be entered whenever it wasn't crowded.

Once the building was complete, it was surrounded with a bamboo fence and a little garden. Someone had managed to get a hold of some roses and placed them by the pergola over the gate. Lucia Bach offered to care for the garden. Ethel thought her perfectly suited to the job, not only because of her horticultural knowledge but because her quiet, slow-moving demeanour reflected the spirit of the hut. Unfortunately her garden was soon pilfered for all the edible bits, including the rose petals. One last decoration Ethel had for the hut was the orchid she had been nurturing since the previous Easter. She placed it on the back wall where, protected from the direct sun, it bloomed prodigiously and gave her heart.

It was time to celebrate their achievements. Eighteen-year-old Sheila Allan describes opening day on Saturday February 13, 1943, in her secret diary:

> This morning the Red Cross Hut was officially opened—we
> had a coffee party—50 of us present we all contributed in
> some way to make this Hut attractive and comfortable as it is
> going to be a place of quiet retreat where we can escape to read
> and relax, whatever! Mrs. Mulvany made it possible with the
> arrangements of the building of this Hut—there were plenty of
> helpers including the men who built the Hut and guess what—it
> only cost $8.50 in actual cash! It is a good place to get away from
> all the congested space and noise around us.[5]

Like the society pages of a local rag, the women's camp news-paper reported on the grand opening. Not only were coffee and cakes served but guests were entertained with music played on the camp gramophone. In the future, of course, even music would be hushed around the hut. The popularity of the private cubicles quickly proved itself. Waiting lists grew to two months in length, but no one objected, even Freddy was impressed with the outcome. "A retreat much needed in our very congested and overcrowded living space. There are several books and magazines, beds for reclining, and chairs made easy, and it is delightfully cool and quiet."[6] After the speeches were made and the thank-yous extended, the Red Cross Silence Hut was open for business. For Ethel, not even the finest suite at Toronto's Royal York Hotel could compare. She knew, though, that solitude and silence were only blissful when they were freely chosen. The solitary confinement she would later suffer through was misery.

Imagination played a key role in creating the silence of the Red Cross hut. Burlap and attap could do little to even muffle sound, especially the nightly Japanese broadcasts. Each evening, the camp loudspeaker pummelled the internees with what Ethel considered to be "utter tripe," such as cases of the British winning two hundred yards at some battle only to be knocked back ten miles inside half an hour by the glorious Imperial Army. Sometimes reports came from Tokyo Rose, the infamous English-speaker who turned out to be many different women, broadcasting Japanese propaganda to undermine Allied morale. All of it could be heard from within the curtained walls of the hut, but when Ethel was inside the words had no power over her thoughts.

In response to the Japanese propaganda the women honed their own deliciously satisfying stories about what they would do when the war was over and, more immediately, about how well their troops were doing. Sometimes a kernel of truth sat at the centre of their war stories, but rumours flew regardless of the availability of hard facts. News, real or fabricated, was essential food for the spirit and a way of combating the negative effects of the broadcasts, which could leave the prisoners wondering what would be left of their lives however the war ended.

One good rumour, though, just like one good meal, and the world looked brighter. The most exciting ones skittering around the camp were about the possibility of repatriation. For sure the ship was coming for them, but when? How many would it take? Who would be chosen? How could you best your chances of getting on the list? There were so many compelling questions to endlessly dissect. The women's camp newspaper got caught up with the idea of ensuring that everyone be prepared. "In case there is a sudden move towards repatriation, collect addresses from those you wish to stay in touch with." And with even more foresight, the women were advised to "pack a small tin in your luggage in case you are in a small boat in a rough sea and need to be sick."[7] Other very satisfying stories told of the terrible losses suffered by the Japanese. Ethel was certain the women had sunk thousands of ships in the Japanese fleet. While being interviewed by Sidney Katz in 1961, she explained:

> It's a wonder there was a ship floating in the world, we put
> so many to the bottom of the sea. Davy Jones' locker was just
> full of them. And the planes that came down! And the losses,
> and the people in Japan that we starved. Oh it was just terrific,
> our boasts, you know. The grapevine of untruths that we sent
> around. And how it would gather momentum! You could start
> one off, it was added to and added to, and I heard my rumour
> come out at the end, and I didn't recognize my own yarn. It'd
> been just so nicely embellished.

Mint Humbugs

1 lb soft brown sugar

½ lb butter

¼ lb golden syrup

Oil of peppermint (English NOT Japanese)

Put sugar, butter, and syrup into a saucepan with 2 tbsps of water. Bring to the boil and continue boiling until the toffee mixture when dropped from the spoon into cold water becomes brittle. Then remove from heat and pour mixture on a well-greased marble slab. Pour into centre a few drops of peppermint and using a knife turn the edges of the toffee onto itself, until it is cool enough to handle. Then knead and pull well and just as it begins to harden pull into strips and cut pieces size of humbugs with large scissors.

Miss Joan Margaret Boston, a British nurse (b. 1914)

Boston worked at the General Hospital, Singapore.

Changi POW Cook Book

CHAPTER SIXTEEN

THE GAMES PEOPLE PLAY

The women's stories may have gained colour and sparkle through their many tellings, but their clothes were fading from over-exposure to sun and sweat, and the effects of malnutrition made their complexions just as dull. The days, weeks, and months slouched by, and it became harder and harder to have faith that they would ever get their lives back. They were constantly in need of a pick-me-up, and what better way to lift the spirits than to mix pretense with frivolity and shape it into a fashion show. Women with design talents, sewing skills, or just plain good humour began working out a plan. They divided themselves into different fashion houses, each of which was to come out with their own collection. Many hands then set to work translating visions of Schiaparelli and Chanel into Changi creations. Some aspiring haute couture designers occasionally interwove coir with scraps of paper, adding a little finesse to their scratchy gowns. Tablecloths wrapped up nicely into elegant turbans, shirts worn back to front made for the latest in necklines—there were so many ways to change the view, if only for a moment. Some twisted course threads of coir to make long straight necklaces. Others rolled it into beads and gave them a splash of colour by soaking them in the washing water of one woman's dress famous for bleeding red dye.

To showcase the clothes, they built a runway out of leftover timber from the dungeon. Iris Parfitt, who had a well-acknowledged gift for stringing along a good tale, was the obvious choice for emcee. When the day came, she sat in grand dame style with an elegant cloth-covered table by her side for her cup and saucer and the ashtray into which she occasionally tapped imaginary ashes from her exceedingly long paper cigarette. Beside her, lending a certain gravitas to the proceedings, sat the acting mayor of Paris attired in a borrowed pair of pants and a chain around her neck from which dangled the key to the city of lights. After welcoming the audience to the centre of the fashion world, the mistress of ceremonies introduced the houses and their creations. Audience members oohed and ahhed as the models sashayed down the runway. Ethel was entranced by the retro-styles from the Roaring Twenties. "Oh you should've seen them. Canvas bags, dresses frayed at the bottom, the hats and beads, you know those Charleston-day beads."

Successful play added spice to the women's otherwise empty days and inspired other creative activities such as the circus that came to Changi. Freddy Bloom conjured up the idea and started planning for it in October of 1942, with the help of the Palomars, a family in the trade who had moved to Singapore in the 1930s to join Harmston's circus. It was by all accounts another raging success. Sheila Allan was captivated right from the start when, just as the audience had assembled in the carpenter's shop, three reporters strode in flashing their notebooks around to let everyone know that they were covering the event. Robbie Worth wrote for the *Syonan Slimes* and Norah Jones and Betty Buchnan for the *Rumour Monger*. Strongman Leonar Palomar accomplished great feats, tightrope artists Sue Williams and Doris Kent artfully practised their balancing acts, and Isobella Bentley, as a fairy queen, brought a little magic into the midst.[1] Throughout the show, lions roared and scared the children, elephants lumbered, seals clapped, and the five dogs who lived in the camp, including Judy, raced around yapping in delight at the strange animals.

If the dogs had known how close they had come to being exterminated just weeks before, they might have been even more excited. Freddy didn't mince words explaining what had happened: "four nasty, bitter, frustrated, inhibited bitches" in camp wanted to have the dogs put down.[2] Uproar ensued. Lines were drawn. Votes were cast. Accusations of fraud erupted and ballots were recast. The final tally showed overwhelming support for the dogs and they lived on, for a time.

By far the best part of the circus for Ethel was the boxing match. It brought back vivid memories of being in the stands at Toronto's palatial new Maple Leaf Gardens in the early thirties. The women got the idea for the match from the men on the other side of Changi, who had already begun putting on their own matches. While the men may have had visions of boxing greats dancing in their heads, in reality their own rounds became shorter and shorter as the lack of nutrition took its toll on the contestants. The women had no illusions about their power in the ring, but they wanted to look as if they could throw a knockout punch. For that they needed to artistically beef up their muscles. Canvas bags were folded and tied on to the women's legs to give a burly look. More canvas was dampened and shaped into sturdy-looking gloves. When their costumes of strength were completed, the pugilists and their seconds strutted through shouting fans up to the ring. Wagers were laid and at the clang of the meal bell the fight began. Contestants parried, punched, twirled, and danced around the ring to roars of excitement and laughter.

Then everything went quiet. In the time it takes for a dream to vanish, the boxers dropped their arms and stood down. Japanese guards had slipped in wanting to share in the fun. The women had no desire to entertain their enemy. They felt they had been caught in a make-believe realm of pleasure that the guards had no business entering. With their silence, they slammed shut the door to their imaginary world right in the guards' faces.

* * *

Play and games varied widely in the jail. As Ethel remembered it, the children's games were all about war. One in particular, played with a red sweater, was a constant reiteration of the battle on the night before capitulation. "They would pile themselves in heaps of 'dead' bodies while others hid and fired from imaginary guns … They had a red sweater which was a 'must' for this battle. It was always stretched out on the ground near the largest heap of 'dead' men. This meant blood."

While children play war games no matter what their lived experience, context shifts the meaning and purpose of these activities. Dr. George Eisen, an expert in education and sports played in European concentration camps, found that both adults' and children's play became a defence mechanism. For adults it was planned and rational and served as an escape from the surrounding horrors. Children's play, however, was about adjusting to reality.[3] From what Ethel saw, the Changi reality was that "You were cornered, you were a rat in a corner and you were ready to spring. And your nerves just tensed. And the children bore with it in prison. They were the strangest little children."

The number of children in Changi nearly doubled as new European, Asian, and Eurasian internees were squeezed into the jail. Eventually there were 328 young ones falling over each other and their mothers, playing, laughing, crying, fighting, absorbing, questioning, and making sense of their reality.[4] One small group wanted to know what a body hanging from a noose really looked like. Was it true that they kicked? Did they really pee their pants? There was only one way to find out. They constructed a frame in one of the cells with three bamboo poles. Two uprights were fitted into notches at either end of a horizontal pole. With a couple of children holding each of the uprights they slung a rope over the top. Through who knows what promises of future pain or pleasure, they convinced little Johnny, the smallest of their gang, to accept the noose. Knowing what would happen if they were discovered, they worked quietly, but that's what gave them away. A woman walking down the hall noticed the muffled voices inside the cell. By the time she opened the door to check on them Johnny's face had already started to darken from a lack of oxygen.

The instigators, far from being repentant, were furious that the woman had interrupted their hanging. All they wanted to do was see if he kicked. Ethel knew that six-year-old Johnny was small for his age and despised by the others.[5] A difference in size may have been all that it took to inspire hatred in this *Lord of the Flies* kind of world. The horror of what the children had lived through, the position they had been put in between warring adults, and the games they created to make sense of it all never left Ethel. Their play was the by-product of war, and she wondered how many would later suffer from its effects. Both children and adults were capable of great acts of creativity and largess, but their imaginations were also capable of taking them into dark places or, as was the case for young Genevieve Logan, completely obliterating all memories of those years. Only from stories told to her later by her family did she know that she was in Changi with her mother—Diana Logan—two aunts, and her baby cousin. "I was four and a half when I came out, but I just blotted the whole thing out."[6]

Ground Rice Porridge

for 400 persons (1 pint each)

60 lbs ground rice

5 gallon container crushed soya beans

1 lb salt

10 lbs sugar

10 lbs peanuts

Cook soya beans separately. If desired, roast peanuts. Boil water, add salt and sugar. Add rice flour steadily stirring continually. Add cooked beans. Allow to boil, stirring continually until thick. Add the peanuts ¼ hour before serving porridge.

Changi Cookery Book.

CHAPTER SEVENTEEN

DOUBLE TENTH

George Peet kept note of the food in Changi with careful, hungry, and at times humorous attention to detail. The former acting editor of the *Straits Times* and director of information in the Straits Settlements government pragmatically divided the prisoners' culinary experience into different periods. For the first six months the prisoners clung to their old eating habits supplementing their rations with food from town, such as Ethel was buying. As the months wore on however, Peet said wheat flour vanished, "cheese became but a happy memory" and "milk disappeared from the tea."[1] When the extras were unavailable, the meals became completely Asian but, he maintained in a tone unusually cheery for any prisoner, they were perfectly delicious and healthy. Few, and certainly not Ethel, were able to look so positively on a diet they did not choose, the staple of which, rice, belonged to the culinary culture of their overlords.

The breakfast they had every day during the second phase of internment was tea and rice porridge (kanji). The meal was healthy enough when it came with soya beans and peanuts, containing the protein and vitamin B1 necessary for the digestion of rice starch. Soon enough, however, amounts of the necessary fats, vitamins, and proteins fell short. Peet was likely unaware that as early as April 1942 beriberi and other deficiency diseases began appearing.[2] Like many others, Ethel would come to suffer from beriberi. The numbness and weakness in the limbs that it causes may have slowly crept up without her paying attention, but she knew when she saw her arms and legs swell that her body was failing. Even the gentlest pressure from her finger on the swollen tissue caused her flesh to cave in and hold the indentation, a chilling sign of how her heart was labouring.

A recipe for the nutritious porridge (as seen at the head of this chapter) that would have kept this disease at bay is included in the *Changi Cookery Book*. This collection of 84 methodically typewritten pages, now held in the Changi Museum in Singapore, gives directions for how to make dishes that the prisoners likely ate in the camp, unlike the recipes for dream food in Ethel's *Changi POW Cook Book*. No author is named on this gathering of 232 recipes, but probably many of the so-called "Asia boys" collaborated in its production. These men had been merchant marines on board the Canadian Pacific liner troop ship *Empress of Asia*. Just ten days before capitulation the ship was sunk off the coast of Singapore, stranding about 100 members of its catering crew in the city.

Ingredients for these practical recipes were culled from what was usually available in Changi: a revolving offering of rice—boiled, fried, dried, ground into flour—as well as soya beans, sago flour, maize flour, potato yeast, and tapioca root. There are a few vegetables listed and a sprinkling of spices: chillies, curry powder, and garlic. Although Peet never mentions eating desserts there are recipes in this collection for sweets indicating how inventive the cooks were. Amazingly, there is even a recipe for "1943 Changi Xmas Pudding for 50 Persons." The substance of it was boiled rice and sago, maize and rice flours, sweetened with Chinese dates and brown sugar, spiced with lemon, green ginger, and cinnamon, all kneaded together with six tablespoons of coconut oil and four duck eggs. The ingredients are creative but the most astonishing aspect of this recipe is the date. By this point, the quality and quantity of the prisoners' food had sunk dramatically. This was due to what became known as the Double Tenth Incident of October 10, 1943. From that time on, the prisoners never had enough food of any kind.

On the morning of that day at 8:15 the internees were marched out into the central square of the prison. No explanation was given, all gates were locked and bayonet-wielding military police stood guard. For over ten hours, the men and women were forced to stand in the beating tropical heat while they and their cells were thoroughly searched. Only later did news seep through the prisoners' ranks that six Japanese oil tankers had been blown up in the harbour on September 28. No one knew, least of all the Japanese, that a small group of British and Australian officers had sailed from Australia on a small fishing boat and, under cover of night, had placed mines on the ships. Already, Japanese frustrations had been growing for months because of their inability to keep up with their early successes in the war. This was yet another sign that things were not going well. Camp officials were convinced that civilian prisoners, in collaboration with Singaporeans, had been transmitting information to the Allies. The bombings merely confirmed their beliefs.

Determined to find out who was involved and how the prisoners were communicating with the Allies, the Japanese secret police, the Kempetai, took close to sixty internees into custody for questioning. Three of those rounded up were women prisoners: Dr. Cicely Williams, Freddy Bloom, and later, Dorothy Nixon. Freddy Bloom was held for five months with fifteen men in a wooden cell with a toilet in the corner that doubled as a washing facility. She was taken out and questioned, but was never tortured, as her male cellmates were. Their screams of torment filled the ears of those next in line. Singaporeans also incarcerated included Elizabeth Choy and her husband, Choy Khun Heng, who had smuggled money and radio parts into Changi Jail. The couple were severely tortured and, with an added twist of inhumanity, were made to witness each other's agony.[3]

Because of the intentionally miserable food rations, Freddy suffered two heart attacks brought on by malnutrition. After the second, the Kempetai, seeing she was no longer of any use to them, returned her to Changi Jail on March 24, 1944. Fifteen men died as a result of their sadistic treatment by the Kempetai.[4] Even prisoners remaining back in Changi Jail felt the change after October 10. The Japanese officers made sure life in general was much more painful. Mary Thomas succinctly summed up the new regime: "In a thousand petty ways, our lives were deliberately oppressed and made burdensome."[5] No more than four people were allowed to meet at any one time, effectively ending camp entertainments, school for the children, lectures for the adults, and church services. Ethel's shopping trips into town were over. Rules governing communication between the men and women were minutely enforced. Japanese soldiers and the Kempetai habitually searched through the women's things, often stealthily entering their quarters two or three times a night, then scaring the sleepers awake with glaring flashlights. A sense of utter insecurity pervaded the jail, worsened by harsh and continual reductions in food rations. From this time onward, it became worthwhile for the prisoners to count each grain of rice.

Cheesy Eggs

Grease ramekin, put tablespoon hot milk, piece of butter, grated cheese, one egg, salt, pepper. Bake.

Joan Draper (b. 1909)

Draper was a pharmaceutical chemist. Her husband was also in Changi.

Changi POW Recipe Log Book

CHAPTER EIGHTEEN

TORTURE

Most of the prisoners' small pleasures were squeezed out of their lives after October 10, 1943. For some, the most difficult situation to cope with was the move out of Changi Jail in May 1944. The prison was now needed to house military prisoners. The civilians were ordered to pack their belongings so they could be trucked across Singapore Island to what had been the headquarters of the British Army and Royal Air Force on Sime Road.

After the fall of Singapore, the Japanese had ordered the British and Australian POWs to clear out what had been this symbolic site of British strength and build huts for themselves for short-term use, while they waited to be sent to Siam or Japan. When the civilians stepped off the trucks at Sime Road, they were faced with a filthy, dilapidated, overgrown mess of buildings. Still, many breathed in the fresh air with relief. Here the gaze was free to roam across acres of green grass mixed with wild rhododendrons and through stands of rubber trees. Instead of the constant echo of human voices within cement walls, they could relish the sound of rustling leaves and singing birds, at least until the latter were added to the cooking pots.

The camp was circumscribed by barbed wire and beyond that a six-foot high thatched fence to prevent anyone from seeing out or in, but it wasn't cement and it wasn't twenty feet high. The attap huts did not keep out the rain or malaria-carrying mosquitoes as effectively as the prison, but they let in the light.

Adjusting to the move, though, was traumatic. Changi was no palace, but they had settled in, fought for their plot of space, and made it home. They were prepared to grit their teeth within the jail's echoing walls until the nightmare was over. Many feared they would have to make choices about what to leave behind and what to take. Facing change requires energy and few prisoners had much of that to spare. Then there were the sick and hospitalized. For them the May 1944 move was a shattering upheaval, and the rate of prison deaths increased. Even though the Japanese supplied ambulances to transfer them to Sime Road, the bumps and jolts of the drive would have been hard to bear. Certainly Ethel's dear friend Euphemia suffered from the experience. She had been sick for more than half a year with tuberculosis, a disease that commonly afflicts those who are starving. At Changi and then at Sime Road, Ethel visited Euphemia in the makeshift camp clinic, watching each day as the already small Australian woman shrank ever further in her hospital bed.

Ethel wanted more than anything to transport her friend away from Sime Road. So she did. She took her to Manitoulin and toured her all around her favourite spots. Sitting by Euphemia's bedside, she recited their names like lines in a poem: Sheguiandah, Mindemoya, Gore Bay, Sheshegwaning, Wikwemikong, and Manitowaning. Each place took them a step farther from where they were. They agreed that Euphemia's son Billy should come too, especially now that she was alone since her husband had died, just two months after he entered Changi Jail. Neither of them knew then that young Billy had already been killed in combat. Ethel and Euphemia stretched out their magic-carpet travels for as long as they could, taking time to imagine what they would eat along the way. Euphemia had a particular fondness for omelettes, so Ethel cooked up all kinds of fluffy, rich, delectable fantasy egg concoctions for her, as well as one or two real eggs.

Despite Ethel's constant attentions, Euphemia died on Thursday, June 1, 1944, just weeks after the prisoners had been moved to Sime Road. Ethel remembered it being a Tuesday, so for years after, that day was tainted with the pain of death. She dressed Euphemia's body with care in her own pink nightgown that she had been keeping for a special occasion. It might have been perfect for her first night of freedom shared with Denis, but just then Ethel felt that her friend, "Toughy," needed the gown more. Together Anne Courtenay, Eileen Pearson, Jean Bales, and Ethel placed Euphemia's emaciated corpse in the grey box with the removable bottom that had been used to transport all the dead from prison to grave. Ethel made a wreath and tucked messages into it that she thought Euphemia would have liked to have shared with her Chinese friends.

No one can fill the place of a best friend lost. Euphemia had been a steady companion who smiled on life. Whenever things had looked particularly gloomy in Changi she had been a great one to talk to. Ethel considered her one of a number of "wandering psychologists." There were a few women like this on whom she depended. Knobbsie was one of them and Lucia Bach was another. Lucia was only six years older than Ethel, but Ethel thought of her as a slow old soul with a quiet, sensible attitude toward life. Ethel arranged all the prisoners she knew on a hierarchy of inner strength with herself somewhere in the middle. She saw herself as a sounding board for those who were weaker. After listening to their woes and consoling them she felt drained of energy and in need of the company of someone stronger than herself. When Euphemia died, Ethel lost a cornerstone of her world, and she was about to lose another. Reports would circulate in the camp that Ethel became completely unbalanced for some unknown reason and had to be segregated for everyone's safety. Her version of what happened had to do with the grandson of Seong, the man dressed as a beggar in the market who had told Ethel to buy pumpkins in stall 38.

The move to Sime Road meant that the prisoners had to devise new black market locations for the exchange of food and news. This was a hardship for Ethel who'd had her surreptitious lines of communication with the Chinese community in place at Changi. But eventually she got a system going at Sime Road and was able to meet secretly with Seong's eighteen-year-old grandson, whom she affectionately named Seong the Third. She found a place for their meetings where the road on the outside of the camp came close to the fence. Knowing that to avoid suspicion she needed a good reason for repeatedly going to that particular spot, she had a hen house built nearby and installed two hens she had bought on her shopping trips into Singapore while at Changi. Miranda and Sunshine's precious eggs were reserved for those who were hospitalized and in dire need of protein, vitamins, and a decent supply of calcium from the ground-up shells. The hens did a fine job producing on a diet of mainly flies and fat grasshoppers.

To meet with Seong the Third under cover of darkness, Ethel pretended she was a sleepwalker. Although sleepwalkers unnerved her, she reasoned that this behaviour gave her a good excuse to be out at night. She and Seong devised a system whereby he would throw a stone with a message attached to it towards the hen house, telling her when he would come to meet her. By her reckoning, she and the young Seong met five times by the barbed-wire fence circling the camp. They lay on the ground, each on their own side of the boundary, and he passed her bits of food and told her of the Allies' progress. News of strikes on Japanese military objectives were "mercy to my soul." Each time she could hardly wait to get back and tell her friends, although it wasn't the same after Euphemia died. At the end of their meetings, in an effort to adopt a tone of normalcy, they would bid each other goodbye in the usual way, *salamat jalan*. For Ethel this expression contained an element of the divine, "Go, God goes with you—As you go on the road, God bless you." That it was an everyday expression was also significant—"You didn't say anything very special or if you did you might want to cry."

Ethel was caught more than once by guards, but continued with her meetings. News of her nocturnal wanderings and disregard for camp regulations were reported to the doctors in camp who attributed them to her mania. On their last rendezvous young Seong was a half hour late. As the minutes ticked by Ethel became terrified of what might have happened to him and of what might happen to her if she were caught again. Her fear was so strong it had a flavour all its own, tasting like the colour green. She felt and heard a buzzing in her head, almost as loud as the pounding of her heart. When Seong finally did turn up he told Ethel this would be their last meeting and he couldn't stay long. He had been caught in his clandestine activities by the Japanese but had been able to slip out when a friend agreed to stand in for him just long enough for him to come and say goodbye. He was to be executed at dawn.

Ethel never questioned the likelihood of someone standing in for Seong, but Sid did during their conversations of 1961. She insisted, "The Chinese are like that. There is nothing that can be compared to just how the Chinese will stand by you ... A friend is a dear thing to the Chinese."

After Seong left that night Ethel felt as if every boil on her skin, each infected sore that ailed her body, now had a sword slashing through it. She crawled back to the chicken pen then stood up and walked back to the hut. It was impossible to lie down so she paced the room. She woke up her neighbour, Clara McLeod, who warned her she would get in trouble if the guard came around. "If he comes," said Ethel, recalling the death of the soldier who sat beside her as she drove the ambulance, "I'll put my fingernails right in his jugular vein and it'll just pump out on me and I'll just love to feel his blood ... It'll be the blood of Japan." Then she did the only thing she could think of, she prayed. She begged for the darkness of an arctic night to descend and blind people so they couldn't fight anymore. For a moment she almost believed it would happen. Then, opening her eyes just a crack to see if it were true, she saw the weak yellow light of dawn in the sky and soon after heard the crack of guns.

Ethel could see that people in the camp thought she was different after that. She agreed: a light within her had been extinguished. Lucia Bach thought the changes she saw in her dear friend had been set off by what happened to J. S. Long, who had gone on some of the shopping trips with Ethel. Long had been taken into custody by the Kempetai after the Double Tenth episode and executed November 27, 1944. Barbara Glanville (nee Bruce), a ten-year-old child at the time, thought someone had informed on Ethel and under torture she had become unhinged. These opinions, voiced in formal interviews decades after the event, contain a few obvious errors, but there is much in each that rings true. Together with Ethel's version of what happened they give a fuller picture of her breakdown.

Barbara Glanville's story:

> With us in camp was a lovely woman we all liked. She was in
> her forties, was Canadian and worked for the British Red Cross,
> which was why the Japanese interned her. She was a very tall
> woman and always very positive and optimistic. She had a tiny
> radio, which she kept in a matchbox. She used it to keep in touch
> with the progress of the war and used to tell us not to worry,
> that things were going well and it wouldn't last much longer ...
> One of the other women split on her in return for extra rations
> and the Japanese took her away. We heard that they'd tortured
> her. I dread to think what they did to her.[1]

Of course Ethel didn't work for the British or have a radio, but she was bringing news into the camp and possibly someone had informed on her secret conversations with Seong leading to his execution.

According to Ethel's good friend Lucia Bach:

> Mrs. Mulvaney [sic] at one point seemed to be behaving rather
> queerly ... She was extremely upset because one of the men
> who always went with her on the shopping expeditions was
> shot by the Japanese ... I think she was very much upset by that
> but what upset her mentally it is difficult to know. There were

many theories but it was clear to us that her mental ability was waning and that her mind was beginning to fail.

I was one of those who was very much aware of it. And I was in touch with other prisoners who were from the Mental Hospital in Singapore. One particular nurse [Nina Catherine Daisy Banks] said, "I want you to watch her because at any particular moment she might become dangerous."

Well as I was very fond of Mul I stuck around her cell ... But she knew ... I was watching her. She knew she was going mad and that my affection for her ... was because I was watching her ... She was busy ironing outside her cell and she suddenly screamed out "Bach, come here. You see this red hot iron? I will attack you with it if you don't sit down on that stool and stay there. If you move from there you'll see what's coming to you."

I was terrified but obeyed her instructions. I knew that other people were passing to and fro and that they were watching ... But suddenly things broke and she did go mad ... She rushed through the camp madly and she attacked the Japanese General. She rushed into his office and tried to attack him. She was overpowered by the Japanese and she was held ... And they sent for men from the camp—Englishmen. And there were 10 men to hold her down and strap her and fasten and chain her to a table top. She was brought back to our camp by the men and remained chained like that until the Japanese had erected a cage—a great big cage in which they could imprison her; very strong bars.

... what triggered the whole matter off is very difficult to say ... It was towards the end of internment.[2]

Katherine de Moubray wasn't at all interested in what had triggered this episode, she merely wondered why it had taken so long to happen: "we were all expecting it, and almost hoping for it in the first six months as the only thing that could call a halt to her very agitating activities." In an attempt to squeeze out a wink of pity for

Ethel she went on, "having had her Red Cross uniform removed by the nips,[3] and having sunk into the fairly harmless position of a bag woman, it's very sad." In Katherine's opinion, Ethel, because she had a history of mental illness, was not as deserving of empathy after her breakdown as was Richard Stanton Nelson, imprisoned on the men's side of Changi. "I cannot feel," she continued, "it is approaching the tragedy of Nelson for instance, who seems to have had not the slightest tendency to madness before he came in here."[4]

Richard Nelson had gone to Malaya as a young man in 1910 to work in the rubber industry. The place suited him well, and over the next three decades he settled down into a pleasant middle-aged bachelorhood, only venturing as far as Singapore in 1940 to become a municipal commissioner. The war destroyed the home he had made for himself and, according to Katherine, his experiences in Changi and Sime Road drove him mad. He would later die aboard the *Empress of Scotland* (formerly the *Empress of Japan*) while returning to Britain, a place he hadn't called home for thirty-five years.

For Katherine and many others at the time, condescension and dismissal were the most appropriate responses towards those with mental illness. Although she was not interested in discovering the cause of Ethel's breakdown or how to help her she dismissively reported the views of one of the nursing sisters who was. "Sue Williams says that Ethel has been persecuted into this by criticism and antagonism (... of course we are on the list of persecutors, beginning with our accusations of her swiping our stuff ...) Sue seems to think that if only people had known she was liable to go mad, she should've been given her head absolutely, not crossed or thwarted in any way." Katherine wryly summed up her view of this position: "Seems an odd philosophy that the world should be run by lunatics, for the sake of keeping said lunatics from having an acute attack."[5]

Under different circumstances Ethel, who was quite capable of laughing at herself, might have been able to appreciate Katherine's humour, but at this point she had gone past the end of her wits. As for the torture Barbara Glanville mentioned, the Japanese did try to get information from her about Seong. The process began innocently enough, "but often times," Ethel later noted, "the more gentle a thing is the more wearing it is ... the way water hollows out stone." What started as short interrogations gradually grew longer. The sessions began at all different times of the day and night, which Ethel reasoned was to keep her off-balance. During her questioning she was forced to stand within a white-painted circle in front of the commandant's desk, just as she had done when petitioning for favours. Weakened with dysentery and having no control over her bowels, bloody unstoppable diarrhea trickled down her legs as questions were fired at her from all directions. At first Ethel was completely baffled by their line of questioning, but she soon realized they always circled around to the same subject, music. Ethel had had plenty to feel anxious about during these interrogations: the secret messages she had tied up in the funeral wreaths and all the money she had brought into camp in the pumpkins. However, the constant referral to music convinced her that the Japanese were instead looking for information about the young Seong, who played the *veena*, a stringed instrument with a hauntingly beautiful sound. After the sessions were over she went straight to the toilets and vomited, the thin milky vomit of an empty stomach.

The second phase of Ethel's interrogation began with her being told to sit in what looked like a dentist's chair. Ever since she was a young girl, Ethel had had a desperate fear of dentists. She figured she had "likely been holding forth" on this fear while in prison, and the Japanese caught wind of it and used it to their advantage. Her theory was not farfetched. In the introduction to *The Double Tenth Trial*, a record of the trial proceedings of the Japanese officers accused of war crimes during the Double Tenth episode, it is noted that "the Kempei Tai were adept at discovering each prisoner's weaknesses."[6] Ethel sat silently and watched as a man sharpened some scissor-like instruments on a whetstone. Gradually as he pulled the tips of these tools over the stone he started his questioning. How many teeth had she had removed, when had that happened, and with a quick change of subject, what did she know about Malayan music? She insisted she didn't need any dental work but was told to open her mouth. She screamed and fired out all the explosive obscenities she had learned from soldiers.

With her head held back and her mouth forced open, it felt to Ethel like her wisdom teeth were being smashed with a hammer and chisel, the nerves repeatedly prodded and splinters of teeth extracted. "By this time I was to the point of just jumping up and down outside of a house kind of thing. Oh it felt like Hades ... like shafts of sunlight striking through you ... every corner of your body ... You know pain has a terrible warmth to it." The pain of un-medicated dental work is excruciating, as anyone who has lived through it knows, and Ethel's unusual descriptions of the agony carry with them the vivid clarity of lived experience. Whatever happened during her inquisition, it was anguishing and was followed by more pain when someone, she assumed it was a man, proceeded to put an electric needle in her back. She lost consciousness for a time and was told afterwards that the bump she received on her head was caused by her own knees jerking upward with the force of the electric shock.[7] Then once again she was asked if she had ever heard Malayan music.

Ethel claimed that her questioning extended over three months, but far worse than her own torture was witnessing that of others. She was forced to watch two male prisoners being interrogated. She thought the two had been intelligence officers. Whether military or civilian, she was sure she had been directed to watch them being whipped to scare her into revealing something incriminating about Seong. The tactic made her vomit, as her own questioning had.

On yet another occasion when she was being questioned she overheard screams of agony emanating from the room next door. She was later told sharpened bamboo slivers had been worked under the prisoner's fingernails. The image twisted itself so deeply within her that after the war Ethel turned her own knitting needles into instruments of self-torture to quell the tumult in her head.

But for now there was one final step in Ethel's interrogation. This time she was faced with two men. One held her arm while the other heated up a branding iron on an electric burner. They asked her about Canadian cattle and how they were branded and, again returning to music, about what western songs she knew. It was clear to Ethel there was something they didn't know about Seong and his grandfather, and they were sure she did. She watched in horror as the iron was held to the stove, heating up each of the four removable end pieces slotted into its handle. When it was hot enough her prison ID number, 2665, was pressed onto the soft flesh of the inside of her left forearm. She heard her flesh sizzle, smelled it burning and, when she looked up, saw four brown eyes looking straight at her. They were "eyes that can do this to you … and feel not a pang."

After the war, Ethel had the number burned off with caustic chemicals. It was a painful process, but she was sure that ridding herself of that physical reminder of her prisoner identity was worth it. "I was kind of a number until I did. If you call a person Mary, they become Mary. But if you call yourself Billy, you're Billy. Well if you call yourself 2665 and you were willing to live under it, then you're 2665."[8]

Damper

About one mug flour, dessertspoon baking powder, mix with water or sour milk. Flour the frying pan (no fat). Cook until slightly brown.

Rose Anne Courtenay (b. 1893)

Courtenay, British, was a great help to Ethel Mulvany with her Red Cross work. Her husband, Christopher Early Courtenay, a businessman, was interned in Changi.

Changi POW Recipe Log Book

CHAPTER NINETEEN
SOLITARY CONFINEMENT, FEBRUARY TO AUGUST 1945

Barbara Glanville, just eleven years old in 1945, was so frightened by the changes she saw in Ethel that the image of the broken woman was still vivid in her memory decades later.

> I saw the empty, glassy look in her eyes as they walked her
> down the steps. She was a pitiful sight. She had lost her mind.
> She couldn't hold a normal conversation any more. She was
> such a wonderful person, it terrified us all. All she did was sing
> at the top of her voice—patriotic songs like "Rule Britannia." It
> infuriated the Japs. They put her in a padded cell. Her singing
> seemed to intensify when the moon was full.[1]

In the language of medical records, Ethel was "violent, abusive, dirty, self-harming and confused."[2] Her condition worsened throughout February 1945 such that she was put into solitary confinement in March. The only belongings Ethel was allowed to have with her were her sarong, her bible, and a pencil. While she was in isolation, her friends took care of her other belongings. Mary Thomas said they were all surprised to discover among her possessions:

a great number of articles which she had undertaken to sell for needy internees and which, when she could not find a buyer, she had quietly bought with her own money at the seller's price. At the time she was herself quite short of money and the articles were of no use to her. Those who had given her the things to sell had no idea of what she had done to help them.[3]

Ethel's home until liberation had a cement floor, a wooden door, and a high barred window. She had a pail for a toilet and another one for food and water. Reflecting on this time in her senior years she drily recalled, "I was in solitary for a hundred and eighty days, so I had a chance to think of quite a few things." She knew that her fellow prisoners thought her behaviour was wild, but however she may have appeared to the world, in her own mind she did not consider herself to be so different. She did what she had to in order to survive, including making friends with the creatures around her, among them two big spiders. The larger one she named after the British prime minister and the smaller "yellow bellied insipid looking" one she called Tojo, after Tojo Hideki, the prime minister of Japan. She decided that under her tutelage Churchill and Tojo were going to learn how to fight like the enemies they were named after.

Ethel had seen trained fleas in a Paris market doing circus tricks, so she thought it must be possible to school these spiders in hatred. Knowing how bad tempered people could become when they felt their meagre resources were in jeopardy, she began by teasing them with food. One day when her *bayam* soup arrived at her door, there was a tiny bit of, what she assumed was, rat meat in it. She stuck a portion of it on a sliver of wood that she had pulled off the edge of her cell door and proceeded to gently wave it back and forth between the two prime ministers. Eventually her own hunger won out and she ate the meat. She then sat back and picked up her bible, but before even opening it she burst out laughing at her own hypocrisy. What kind of a Christian incited hatred in others for her own entertainment? Ethel's better angel did not visit for long. Air raids were coming thick and fast during these final months of war and she didn't want to take any chance that something might happen to her, allowing little Tojo to survive. That would not have been a good sign. Tojo thus came to a dramatic end during a particularly loud air raid, adding a little crunch to Ethel's dinner.

Luckily there was no shortage of spiders in Ethel's cell. Not only did they provide food and entertainment, she used their webs to bandage the jungle sore that had developed on her ankle. These wounds, which began with the slightest of cuts, easily became infected in malnourished prisoners whose natural immunities were low. The infections quickly become gangrenous, for which amputation was a common solution. Whether it was the spider web, long used in traditional medicine, or the enforced rest she got in solitary, or a combination of both, her wound healed.

After the death of Tojo, Churchill, having accomplished his purpose in life, was allowed to wander away, and Ethel turned her attention to ants. A group of them came each day to her cell, and she made herself believe they were the same ones returning to visit a friend. Watching them day after day, she wanted to know more about their behaviour. Did they play at the game of war as she had heard? Was it true that they had generals and casualty clearing stations? When Kawazue, the guard patrolling the women's quarters, came by and asked if she wanted anything, she quickly asked for something to read about ants. She wasn't sure what to expect from him though. He was an interpreter who had learned Malay as a resident in Singapore before the war. Nicknamed Puss-in-Boots because he swaggered around in jackboots, he was best known for beating both men and women when he was drunk. On one night alone, he was responsible for beating seventy internees for failing to bow when he entered their quarters unannounced.[4] However, two nights after Ethel's request, she saw pieces of paper flutter down through the bars of her window and heard his voice telling her to eat them if she got caught. In the light of day she discovered he had given her a *National Geographic* article about ants. As most do, she enjoyed the pictures first, then set about reading the article. She just had time to finish it before hearing someone approach her cell. Obeying her orders, she began eating. The pages turned into a gummed-up unchewable mass in her mouth, but with each bite she willed herself to believe it was soda biscuits. If she imagined something tasty she knew the saliva would flow and the mouthful would be easier to swallow.

Ethel's imagination could expand to create magnificent dining tables laden with invisible feasts, or plan a house where the bliss of intangible silence could live, and she was always eager to join with others in the pleasure of make-believe worlds. Ethel suffered an agonizing breakdown during the final months of her imprisonment. Whatever impression Ethel's activities gave anyone witness to her during her solitary confinement—singing patriotic songs long into the night, egging Prime Ministers Churchill and Tojo into battle, and enjoining her new ant friends to visit her again—the logic of the inner world she created for herself helped her to survive.

Part Four
Breaking Out

Sour Milk Cakes

flour

½ teaspoon baking powder

sour milk

Sift flour, baking powder, pinch of salt. Mix with enough sour milk to make a stiff paste. Fry in boiling lard, dropping paste from a dessertspoon into the pan. The small cakes must not be turned until the one side is well browned. Turn and brown the other side. These cakes must be eaten hot with fried bacon or can be used as a sweet served with sugar, jam, or syrup.

Toosje de Jager, Dutch (b.1909)

Jager was married to Hendrik who was imprisoned in Changi on the men's side.

Changi POW Recipe Log Book

CHAPTER TWENTY
SHAMEFUL HUNGER

News of war's progress was essential nourishment for the prisoners' mental wellbeing. While hard facts were not always available, overhead air raids were an exquisite indication that the Japanese were in trouble. On February 1, 1945, the prisoners witnessed the biggest raid to date. George Peet, on the men's side of Sime Road, counted more than ninety bombers. Although wincing at his own words he admitted, "It was an incredibly lovely sight."[1]

The raids occurred with increasing frequency until April, when the skies fell silent and prisoners' hopes plummeted. For long, hot months there was nothing. Then, in early August rumbles followed by crashing bombs and billows of dark smoke rocked the earth and filled the sky. Excitement and fear ran wild when the raids resumed. The prisoners knew it wasn't just their enemies who were in danger. Until they were liberated, they stood in a far more precarious position than the Japanese, squeezed as they were between Allied shells and possible enemy retribution. The latter they could only be wary of, but for the former, they developed their own Air Raid Precautions. These, said Mary Thomas, "consisted, on paper, of an elaborate organisation of stretcher-bearers, aid-posts and fire-fighters, and in practice of some open roofless slit trenches and a hopeful trust in Providence."[2]

Ethel was released from her solitary cell during the worst of the air raids. She saw prisoners digging trenches around the camp and was hurriedly ushered into one. The rush, confusion, and terror of these raids blurred all but one of them together. Ethel was crouched down with five other women all trying to make themselves as small as possible when she saw an Allied plane come down in flames. Parachutes sprouted out of it and began floating down like milkweed seeds. As the women gazed skyward they noticed one airman whose chute had caught fire. A whinging little voice among them said what they were all thinking: "I wonder what's in his knapsack." All eyes were trained on the pack hanging off him as he came tumbling to his death. Their only thought was for the food being consumed by the flames. Later it occurred to Ethel that this soldier was their Christ come to deliver them and they, like the disciples in the Garden of Gethsemane, didn't give him a moment's consideration. She was stunned at just how low she had been brought for want of food.

In the months leading up to liberation, George Peet marked down the decrease in prisoners' rations with ravenous precision:

February 6: Rice ration is to be cut by 20%.

March 8: The rice rations have been cut again. Four-hour workers, of which I am one [in the camp gardens], a cut from 17 ½ ounces (nominal) per day to 10 ½ ounces. Part-time workers 8 ½ ounces, non-workers and women 7 ounces.

April 8: The rice ration has been cut again, this time by 6%.[3]

This downward trend was only relieved when the prisoners each received Red Cross packages. The packages came, however, at a heartrending cost, one that caused Freddy to cry all the tears she had held back behind her cool wit for the last three years. The dogs, they were told, would have to be killed. No food could be wasted on them.

Hunger was pitted against love, and on April 16 Judy and the other dogs were killed. The packages were handed out on the twenty-third, the first ones since Christmas 1943.[4]

Relegated to her cell except during raids, Ethel knew nothing of the Red Cross delivery or the fate of little Judy. Not only was she cut off from camp activity, she missed out on the delicious swirl of rumours that were being dissected down to the minutest detail. Mary Thomas clearly remembered the talk. "On the evening of 15 August 1945, an extraordinary rumour began to circulate in the camp. It concerned the collapse of Japan and some unheard-of-catastrophe."[5] Had someone with a secret radio heard about the emperor's "Jewel Voice Broadcast" that day? In far-off Japan the recorded speech of Emperor Hirohito accepting the Joint Declaration of the United States, China, Britain, and the Soviet Union had been broadcast despite much controversy. Even in the wake of the Hiroshima and Nagasaki atomic bombings, Japanese military and government leaders had been arguing fiercely with each other about the surrender. Some had insisted on carrying on the fight, no matter what the civilian cost. Because of this internal battle the recording of Emperor Hirohito's four-minute speech barely made it on air. Nationalist militants tried to smash the record and when that failed others tried to hold up the radio station. For those Japanese who listened to the voice of their emperor they never once heard him mention "surrender" or "defeat."

"The war situation," he explained with obfuscating delicacy, "has developed not necessarily to Japan's advantage." In a face-saving measure, he transformed Japan's status as loser into the magnificent and selfless role of peacemaker, claiming "it is according to the dictates of time and fate that We have resolved to pave the way for a grand peace for all the generations to come by enduring the unendurable and suffering what is unsufferable."[6] Horrified by his speech, a group of young kamikaze pilots took off from airfields near Tokyo and scattered leaflets over central Japan. "Do not obey the false orders to surrender ... Resist to the end!"[7]

Robert Guillain, a French journalist who was trapped in Japan throughout the war, believed that the Japanese people first received a clear picture of the war's shattering news and the power of the atomic bomb through American broadcasts in English and Japanese that were being sent from a new transmitter set up on the island of Okinawa, captured on June 22. They were inundated with information about this weapon for which their language had yet no name. The confusion and tension in Japan was mirrored in the far-flung Japanese prisoner of war camps. Even though the next morning, Sunday, August 16, when the women at Sime Road were served "fried cakes of rice with a V for Victory stamped on each one," this victory brought neither freedom nor peace.[8] The following three weeks were filled with uncertainty; no one knew who was in control. In the days after the emperor's speech Lord Louis Mountbatten, supreme Allied commander of South East Asia, tried to communicate with General Itagaki Seishiro, Japanese commander of the 7th Area Army in Singapore, but his efforts were met with silence. Mountbatten was worried the British takeover of Singapore might end up in a battle, and the prisoners of war would be massacred. As it turned out, he was right to be concerned. Itagaki, with his long military record in China and Korea as well as his service as minister of war, was one of those who had strenuously objected to the surrender. On August 18 he went to Saigon to see his superior Field Marshall Count Terauchi Hsiaichi. Terauchi was not interested in Itagaki's arguments and told him there was no choice but to obey the terms of surrender.

On August 19, when there was still no word from Itagaki, Mountbatten ordered a small team of doctors led by British Signals Officer Captain Frank O'Shanohun to be parachuted into Singapore to bring aid and to find out what was going on. They landed at daybreak on an empty racecourse in a silent, darkened city. O'Shanohun later described this first official face-to-face meeting with a defeated but armed enemy. "I began to walk towards the main stand, I saw movement as a Japanese officer stepped out of the shadows. This was it! I kept on walking towards him and as I drew closer I saw a white band around his sleeve."[9] Relieved to see this mark of surrender, O'Shanohun let the officer know his intentions. One of the first places the team went to distribute the food and medical supplies they had brought with them was Sime Road camp. Ethel, still in solitary, would not have known about this visit which, as it turned out, was abruptly put to an end almost as soon as it began. "I was soon told quite sharply by the crusty civilian doctors that I could take my medical team away," reported O'Shanohun. "After more than three years in a Japanese camp, they knew all the internees' medical problems, I was told. 'Just give us the medical supplies,' they said, 'and we can do the job ourselves.'"[10]

The next day Itagaki met with O'Shanohun to give notice that he was ready to receive instructions for the surrender. Two days later, on August 22, the Japanese commander gathered his generals and senior staff to tell them the news. That evening, devastated by the surrender, over three hundred Japanese officers and men held a sake party at Raffles hotel, then did what they believed was expected of them and what they had expected from the military prisoners they had captured in 1942. They killed themselves, some with their swords, and others with hand grenades.[11]

For the prisoners, victory brought medical supplies, an increase in food, and control over the rice store, but not liberation or even any official word from the Japanese in camp. On August 20, Major-General Saito Masatoshi, commander of prisoner of war camps, met with the men's representative at Sime Road to say that negotiations were continuing but the Japanese were still in control. They brought in more food for the prisoners and told them the Royal Air Force would begin to drop food parcels on the twenty-fifth. The emotional strain on both sides was palpable. Prisoners tiptoed around the gun-toting Japanese who, Mary Thomas noticed, were "sulky and inclined to burst into tears."[12] George Peet remarked, "The Japanese camp commander, Lieutenant Suzuki, has strictly forbidden us to cheer. The Japanese officials here are very nervous lest we provoke an incident with their military."[13]

Finally, under the watchful eye of Lord Louis Mountbatten, Itagaki signed the surrender papers on September 4, aboard the HMS *Sussex*, within hours of the Allied leader's arrival in Singapore. Mountbatten did not want to take any chances while he waited for the formal and very public signing in Singapore's imposing Municipal Buildings on September 12. Nor did he want news of this initial secret signing to get out and upstage all the pomp and ceremony that the sagging British Empire could muster to show the world they were striving to retake what had been so ignobly lost.

The first sign of freedom for Ethel was the changed atmosphere when a contingent of Allied soldiers entered the camp. Much like after the Japanese had taken over Singapore three and a half years before, all was quietness. "It was a dead still quietness everywhere … They have to be careful not to let this become emotional or people would start to cry and there's a lot of tears had been pent up all this time." Ethel, now free to come and go from her solitary quarters, saw her world anew, much like what the liberators were seeing for the first time. Men stood, if they could, wearing just their G-strings and nothing on their feet. Women too, were scantily clad in thinned-out dresses and shorts whose hems had gradually risen over the years, snipped off for need of fabric elsewhere. The prisoners' apparel allowed a clear view of raw, suppurating sores. Ethel overheard one of the liberating soldiers saying, "This is like coming in to a valley of bones with a bit of flesh hanging here and there."

He wasn't the only one to be stunned by what he witnessed. Ethel kept her eyes on one of the musicians in the brass band that later played for them. She could see that this old, hard-nosed sergeant was himself watching another. The subject of his gaze was a bedraggled prisoner who was doing his best to stand for this momentous occasion. The old sergeant never missed a beat of his music but tears began to roll down his cheeks as he watched the prisoner' legs crumple and his whole body slowly sink into a roadside ditch. The sergeant appeared to Ethel as if he were standing over his own son's coffin.

At noon on September 5, the British soldiers enacted the simple, time-honoured and deeply symbolic flag raising ceremony for the prisoners. As internee Harry Miller, a pre-war reporter for the *Straits Times*, gazed at the rag-adorned women and children gathered to sing around the flagpole, the quality of their voices took him back to the start of this war saga.

> It was with broken voices and choked throats that we tried to
> sing the national anthem. But the loudest voices in praise were
> from the women who, three-and-a-half years before had, with
> faces held high and shoulders firmly back, marched into Changi
> singing, "There'll Always Be An England." Now they were
> singing victoriously.[14]

Ethel watched this flag raising filled with pride and a sharp desire for revenge. She grudgingly appreciated the diplomacy involved in folding the enemy flag after it was lowered and its hand-over to a Japanese officer. She was sure she was not alone in wanting to torture the man she held responsible for the mistreatment of prisoners, the much hated Major-General Saito Masatoshi, commander of all Malayan camps from March 27, 1944, until the end of the war. Ethel imagined a slow cooking recipe for this act, carefully flavoured with loathing. Each day she would carve off bits of his fingernails and toenails until she arrived, ever so gradually, to the quick. She wanted him to feel the same agony as the men she had overheard being similarly tortured. There would be no torture for Saito, but he did get his day in court. After his surrender he was accused of war crimes and arrested on September 11, 1945. He was later convicted and hanged in 1953.[15]

* * *

During these early days of September, the liberators had been working behind the scenes to bring families and separated spouses together. Labouring under a flinty relationship with the Japanese and with so many prisoners to see to, it took time and care to coordinate.

The first step in the process for Ethel was receiving a letter from Denis. She was overjoyed and to respond immediately got hold of some of the Australian Red Cross Society onionskin paper that had appeared in camp. "Darling Husband ... It is so wonderful that you are coming to get me for keeps." She knew he was aware of her breakdown and straightaway wanted to allay his fears. "Bless you darling this has been no picnic, but I will be fine as soon as we are together again." Of greater concern to her at that moment were his own health problems and the welfare of the wounded soldiers. Apart from these worries, she just wanted to be with him. As for the future, if they could make a quick visit to the cabin on Pulau Shorga it would be wonderful, but if not, it didn't matter. "I shall be happy as a sand boy when I see you and there is much that we can do together ... Come as soon as possible, my darling, my love."[16]

Her sentences trip along with an excitement in keeping with the new world of freedom that they faced. When Denis received a letter from Ethel's friend Audrey Goodridge written two days later, assuring him that "Mul is very much better," he might really have thought Ethel was well and as relaxed as she could ever be, particularly after all that she had been through. But then he received her Sime Road medical report of September 5 stating, despite occasional improvements, she was very sick and required sedation to control her moods.

Ethel's friends knew what Denis would be up against when he came to collect her, but they acted almost as a defence team representing their client against charges of being mentally unfit, charges made by prison doctors who, from their point of view, had never been Ethel's supporters. Denis, as a husband and a doctor, would ultimately be her judge and keeper, and they wanted him to be aware of mitigating details that would never be included in any medical report. Sue Williams, a nurse whom Ethel had befriended marching into Changi Jail three and a half years before, got together with Lucia Bach to compose a letter to Denis the day after the report was sent out. They were sure Ethel's breakdown had been caused by overwork.

"She did the work of ten persons herself," explained Lucia. "The speed and energy and constant strain were bound to tell and despite anything we did to prevent it, she persistently overworked."[17] To prove the point and make a case for Ethel's character, she described what their friend had taken upon herself to help alleviate the miserable conditions they had lived in. Anne Courtenay also wanted to be on record as a witness to Ethel's efforts in the camp. In the chaotic excitement of those final days her letter to Denis streamed out onto the page unfettered by punctuation or paragraphs. She never mentions Ethel's mental state, but her words are telling of the unrelenting energy Ethel applied to the projects she dreamt up and made happen. Together these women were offering a sympathetic understanding of Ethel's state of mind similar to what Daniel and Mira Mulvany had, back in 1939.

Ethel had long dreamt of the day she and Denis would be together again, wondering where they would start, what words they would say to each other. In the end the habits of lovers took over. After their first fragile kisses she held him and then, as she remembered it, time seemed to take on another character. That moment became a thousand years and in that millennium they exchanged soft words. This man, a doctor, who had spent the last three and a half years fighting disease, malnutrition, and the wounds of torture on behalf of his patients, was shrunken from the burden of his own trauma and physical illness. He was so slight to begin with, her hands surely felt the bluntness of each bone in his back as she hugged him while whispering her endearments. She might have felt the beginnings of a stoop around his shoulders and noticed grey hairs at his temples and throughout that funny little Clark Gable moustache of his. His eyes would have been filled with exhaustion and, perhaps, fear, as he looked at her thin, drawn face.

Gradually the tenderness of their first exchanges was punctuated with questions. Ethel absolutely needed to know what had happened to Ostell, a corporal in the Royal Army Medical Corps and one of her favourite people. Denis knew she was going to ask about him so had braced himself. Corporal Anthony Ostell had died of tuberculosis on August 11, 1945, just days before liberation. Denis tried to soften the news for Ethel, telling her that there had really been no good reason for him to die then, so it must have been that he had been overcome by the great joy of what they all felt was coming.

Denis knew that she would ask about Kelly, too, an Irish orderly in the medical corps. He had been shot in the back escaping the Japanese. They both agreed, knowing Kelly's unstoppable personality, his fate was hard but not a big surprise. There were many more that Ethel wanted to know about but Denis refused to go on. The losses were too great to hear. Knowing Ethel was in a delicate frame of mind, he tried to redirect her thoughts to something happier. So they talked about her brother Harv and sister Marg and Aunt Susie and mused about how Canada and England might have changed. Then, for some reason, Denis asked a painful question, and the conversation went spiralling into blackness. Maybe he had been trying to manage Ethel's high hopes, but instead she came crashing down when he asked her who would be the hardest person for her to lose. She didn't need to think twice, it would be Keith Greenaway, her adored younger cousin, whose photo she had kept tucked in her bible throughout the war. Denis warned her that the life expectancy for air force pilots like Keith was very short. He thought it probable Keith had been involved in the fighting over Thailand and Malaya and, like so many others, would have been killed. He cautioned Ethel not to get her hopes up too high, knowing how easily her heart could break and what the consequences would be. Still, Ethel was sure Keith had survived the war, and it later turned out she was right. To Keith's great frustration, the Royal Canadian Air Force considered his service as an instructor in Canada far too valuable to let him go overseas to fight.

There was another name that came into Ethel's mind. He'd had nothing to do with the war or Singapore but the pain she felt from his death poured out when she thought of the young soldiers who had died or might be dead. It was Paul, their unborn son. Denis understood and could see how her mind was working, how she had made Keith her Paul and a lot of other young men as well, and that was why her heart broke so often. To prevent more heartache, he urged her to let the subject go for now and turn her attention elsewhere. But there was one more question she had for Denis.

"Where did the Canadian Red Cross quilt go?"

Denis assumed she was talking about the British quilt. "It's with one Colonel Collins. I think he's going to take it home."

"Like heck he's going to take it home!"

"Well, Ethel, what can you do about it? The war's over. Don't you start another war."

"I'll fight for that quilt."

"When the war's over you'd fight one of your own for that quilt?"[18]

He was right of course. This was no time to quarrel. She held back her frustration and confusion over the quilts, and let the topic be for now. She and Denis stepped out of her cage into a new world. Seeing her out in the open, friends came over to greet her. She could tell from the looks on their faces that they had been warned not to make too much of a fuss, otherwise she could easily become overwrought. She wasn't the only one whose emotions were flaring. Women all around her were weeping, seeing their husbands for the first time in far too long or discovering that they would never see them again. As they walked through the camp Ethel saw little Reggie Stuart sitting at the side of the road convulsed in tears. She had only seen this tough little boy crying in such a fit like this once before. Reginald Stuart had been born September 1, 1941; all he had known was war. Still, when they had all moved to Sime Road camp from Changi, he like many of the other children, had been terrified. There were no protective walls at Sime Road, and the air was filled with the unnerving sound of wind rustling through leaves.

When she asked him what was wrong, he said he wanted to know what they were going to do, now that all the guards had been taken away. Ethel understood. She approached an airman who was carrying a side arm and explained there was a little boy who needed to know there were men with guns who would take care of him. The airman agreed to sit with Reggie and try to console him. Ethel could see there were other, even bigger, adjustments that many children at Sime Road had to make. There was suddenly a man in their lives. For some, their fathers were almost complete strangers who now monopolized their mother's attention.

Possibly to the relief of some children, the fathers were not allowed to spend the night in the women's camp because of limited space. Ethel's unique situation meant Denis was permitted to stay. She did not speak of what they shared when they lay together for the first time in three and a half years.

The next morning, they went to stand in line for their bayam soup, she with her old tomato tin and Denis with his army medic can. Denis was excited—this was about the last time they would have to queue for food. They took their ration back to her cell and sat on the doorstep, relishing, if not the food, at least the moment. For Ethel the only other day in her life that had given her such pleasure had been their marriage day, and she didn't suppose there would be any other day in the future that could compare to the bliss of "sitting there with that cell behind you and everything ahead of you."

Ambrosia Dessert

1 cup mashed bananas

1 cup granulated sugar

3 tspns lemon juice

¼ cup orange juice

¼ tspn salt

2 beaten egg whiles

1 tspn grated orange rind

½ tspn grated lemon rind

mandarin oranges slices

Mix mashed bananas with sugar, lemon juice, orange juice, and salt. Beat well, add beaten egg whites, grated lemon, and orange rind. Chill for several hours. Place in sherbet cups and serve with mandarin sections.

Euphemia Redfearn, Australian (1896–1945)

Redfearn was married to jockey and horse-trainer William Wyatt Redfearn (1878–1942). Both died in internment.

Changi POW Recipe Log Book

CHAPTER TWENTY-ONE

FIRST FEASTS

E thel was desperately disappointed that even after British forces had taken over the camp, the food being served was the same wretched slop. She realized they weren't allowed to give the prisoners so much as a candy, but her frustration was keen all the same. Their liberators were dutifully obeying orders informed by the recent experiences of the Allies, who had freed tens of thousands of prisoners from the German concentration camps. There they quickly discovered that providing food in the amounts yearned for by the prisoners actually killed many of them. The body does not readapt evenly to a normal diet after having been starved. The metabolism reacts quickly to the increase in food but the circulatory system takes much longer to adjust. Already weakened hearts became overly strained, resulting in heart failure.[1]

Ethel didn't know of anyone dying from overeating during those early days of freedom at Sime Road, but she heard rumours that some died that first night at different camps. This may have been because of the generosity of locals who offered food to their friends and those they had worked for or with before the war. Many Chinese arrived at Sime Road bringing hard to carry food, like eggs and milk, in big glass bottles. The medical staff responded by setting up an armed guard around the camp.

Mary Thomas found out about the food restrictions from flyers released by planes after the Japanese surrender. Addressed "To All Allied Prisoners of War" they requested:

> If you have been starved or underfed for long periods DO NOT eat large quantities of solid food, fruit or vegetables at first. It is dangerous for you to do so. Small quantities at frequent intervals are much safer and will strengthen you far more quickly. For those who are really ill or very weak, fluids such as broth and soup, making use of the water in which rice and other foods have been boiled, are much the best. Gifts of food from the local population should be cooked. We want to get you back home quickly, safe and sound, and we do not want to risk your chances from diarrhoea, dysentery and cholera at this last stage.[2]

All this meant more bayam soup. Guy Howard Bedford described this concoction for readers of his local paper back home in England. As a serving member of the Fleet Air Arm aboard the relief ship HMS *Sussex*, he arrived in Singapore on September 4 and was taken on a tour of Changi Jail. One of the cooks led him to the galley where the evening meal was being prepared and showed him what was brewing.

> It consisted of ... a yellowish looking mess with pieces of dismal looking vegetable floating like scum on top. "This is much better than the lot we had last night," said the guide, "You can see the stuff is there—last night you could see the bottom of the tub."

Bedford was not impressed. "At home a farmer would think twice about feeding such a mess to his pigs." While arrangements were being made for HMS *Sussex* to transport the newly liberated prisoners now milling around the docks, the cooks on board worked tirelessly. The *Hotel Sussex*, as it became known, served as many of the semi-starved internees and former POWs as possible. In the beginning, bread was all they cared about, it was "far more precious to them than gold."³

Ethel would have to wait until she was on board ship and out to sea for her first taste of that most desired food, the one that had begun all of the women's recipe discussions. She and other very sick women and men were taken by ambulance on what seemed like an excruciatingly long trip over bumpy, war-torn roads to the awaiting hospital ship SS *Rajula*. When they arrived at the docks, they were met by a party in full swing. Looking up at the crowd from the stretcher she lay on, Ethel could see throngs of well-wishers alternately chatting with one another, saying goodbye to those who were leaving, and singing along as the band played the 1910 classic "When You Come to the End of a Perfect Day." She saw her friend Yap Pheng Geck of the Chinese bank among the throng and begged her stretcher-bearers to slow down. Dr. Yap knew a lot of people in Singapore through his work as an officer of the Singapore Volunteer Corps and as an active member of the Singapore Municipal Commission. If anyone had known the fate of the Seongs it would have been him. However, her stretcher-bearers had a mission and didn't want to get swallowed by the crowd. She was whisked up the gangway, onto the ship, and into her bunk, comforted at least by the knowledge that Denis was somewhere nearby.

As soon as she was settled in her bunk she gave her full attention to the orderly who arrived at her bedside with half a glass of milk. She gulped it down, reached her finger into the glass to catch any stray drips and then asked for water so she could rinse out the remaining essence and drink it. Next on the menu was more bayam soup. She didn't object this time, knowing that real food was coming soon. Before then she had her blood tested and due to low levels of iron, she was given a transfusion. Feeling safe and somewhat sated she fell asleep. In this moving picture of her life, the next thing she knew, Lady Mountbatten, dressed in her St. John's Ambulance uniform, was leaning over her, thanking her for the work she had done for the Red Cross. Before Ethel could respond she had whisked off to the next person. While she didn't really care one way or the other about Lady Mountbatten, the commemorative plates the patients received after the entourage left made a deep impression on her. The one Ethel received had flowers on it. She adored blossoms of all kinds, but in her present state found those flowers confounding. While devouring the first morsels of food served on the plate, she ended up scraping away at the flowers, only to discover, to her profound frustration, they were inedible images.

The next morning the patients were served milk, egg, and sugar beaten together. Ethel wanted to linger with the heavenly flavour of it but just couldn't keep it in her mouth long enough. There was only one fleeting chance to taste her food, and that was when it was on the way down. After the eggnog she had an injection of what she thought was iron and ate some of her daily ration of pills before falling asleep again. The pills Ethel assumed were vitamins, were barbiturates. She was being given 12 grams of luminal per day, a common "sleep cure" for psychotic disorders.[4] Between the drugs, exhaustion, and relief, Ethel spent much of her time dozing.

When conscious though, she, like all the other patients, begged for more food. When her first real meal finally arrived she was sure it was worth the wait. In her interview with Sidney Katz she said that it smelled just like she imagined Ned Pratt's table in the skies, "Like chicken. Real, rip roaring, live cooked chicken." Beside the roast chicken was a tiny helping of mashed potatoes smoothed out with milk, no butter, because that would have been too rich. The cook had taken care to place the fluffy white mound just so on the flowered plate and score the top. By then Ethel was wise to the flowers and paid no attention to them. Instead she noticed the colourful teaspoonful of pureed carrot that balanced out this most glorious sight. Not that she spent long just looking at the food.

The carrot made some of the patients sick to their stomachs but after vomiting they immediately asked for more. That Ethel wasn't sick to her stomach was something of a miracle because her serving of roast chicken came on the bone, and she ate that too, as did about ten others. When the orderly came back for the plates he could see that they had all been licked clean—"with our tongues and no pardon me or anything"—and there were no bones in sight. He was convinced they would all die, but Ethel assured him she wouldn't. If she didn't have enough juices in her stomach to dissolve that bone, then she told him she wasn't worth living. She even bet him a cent she didn't have that she would live. He called the doctor anyway. Ethel was terrified that they were going to pump out her stomach and deprive her of the first real meal she'd had since before the fall of Singapore. With the same spirit she'd shown when she first met Denis while on her sickbed, Ethel let the doctor know she would raise Cain if he went near her. He laughed and told her there was no use in pumping out a stomach for bones. Fortunately the barely chewed chicken bone made it through her system, and after that episode no more bones were served to the patients.

The only thing Ethel was able to linger over during that voyage was a glass of ginger ale. The sparkling bubbles made her think of the champagne served on her wedding day.

Fowl Badum or Dry Curry

1 fowl

1 tbsp sliced red onion

4 cloves garlic chopped

green ginger chopped

pinch of ground saffron (dry)

20 dry chillies roasted and ground

¼ tspn fenugreek

1 tbspn coriander seeds

1 tspn white cumin seeds

½ tspn sweet cumin seeds (roasted and ground together)

1 tbspn ghee

salt

2 inch piece of cinnamon

1 inch piece daun pandan

¼ stem lemon grass

small sprig curry leaves

1 wineglass of vinegar

3 teacups coconut milk (extract)

Cut the fowl into meat joints put them in a chatty with the coconut milk and the rest of the ingredients except the ghee. Boil slowly until the fowl is tender and the gravy reduced to very little. Remove the fowl from the gravy and fry it in the ghee. Pour back the gravy and keep on a slow fire for a couple of minutes longer.

Rosalind von Hagt, a widow from Ipoh, Malaya (1886-1946)

Von Hagt was interned with her family of one son and eight daughters.

Changi POW Recipe Log Book

CHAPTER TWENTY-TWO

THE HORRORS OF HEALTH CARE

The SS *Rajula* was met by a flowing crowd when it arrived at the docks of Madras (Chennai) on September 16, 1945. Women, in a profusion of brightly coloured saris, carried armloads of gifts. There was "soap, powders, towels, toothpaste, cotton wool," all mundane items that had been transformed into luxuries.[1] Josephine Foss, the former headmistress who had been so helpful in arranging clandestine meetings between husbands and wives in Changi, was in awe of the sight. Although so weak she could barely walk, she took in the view from the bridge. There was only one thing that was missing among all these offerings—food. It was disappointing, but Fossy assumed they had been told the former prisoners couldn't handle it.

Despite the vibrancy of the scene, Ethel felt it was shot through with sadness. She was sure the women were waiting, not for these British, but for their own loved ones to be returned from Singapore. The SS *Rajula* had long provided the Straits Service between Singapore and Madras and was a favourite of the many Indians who had travelled on it, but there were no Indians on that ship. It was, she thought, "another mistake in the line of terrible mistakes made by

England towards India." Even though she was sure the onlookers were disappointed, they were prepared to give the ex-prisoners the garlands they had brought. Unable to get near the protected patients to hang the flowers around their necks, they spread them out all along the road leading up from the docks. As the ambulances drove over them, the crushed flowers sent up an enveloping perfume through the sultry air.

A part of Ethel felt at home at that moment. On September 30 she wrote to her brother Harvey, "We are free! After a long and terrible nightmare. None can imagine, who has not been a prisoner of war, just what joy it is to be alive after these gruelling times." Harvey notified the *Manitoulin Expositor* of the great news, and the paper wrote a spread on Ethel, reprinting her letter. They recounted that their island girl's fondest dreams, "are centred upon food, particularly she is longing for Morelles [sic], bread and butter, rabbit stew and raspberry pie."[2] For Ethel, though, few of these dreams or any of her others would come true any time soon. The next year would prove to be one of anguish and horror with challenges every bit as devastating as those she had faced during her years of imprisonment.

From Madras, Ethel and Denis boarded a hospital train heading inland to the city of gardens, Bangalore (Bengaluru.) There she was to receive a relatively new form of treatment for her mania at the British Military Hospital in Jalahilli on the outskirts of the city. Insulin coma therapy had been developed in Vienna in the 1930s by Manfred Sakel, who was convinced his experiments showed that insulin helped calm psychotic patients. By the late 1950s his theory was disproved but not before it had gained great international popularity within the medical community. The treatment was horrendous and dangerous for the patients. From the doctors' point of view, having little else they could do for those suffering from debilitating mental illnesses, it seemed to provide a glimmer of hope.

Ethel was given her first of nine daily doses of insulin on September 20. Each day, as per protocol, the dose was increased by ten units with the aim of bringing her to the point of severe hypoglycemia.[3] Comas would be induced in the patients and then the doctors would administer glucose to revive them. Ethel never forgot the terrifying feeling of not being able to breathe and then passing out during this procedure.[4] By the third day, the effects were beginning to show. She was even more restless than when she had arrived. Other reactions to the treatment regularly ran the gamut through pouring sweat, loss of bowel control, terrible anxiety and confusion. To whatever extent she suffered from these side effects, Ethel could not be blamed for feeling she was being given an injection of distilled prison camp experiences—the loss of control she suffered from dysentery, the profuse sweating from fear, and the anxiety generated from malnutrition. Even more torturous was the seething hunger invoked by severe sugar depletion during treatment. So powerful was this hunger that in an attempt to relieve it patients often became obese.[5] Ethel's hunger may have been powerful, but at this point, what she wanted most was to be free and reunited with Denis. When she was finally released after four weeks, her doctor remarked that she was cheerful but appeared to have no more insight into her illness than when she had arrived. Another feature he noted that had remained unchanged about Ethel was she continued "to entertain" what he considered to be "irrational prejudices, as for example against the medical profession."[6]

Ethel and Denis moved into a hotel in Bangalore. For a few weeks they ate good food, slept in beds, and kept each other company while trying to decide where they would live their lives. Ethel wanted to stay in India and Denis was pushing for England. Before they could settle on which it was to be, Denis received word that his father in England was very ill. After consulting with Ethel's doctor to see if she was stable enough for him to leave her alone, he flew to England on November 25. To be separated from him so soon after her treatments, and just two months after having being reunited with him after the war was more than Ethel could bear. Three days later she was back in hospital where she stayed, with the exception of a bleak Christmas spent at a Red Cross Reception Centre without family or friends.

When Denis returned on January 4 he found her in a bad way. She was dirty, disorderly, exhibiting violent behaviour toward hospital staff, and had developed a habit—understandable for a former prisoner of war—of hoarding. What was surprising, given her health, was that she had to be force fed. Why, when she had just gone through the rigours of insulin treatment which balloons the appetite, and years of desperate, fearful hunger, would she refuse food? It would take her many more years to finally be able to satisfy an appetite that went far beyond the need to fill her stomach. Eating disorders are so complex and deeply fraught with emotions, it is impossible to know what was going on in Ethel's mind, especially from this distance. But in her later interviews with Sidney Katz, she agreed when he said, "Food became a real obsession for you, didn't it?" Having it or not, eating it or not, both are about control. Ethel deeply wanted to experience some control in her life and to savour what she had had before the war, the pleasures of a home and a marriage.

She did not begrudge Denis for having left. When he returned she reached out to him from deep within her broken state to offer loving affection. In spite of her welcome, he knew from her psychiatrist that all was not well. The medical board recommended that Ethel be evacuated to England and remain in care for an indefinite period. In mid-March Denis convinced a reluctant Ethel to board a hospital ship, telling her that he needed to return home to be with his newly widowed mother. The ship's doctor kept a close eye on Ethel, and by the time they arrived in England, he was convinced that she was fit enough to stay with Daniel and Mira at their house, Rosecroft, in Haywards Heath. Denis disagreed with the doctor's opinion and maintained that Ethel was certifiable. After a few weeks during which all was well, some unrecorded event caused Ethel's nascent peace of mind to shatter. Consequently, on April 25, 1946, the wheels of the car carrying Ethel and Denis crunched up the gravel drive to the front door of one of the most prominent mental hospitals in the world, Bethlem Royal Hospital. Denis signed the committal papers and gave his consent for more of the terrifying insulin coma therapy and electrical shock therapy, whatever the doctors thought might make a difference.

* * *

In 1946, Bethlem Royal Hospital was not the same house of horrors that had gained infamy under its colloquial name of Bedlam, but it was the same institution. The priory of St. Mary's of Bethlehem was founded in 1247 and by the next century was treating the insane, making it one of the world's oldest hospitals for the mentally ill. Throughout its history the hospital was housed in various locations in London. In the late seventeenth century it moved to the then open land of Moorefield's, London, where it was housed in a weighty baroque edifice, now the Imperial War Museum. The hospital contained large galleries from which the public were allowed to view the inmates as a form of gruesome entertainment. In all, this establishment became a metaphor for a world utterly unhinged.

In 1930, the institution moved again, this time to a semi-rural estate in Kent away from the congestion and smog of London. The hospital Ethel entered that springtime was a collection of smaller modern villa-like buildings, designed for patient comfort. The sparely furnished rooms had verandas overlooking a grassy courtyard. Although rubble from buildings bombed during the war was strewn about the place, there were enough calm vistas of trees and greenery to help soften the frightening truths of mental illness facing each patient upon entry. But when Ethel entered the building, she resisted even glimpsing her surroundings. Instead, she kept her eyes fiercely shut, not even deigning to look at the admitting doctor. When he asked her questions about her history she would only say, "The call from God has come!"[7] All the while she waved her hands violently about her head, grabbing and clutching at her hair, fending off his questions as if they were air-born fiends. When nothing more could be gained from the interview, she was led to her room in Tyson Wing, a section specially reserved for wildly excited patients.

At first the doctors were unsure, was this a case of schizophrenia or mania? Regardless, they decided the best course of action would be electric shock therapy. Although newer and safer than insulin treatments, it presented its own horrors. There were no anaesthetics or muscle relaxants to soften the process when Ethel received this treatment. She was fully conscious as she lay down on the bed and had the electrodes tightly fitted onto her head. For an eternal few moments she waited while the assistants prepared her for the oncoming convulsions. For many patients these were so severe the cracking sound of breaking bones would fill the operating room. Everything was so terrifyingly similar to what Ethel had undergone at the hands of the Japanese—only this time it was British doctors who compelled her to undergo this torture. Finally they turned the knob on the control mechanism beside the bed and 130 volts of alternating current flashed through Ethel's brain for .2 of a second. She was lucky, over the course of six treatments no bones were broken.

Throughout her stay at Bethlem Ethel wrote almost daily to Denis, beginning and ending her missives with endearments. Without a hint of the mental turmoil that she had been suffering, she chatted about his welcome visits, the friends she was making among the patients, how bad the food was, and how nice it would be to take a trip to Canada to see the family. She asked if he would please make sure to return all her mementos that she had so carefully cradled all through prison camp. She knew that some of her belongings were in Worthing at her mother-in-law's house and was anxious that if something happened to him while she was in Canada, Mary Mulvany might not return them. Someone had already thrown out the lipstick container he had given her just before they were sent to prison camp and which she had held onto all through the war. With poignant observation she explained to Denis that these small treasures "sometimes save me lonely moments." Ethel had not forgotten how her father-in-law had treated her before the war. She assured Denis, "I am not filled with hatred towards Worthing but my only way of overcoming past quarrels is to have my own things in my own hands."[8] While she was on the subject, she asked for the second time who had the Red Cross quilts. Would Denis write and ask for them please? She wanted to take them back to Canada to show her Red Cross chapter.

Sure that she was getting much better, Ethel thought it was time to leave. Her doctor agreed that she was improving. He wrote in her file, "She is with the exception of an occasional disconnected train of thought, rational and has a certain amount of insight into her illness."[9] For safety's sake though, he advised that she be kept under observation at the hospital, at least until the end of June. Meanwhile, Denis wrote to Aunt Susie to see if Ethel could stay with her in Toronto. Despite Susie's reply that they would both be welcome, Denis only booked one ticket.

In early July, the discharge committee met and agreed Ethel was well enough to leave. A few weeks later Denis and Brigadier Walker, a friend from India days, escorted Ethel to the docks at Southampton. Wearing her blue coat fashioned from an old blanket and clutching the $14 given to her by a Salvation Army officer, she joined a crowd of anxious war brides and war-calloused veterans waiting to board the *Queen Mary* bound for Halifax. Having been shuttled from the jail house of Changi to the asylums of Bangalore and Bedlam, she was about to return to the colony from whence she came, without her husband. She and Denis had found enjoyment in their years of marriage and he had stuck by her through bouts of mania and depression, but the war, and what he had endured throughout his years of imprisonment, had sapped his resources. At the end of this global conflict fate had presented him with a life of dividing what little energy he had left between a very sick wife and a widowed mother. As a Roman Catholic and a man of traditional views who had been devoted to Ethel, divorce would have been wrong on so many levels. But it's hard not to wonder, if, as he stood on the docks that day, it may have seemed like an act of self-preservation worthy of quiet consideration.

Ragged Robbins

2 egg whites

1 cup of sugar

1½ cups cornflakes

½ cup chopped walnuts

½ cup chopped dates

1 tspn vanilla

Beat eggs stiff. Add other ingredients. Drop in teaspoonfuls on oiled baking sheet.

Ethel Mulvany, from her copy of *A Guide to Good Cooking* (1932) that was retrieved from the ruins of her house in Singapore and which she took into Changi Jail.

Changi POW Cook Book

CHAPTER TWENTY-THREE

IS THIS HOME?

After the *Queen Mary* docked in Halifax Ethel continued on with her journey by troop train to Toronto. At Union Station, Aunt Susie and Uncle Frank Wood gathered her up and drove her back to their house on Barrington Avenue. Manitoulin would always be home, but the house on Barrington was the next best thing. Even when she was imprisoned on the other side of the world, Ethel knew the middle bedroom upstairs was hers. The bed, the desk, the chair, everything was the same as before, all that had changed was her.

As soon as she could, she marshalled her cheerfulness and wrote to Denis, the first of what would be a series of fortnightly letters throughout that summer and fall. She prattled on about the usual particulars of everyone's health and wellbeing and then moved straight to food. "It is wonderful to get the fresh fruit ... how I would love to send you some ... They have what they call rationing here but it is almost comic to hear what the 'rations' are—a lb. of butter a week."[1] In place of the fresh fruit she wanted Denis to have, each month she sent non-perishable food parcels to him and other friends in England, where post-war rationing was not so comic.

Despite the tone of her letter, Ethel was struggling. Years later in her interview with Sidney Katz, she tried to put words to the feeling.

> You're walking as if in a shadow. There's a shadow by you that is you [now], there's a shadow by you that was you [before the war], there's a shadow by you that was you in the prison. And you can't quite endure, you're kind of a triad. There you walk, in a nervous shock, a trauma of types. You know you want the other two to become you, but you can't see them merging.

Being trapped in this wandering triad of selves was made all the worse by not knowing what her future held or even where it would be lived. Was she to return to England to be with Denis? Would he come to Canada? Where would their home be?

Ethel sensed a growing despondency in Denis's letters. She knew he had plenty to be despairing of. Closest to home was his own health. Strained even before the war with his appendectomy, once back in England he suffered blood poisoning and digestive problems which he blamed on the POW diet. Unknown to Ethel, he was hospitalized just weeks after she left. His father's death so soon after liberation had been a hard loss. Then there was her own health, which she knew weighed heavily on him. In reply to his letter of August 25, 1946, she first offered compassion: "Darling, Your letter ... sounds too blue for words." Then she pleaded with him, "couldn't you just try to forget all of our unhappy past and be carefree for a while?" By October her letters to him were forwarded so often she didn't know where he was living, but by then he was already beyond her reach. Unbeknownst to Ethel, Denis had written to Susie, revealing his intentions to end the marriage. Susie was stunned. From what she understood, Denis had been going through a difficult time, but she had no idea that he had come to this conclusion. On September 16, she wrote back with deep sadness, "If you must hurt her please wait until we have a chance to be sure she will not relapse." Denis tried to go slow, at first coolly asking Ethel how she saw the future. Then finally his letter arrived in the mailbox announcing, "I want to be free."[2]

The words crippled Ethel. Why? Why would he ask for a divorce? Surely they could regain their early happiness if only he had faith in her. If he didn't love her anymore, why had he insisted on keeping their wedding certificate and the precious photo album from their honeymoon? These treasures that Ram Bharose had dug out of the ruins of their house and given to her before Singapore fell, they were symbols of their love, weren't they? None of it made sense. She copied his tormenting words all over notebooks, scraps of paper, even in her bible. What was left to hold on to? No war-torn husband. Not even a piece of paper proving that there had ever been a marriage born in India. Her ideas began to twist together. She had written to Denis while in Bethlem, asking for her prison camp mementos. He had complied, handing over the papers and items so dear to her, including her recipe collection, but he had no Red Cross quilts to give her and, for some reason probably even he did not understand, he held on to the photo album. After Denis's request for a divorce, Ethel latched onto the memory of the quilts. She was bent on having them and was terrified that he had thrown them out, thinking they were old junk ... like his marriage. Over time she multiplied the three original Red Cross quilts into four, then five. One was for the Imperial Japanese Hospital, one was for the Australian hospital, one was for the Americans, another was for the British, and the last was Canadian. Numbers and nationalities leapfrogged around in her head. She started a letter writing campaign, claiming that the British quilt had actually been made for the Canadian Red Cross, and it belonged in Canada. She was so persistent that research was eventually undertaken on the British quilt to see if there was any sign that at one time "Canada" had been written on the label. None was found.[3]

There was one Canadian quilt however, an intricate, multi-coloured hexagonal patterned one Ethel's mother had sent to her in India after she got married. It had stayed with Ethel through all her years of freedom and imprisonment and had accompanied her back to Canada. But this was not one of the Red Cross quilts she was fixated on. There were no embroidered dreams on it belonging to her or anyone else. It had never been a means for her to send a message to the man she loved. Within this anguished clutter of ideas, was it really a quilt that was so important to her, or a marriage—a union between a quiet dark-haired Englishman and an effervescent young woman from the colonies? Either way after the war there would be neither a quilt nor a marriage. On November 6, 1946, while stationed in Dover, Denis had met Eileen Lawson-Matthew, a young medical student twenty-one years his junior. Almost as quickly as he had fallen in love with Ethel on the boat from Shanghai thirteen years before, he was declaring his love for Eileen.

Peter Pans

Biscuits

2½ cups self-raising flour

1 tspn salt

½ cup butter

¾ cup milk

Filling

½ lb dried apricots

4 oz prunes

¼ tspn almond essence

2 tbsps sugar

4 oz seeded raisins

4 oz blanched almonds

Sift flour and salt. Cut in butter. Add milk all at once. Stir. Roll out ¼ inch thick and cut with 3-inch cutter. Place half circles on ungreased baking sheet. Brush with melted butter. Place remaining circles on top and brush with butter. Bake in hot oven for 20 minutes. Separate halves of hot biscuits. Spread bottom halves with cooked filling. Place other halves on top. Decorate top with whipped cream, ½ apricot with prune and almond in centre. Serve with a little syrup in which fruit was cooked.

Changi POW Cook Book

CHAPTER TWENTY-FOUR

NEVER ENOUGH

Ethel did her best to fill her emptiness with food. Manners went out the window, all that mattered was how quickly she could consume what was on her plate. At first she ate massive quantities. Breakfasts consisted of four eggs, a half-pound of bacon, slice after slice of jam-covered toast, and as much fruit as she could fit in. Aunt Susie quickly saw Ethel was getting out of control and consulted the family physician. Dr. J.Y. Ferguson, although no expert in all that ailed Ethel, had heard that former POWs initially had to be kept away from rich food and advised Susie to limit the fats and sugars she served Ethel. It was good advice, but Ethel could not be stopped. Sugar was the first restricted item to catch her eye. As soon as her aunt's back was turned she found a bag of white sugar in the kitchen and began eating it by the spoonful. As she crunched down on it the crackling sound in her mouth reminded her of eating ants, like the little friends who had come to visit her in solitary. Cherries were next, six pounds of them. Susie had asked her to pick some, explicitly reminding her that if she ate any as she picked she must be sure and remember to spit out the pips. Ethel did that, but she just couldn't fill the baskets Susie had given her. All she could do was fill her belly. Fortunately she didn't suffer any ill effects and, to even her own astonishment, she managed to eat dinner afterwards.

She was conscious that her eating habits were bizarre, but she couldn't stop. Waste was intolerable, even apple cores had to be eaten, her own and anyone else's. She would pick them off her aunt and uncle's plates and finish the stem, the seeds, and even the hard, thin papery sections cupping the seeds. When she had eaten until there was room for no more, she would take her plate out through the kitchen to the back porch where she would sit on the steps and run her finger over the surface, picking up leftover juices and crumbs that she had been unable to scrape up with her knife and fork. When that was done she would lift the plate and, like an appreciative dog, draw her tongue over it, cleaning off whatever essence of food remained. After returning to the kitchen to help her aunt do the dishes, she would go upstairs and unload all the food she had pocketed over dinner. She saw it as stealing, but instead of trying to stop herself she honed her skills, which she rated as somewhere on the scale between Houdini and a street urchin. She hid her stolen treasure inside her pillow case, in the bottom drawer of her bureau, and in an old shoebox in the cupboard. Although she never stole money or anything from a store, she felt a sense of empathy with thieves incarcerated in the nearby Don Jail. Every time she rode the streetcar down Broadview past the oppressive building, she sent up a prayer for them.

Ethel realized that her aunt and uncle knew exactly what she was doing, and she was always grateful they let her continue to hoard for as long as she needed. Susie never offered to clean out Ethel's room but would try and get Ethel to sit with her elsewhere in the house so she wouldn't be constantly surrounded by the stench of rancid cheese. For Ethel it was a divine scent. Even when there was absolutely no more space in her stomach, she was comforted just by the smell of food; the same was true for the sight of it. She made a habit of getting on the streetcar at Main and Danforth and riding it all the way to Jane Street, where she would put in another ticket and return. The whole point was just to gaze at the fruit and vegetables under the fluttering awnings of the greengrocers' shops, especially the oranges which had come to symbolize pure luxury to her while she was in Changi. In Toronto it was more than just the presence of bright coloured pyramids of produce that delighted Ethel, it was that these delectables had been artfully designed to be savoured first by the eyes and only then by the tongue. This was a world where appetites were courted, not controlled.

Her family refrained from commenting on her odd behaviours and they never let on how distressing her appearance was. Not everyone was so restrained. George Elliot, an elderly member of the congregation where Ethel went to church, was unable to hide his revulsion when he looked over at her one Sunday morning. Ethel caught his glance and was surprised at his reaction. She was confident she looked quite well once her boils and carbuncles had healed. Thinking on it some more, though, she realized she still had a raw look about her that some found startling. At the same time, that look was recognizable and familiar to others who had lived through similar horrors. To them, she presented a kindred spirit with whom they could share their feelings. Hugh Lackie was one of those people. This former Hong Kong prisoner of war and now United Church minister approached Ethel at church. Ethel told Sidney Katz about how she and Hugh had got to talking about the hell they had each been through and, each knowing the other would understand, openly shared stories of the thefts they had committed after returning home.

He told Ethel that one day his wife had come home from the bank after withdrawing her housekeeping money. He slipped twenty dollars out of her purse when she wasn't looking and went downtown to buy tinned goods and sugar, things that he had longed for in prison. Laughing at the absurdity of it, he said he was careful to take the sugar out of the bag and pour it into a jar to prevent ants getting at it, as they would have done in Hong Kong. Now that he had his secret stash he had to think of where to hide it. When he was hanging up his winter coat in the hall cupboard he noticed his wife's spring hats all done up in cellophane-covered boxes on the top shelf. Knowing she wouldn't be touching them for months, he filled each hat with his tins and jars and put them back in place.

He was so comforted by the knowledge of his secret supply that when his wife approached him upset that she seemed to have lost some of her housekeeping money, he didn't let on. Innocently, he asked how much was missing and helped her search high and low throughout the house. As Hugh related this story to Ethel the two of them ached with laughter at the sadness and truth of it. Ethel loved pointing out the hypocrisy of God-fearing Christians she knew, herself included, but here was a minister who stole and lied and went to church the next Sunday to preach to his congregation. Not until the next spring was Hugh forced to own up to what he had done. He came home after a day of visiting a sick member of his congregation and was greeted by his puzzled wife. She had been doing some spring cleaning and had come across his stash. Only then did Hugh admit what he had done to make sure he wouldn't be without food.

His wife sat down on their living room couch and sobbed, "To think you were ever that hungry."

"Oh," he replied, "I was a lot hungrier than that."

Orange Sponge Cake

4 eggs

¼ tspn cream of tartar

1¼ cups cake flour

¼ tspn salt

3 tbspns corn flour

1 cup sugar

2 slices canned pineapple

grated rind one orange

1½ tspns baking powder

¾ cups cold water

1 tbspn lime juice

1 egg yolk

2 tbspns butter

Cake made like any other sponge cake.

Mary Morris, a British student
(b. 1929)

Changi POW Cook Book

CHAPTER TWENTY-FIVE

THE GIFT OF FOOD

Never one to be empty-handed for long, Ethel took up knitting multi-coloured scarves and making brooches out of seashells. She tried selling them to tourists at Aunt Susie's cottage. Realizing that she could no longer rely on Denis to support her, having some income was important, but she knew there was more to it than that. These occupations were contorted with a desire for pain.

"It was the knitting needles. As you flashed them back and forth you could just visualise using such things upon the ones that had used them upon us."

Again and again, as she wilfully looped and tugged each colour of wool around her needle, distinct and dreadful memories filled her mind. The horror of children's death games would have come tethered to red, while blue was the dress she had in Changi, stained with sweat and fear. She knew the memories and desire for revenge were bitterly poisonous, but they constantly gripped her. The only thing that could dull the agony was immediate, attention grabbing, physical pain.

"I wouldn't be bothered doing anything unless there was a sharp point around, where I could think 'Now, I'll do this like I saw such and such done. Putting things under fingernails.'"

She repeatedly stabbed the tips of her fingers with the knitting needles and the pins she was gluing on the back of the brooches. All the while the screams of tortured men played out in her head.

"I was a year and a half in that awful hate business," she claimed, but in fact, the loathing within her lasted much longer and was so powerful she called it "dementia," viewing it as a disease that feasted on her insides. She was sure it could be understood and even excused if she were still a prisoner, but not now. She could only feel contempt for herself when she crossed the street to avoid walking past a Japanese mother and her innocent young child. But at the same time, it was impossible to stop it.

"You'd see your hair just want to stand on end and you'd remember some awful dastardly thing you'd witnessed in the prison."

While she was still in this state of mind Ethel was asked if she would write about her experiences. She always maintained that she was the only Canadian woman in a Singapore prison camp and thus had a unique story to tell.[1] But, she told Sid years later, "I didn't do the book. I didn't take any of these offers. At one period I was offered $3,000, and boy it looked big, 'cause I only had $86 at the time."

It wasn't that she didn't try to write her version of what happened in Singapore. Soon after her return to Canada she paid a visit to her old friend Ned Pratt at his office at Victoria College, University of Toronto. She sat across from him, his desk heaped with correspondence and cold cups of tea, and told him what she could of her stories. He listened patiently for a time, then handed her a stack of yellow workbooks and a collection of pencils. "Write it down," he told her. "I will do the introduction."

She went straight home to Aunt Susie's and that evening, cleared off the desk at the foot of her bed, laid out the pencils and pressed open the workbooks ready to start in the morning. But it was not to happen that way. About 3 am she woke up. "Not the get-up-and-get-busy sort of awake but the lie-there-and-think sort." She remembered what her father used to say at times like these. "Just listen. The still small voice will speak to you when you listen." Ethel knew this piece of wisdom from the bible. God speaks to Elijah not with big winds, earthquakes, and fire, but quietly.[2]

She tried to listen, to order her thoughts, to settle on where to begin her saga. But all her efforts were hijacked by a pure form of hatred aimed directly at her former Japanese jailors. The stream of poison was only halted when an image came into her mind. She saw two children sitting on the floor in front of her, reading her future books. Knowing she could not willingly pass on her hatred, especially to young ones, she got up, closed the workbooks, put the sharpened pencils in the drawer, knelt by her bed and said the Lord's Prayer. The next morning she called Ned Pratt to let him know her decision.

Although she was not yet fit to write her story to raise money, either for herself or any worthy philanthropic cause, Ethel still had her collection of recipes. Each one told a story of longing—for comforting food, for meals shared, for the security and love of home and family. The recipes would be her voice. As she turned the idea over in her head she came up with a plan of how she could sell a cook book and who she could support with the proceeds. She no longer had a husband she could spoil with treats, so she broadened her horizons. There were many other former POWs still suffering in hospitals who could do with the comfort of good food. She convinced the printer at a shop around the corner from Aunt Susie's to make up two thousand copies. The quality was not what she had hoped for, nor was the look of the thing. The oddly sideways drawing of Changi Jail printed on the green blotting-paper cover was downright unattractive, but it suited the grimness of the story of hunger and war which she told in the forward. At the end of her description she concluded: "As from one Canadian who survived the horrors of war and prison camp, may I just say, 'Enjoy your homes. Enjoy your food, there is nothing that can take their place.'"[3]

Ethel knew the cookbook was not "of great urgent appeal" and that buyers would have to hear the origins of the collection before they could be parted from their money. So she decided to drum up speaking engagements. She went to Kiwanis clubs and then to Rotary clubs, to nurses' and doctors' organizations and church groups. She travelled up to Manitoulin Island, around Toronto, out to Woodville, on to Cambray, and down to Lindsay, Ontario. When setting up her tours with local organizers, she was straightforward about her abilities. "I'm no speaker," she admitted, "I just talk." When they asked how much she charged she responded, "I don't put a price on my speech, but it may cost you something before you leave, if you can only manage to see what hunger is." Her scheme was to take a suitcase full of the cookbooks and leave it open at the back of the room where she was presenting her tales of prison life.

Ethel was hard on her audiences. "Here you are," she admonished, "proud and fat and you're looking at me, I weighed 85 pounds. You can see where I've had boils and carbuncles. I've had two hundred and sixty-four boils and three carbuncles, my friends. I've got lots of marks of them on me." She went on to suggest that some in the audience may have sat out the war in rather comfortable circumstances not knowing the meaning of hardship or hunger. But she hoped that after listening to her they would be able to see what hunger looked like and that "at the end, you'll put the money in and help." After pointedly appealing to their consciences, Ethel told her listeners they should decide how much they wanted to pay for a copy of her cookbook, five cents or five dollars, or nothing at all. It was up to them. By the end her little suitcase was always full of money and empty of cookbooks. She went back to the printer again and again. In the end he produced twenty thousand copies and she raised eighteen thousand dollars.

With the funds she raised she sent precious oranges, tea, and cigarettes to ex-POWs still hospitalized in England. They would all be appreciated, but it was particularly important to her that the luscious citrus fruit that had been the stuff of her dreams as a prisoner be a part of the gift. Eaton's shipped the goods and once there, two friends from Singapore and India days made the distribution to the recovering soldiers. Brigadier Walker, of the Royal Army Medical Corps, the man who had seen her off to Canada not so long ago, was one of them. The other was Colonel John Kerr of the Sherwood Foresters. Ethel felt particularly for the welfare of the Sherwood Foresters as the 5th Battalion had arrived in Singapore January 29, 1942, only to be captured and imprisoned within weeks. Many of them worked and died on the Thai-Burma railway.

Brigadier Walker and Colonel Kerr sent Ethel letters of thanks for all that she had done. She saved them for decades. They were evidence of the part she played in presenting a feast to the wounded ex-POWs, one as unexpected as if it had come from a table in the sky.

Part Five
Putting It All Together

Toronto Pie

Crust

14 graham crackers or

28 gold cup biscuits

½ cup sugar

½ cup melted butter

1 tspn cinnamon

Mix and remove ½ cup for the top. Take the remainder to line a pie plate.

Filling

2 cups of milk

2 egg yolks

2 tbspns corn starch

¼ cup granulated sugar

1 tspn vanilla

Cook until thick and spread in lined pie plate. Beat 2 egg whites with 3 tbspns icing sugar and spread on top of filling. Sprinkle remaining crumbs on top, bake in slow oven for 20 minutes. Serve when cold.

Ethel Mulvany

Changi POW Recipe Log Book

CHAPTER TWENTY-SIX

NOT FIT COMPANY FOR HERSELF

As a philanthropic gesture the cookbook was a great success, and selling it as Ethel did gave her a chance to hone her story. She became more adept at encasing her hatred of all things Japanese within the context of the war, but it was still there, lurking. Trying to get rid of it reminded her of pulling out a fish hook: inevitably the barbs catch and rip, in this case, "into the very heart of the 'hater.'" Living with it, however, was worse. Her mind felt warped by her inability to let it go. It wasn't until a year or so later when she and her aunt were at church that things began to shift inside her.

Still leery of crowds after all that she had been through, Ethel led the way up to the church gallery. As she looked around she observed a young man of about twenty-three or four sitting on the other side. She knew right away he was Japanese. As she stared at him she thought he had a lonely look about him. To her aunt's utter astonishment she announced that she was going to go over and sit beside him. Not a word was spoken between the two, but Ethel felt a change. "There was a warmth and a sadness and a forgivingness that went through us at that time. That was a wonderful feeling ... I thought about this young man at my side and wondered just how much kindness there was for him in this country. That, I believe, was my first moment of real forgiveness."

Ethel was right to question how much kindness there was for anyone of Japanese descent in Canada. The War Measures Act of 1942 had infamously uprooted and destroyed the lives of more than 21,000 Japanese Canadians. Forced from their homes with only the possessions they could carry, families were often torn apart and their communications censored. They lived in wretched housing within guarded camps, suffered from preventable diseases, felt the grind of hunger, and were deprived of all news of the outside world. The Act was revoked in 1945, but contempt for the Japanese fostered by wartime propaganda was kept alive by atrocity stories in the press from returning ex-POWs, none of which helped to soften unexamined prejudices.[1] New to Ethel's church, this man might have been one of the thousands of West Coast Japanese Canadians who had been sent to internment camps in BC and Alberta and who, at the end of the war, not being allowed back to live on the west coast, had chosen to resettle east of the Rockies rather than succumb to the government's urging to accept "voluntary repatriation" to a war-devastated Japan.[2] Although racism, fear, and a desire for revenge stretched across the country, there were some who protested the ill-treatment of the Japanese. Many of those who spoke out and wrote letters to the government were members of the United Church of Canada.[3]

After her strangely soothing encounter with the young Japanese man in church, she never made any more brooches. No more stabbing herself under her fingernails with sharp pins while the spectre of the tortured loomed over her, screaming into her thoughts. The memories stayed but the tangle of seething emotions tethered to them started to wither. There was, however, nothing straightforward about Ethel's recovery. Up to this point, the only income she had been earning had come from the sale of the pins and scarves she had been making, and there wasn't much in that. Questions swirled round and round in her head, ratcheting up her anxiety levels with each turn.

She hated being a financial burden on her aunt and uncle but had no idea how she was going to support herself. Middle-aged, unwell, and unsuited to most jobs open to women, Ethel was stuck.

In this state she went to see Dr. Jacob Markowitz. They had met in Singapore before the war when she was working with the Red Cross. "Marko," as she called him, had been responsible for saving the lives of thousands of POWs through skilful and ingenious methods of surgical improvisation—a feat for which he had been awarded the Order of the British Empire in 1946. Ethel did not seek him out for his particular areas of expertise. As a physiologist and surgeon he was not an authority in what ailed her, but they had two things in common. One was a friendship with Ned Pratt and the other was a shared history of being imprisoned by the Japanese. As one of the prisoners on the infamous Thai-Burma railroad, Markowitz knew intimately the kind of experiences that clung like burrs in Ethel's brain. That counted for a lot. As he himself put it, "Prisoners of war smell out each other."[4]

Ethel trusted him, at least she did when she was on a relatively even keel. But in 1949, just as she was beginning to experience some release from the hatred that plagued her, she felt her world unravelling. From Markowitz's medical point of view,

> She was obviously nervous, over-active, couldn't keep her mind
> on any one topic of conversation and she was ill-at-ease in
> herself. She knew there was something the matter and was not
> fit company for herself, is the best way I can describe it. She was
> unhappy ... She was very bright and her conversation had witty
> remarks all the way through. She was in a hyperkinetic state
> when I examined her. She couldn't stay at home long enough to
> sleep and had to do a dozen things at once.[5]

As her state worsened, Markowitz felt the best solution was for her to be hospitalized. But when she found out he had signed the papers for her committal to the Toronto Psychiatric Hospital, she got on a bus and vanished into the city. The police were notified straightaway. On April 17, 1949, they found her or, as she might have put it, "trapped" her. The tale of what happened to Ethel after she was committed to the TPH that day was later told in front of the Canadian War Claims Commission.

The commission had been created in 1952 in no small part spurred on by the American announcement in February 1950 that they would pay ex-POWs one dollar for each day spent in captivity.[6] On October 9, 1952, Prime Minister St. Laurent announced a similar payment scheme for Canadian ex-POWs. Ethel had never doubted for a second that she deserved the same compensation as any military man even though she had been in the Red Cross not the armed forces. Surprisingly enough, R.J. Batt, advisory council for the commission, agreed, reasoning that had she enlisted in the Canadian forces, "With her education and apparent ability, it seems to me that she would have held a rank at least equivalent to a Registered Nurse upon enlistment, that of a lieutenant; possibly by the end of internment, that of a captain."[7] So Ethel made her claim in 1953 asking for her dollar a day, which she received in the amount of $1,274.[8] She was then advised by the Department of Veteran's Affairs to take her claim a step further and request compensation for personal injury and property loss. That the war had been injurious to her health should have been easy enough to prove with medical records. But when asked to provide evidence for her claim, all she submitted were letters about her household goods that had been destroyed in the war.

The most detailed document Justice James Duncan Hyndeman had to consider in support for her case was a letter from Ram Bharose, Denis Mulvany's former servant. Bharose, still living in Singapore, had replied to Ethel's request for help:

> *29 August, 1955*
> *Dear Mulerany [sic],*
> *I am very glad to tell you that I am in the best of my health ... Yes, Mulerany [sic], I know that you own the following in Singapore; and I can remember very well the number of things you own. I give below the list of such things.[9]*

Prompted by Ethel, he gave a detailed list of her possessions destroyed in the war, the things that had shaped and coloured the contours of her previous life: rubies and pearls, fur coats, evening dresses, a new roadster, the beloved boat, *Honora*, silver cutlery settings, Persian and Indian rugs, and much more including the simple cottage on Pulao Hantu so cherished by the Mulvanys. Ethel had estimated, and Bharose had faithfully agreed, that the total value of all the items was $11,200.

The other letters came from Ethel's adored cousin, Keith Greenaway, by then a wing commander in the Royal Canadian Air Force, and Alice Miller, the late prime minister Bennett's former secretary. Both wrote to vouch for Ethel's ownership of a Birks diamond watch given to her by Bennett in thanks for her work in the 1935 Indian Arts and Crafts exhibit. Wanting to keep the record straight, Ethel insisted when she submitted the letters, "there was no political tie to this gift, since Mr. Bennett was well aware that our family was Liberal."[10]

Justice James Hyndman might have realized he was dealing with an unusual character. In the end, the only letter that had an effect on his decision was the one from Alice Miller because, as he put it, "Miss Miller was well known to me for many years as the confidential secretary to the late Viscount Bennett, and I do not hesitate to trust what she says."[11] Hyndman ruled that Ethel should be compensated $750 for her jewellery and furs. As for her other claims, he did not find there to be sufficient evidence to prove that she was co-owner of the household goods, the boat, or car, which he argued "in the normal course of affairs ... would have been purchased by [Dr. Mulvany]." Regarding her health, having been provided with no evidence to the contrary, he believed she fared no worse than any other POW and was therefore not eligible for special compensation.

Livid, Ethel snapped back a response to Judge Thane Campbell, former premier of PEI, who had taken on the job of chief commissioner. She strained to be polite and incorporate a modicum of political savvy at the start of her letter, noting that she had met Campbell's son Alexander two years earlier. If knowing an acquaintance of Hyndman's had made a difference to his evaluation of her claim, it wouldn't hurt her to press her connection, however tenuous, with the chief justice. After this introduction her handwriting bent over and tightened. "Reading the notes by Deputy Commissioner J.D. Hyndman I am forced to state it was and is quite evident that he was not a prisoner and I notice that he has diagnosed my case without even a stethoscope. Rare." Of course, if Ethel had submitted medical evidence Hyndman would have had more to work with, but she was in no mood to consider this while scratching out her response. Next on her list of grave errors committed by Justice Hyndman was his attitude towards property ownership in a marriage. While Hyndman had spoken as a man of his era, Ethel wrote as a woman ahead of her time. She charged that she brought money into the marriage and, furthermore, "I owned my own articles, I was not a chattel of my husband." But the hardest of all for her to swallow was that he questioned her word of honour. "I am glad Miss Miller is <u>known</u> by him to be honest. I may add that I am known to be honest to my friends too."[12]

Ethel couldn't see that there was a different standard of evidence for a court of law than were was for life. She felt she had to defend herself against what she took to be an accusation of dishonesty and for asking for more than she was due, so she demanded a review. This time her lawyer told her she must consent to have her medical files submitted to the commission if she was to make an appeal.

* * *

Jacob Markowitz was only expecting to have to write a letter in support of Ethel, not to have to appear as a witness at her appeal hearing in 1958. He was ready to help but since she was no longer his patient he had destroyed her medical file. This meant he had to speak from memory trying to recall what condition she was in when they had met up again after the war. For the most part Ethel sat quietly as the small group convened at her lawyer's Bay Street office. She listened as the commissioner, this time Justice C.W.A. Marion, her council, Hugh J. McLaughlin, and her witness, Jacob Markowitz, dissected her pathological frailties in front of her.

As far as Markowitz could remember, Ethel had spent many months in 1949 at the Toronto Psychiatric Hospital during which time she received electric shock treatments resulting in severe memory loss. "And you say that she will never have any normal earning capacity?" Justice Marion asked. Markowitz was adamant, if not fully informed. "Not after shock treatments, they don't have the same capacity. Somebody has to sign a piece of paper authorizing the authorities to give those because of this consequence."[13] He went on to point out that not only did electric shock therapy have dangerous side effects but Ethel would have required twenty-one treatments at a time and at twenty dollars per treatment it was very expensive.[14] He stated that although she eventually recovered, she would be susceptible to repeated breakdowns throughout her life, all worsened because of her POW experiences.

Pressing home this last point, he drew Justice Marion's attention to Ethel as she sat in the room. They all must have swivelled their heads to stare as Markowitz explained that she was presently suffering from yet another manic episode. Her "conversation [is] repeated and skipping from subject to subject, and it is very hard to know what she is talking about. She will start on one thing and it will remind her of something else, and the conversation is hard to follow." He reminded the judge that this was many years after her release and, he emphasized, "I believe it is going to get worse."[15]

Ethel must have been devastated to hear such a stark diagnosis especially in public, but there were more indignities to face. Markowitz picked up the sketch of her done in Changi by fellow internee Joan Stanley-Cary. "She looks thin and grim," he said, noting, "The artist tends to flatter a person. I am quite sure this is not as bad as the real thing." Next were her eyes and teeth. Their weaknesses needed to be discussed so any wartime damage could be measured and duly compensated. But for Ethel, the most painful of all their deliberations was over the failure of her marriage.

When Ethel became aware that Denis had met and fallen in love with another woman so quickly, her initial pain over his request for a divorce ripened into anger and bitterness. She adamantly refused. Not until she heard that Denis and Eileen had begun a family did she reconsider her stand. At a time when society frowned upon such things, she did not want to be responsible for marring the future of any child they might have. In spite of her sadness, she found it within herself to write Denis one last time, offering words of peace.

> September 22, 1950
> My dear Denis,
> It seems that this "business" will soon be through ... I pray that Eileen may know peace and happiness. In this closing chapter of our married life may I just say "Thank you for being you." God bless, guard, guide, and keep you for time and Eternity.
> With my love, Ethel.

In her own mind she blamed herself at least in part for the breakdown of the marriage. When her lawyer at the review hearing asked her what she thought was the cause of her divorce, she replied thoughtfully, "Well I think when he saw what I was like [after liberation] and saw what the others were around him, that even he couldn't stand it."[16]

When the hearing was finally over the waiting began. Markowitz's testimony raised enough questions and doubts in this convoluted case that Judge Campbell, chief war claims commissioner, requested that a comprehensive medical summary be written by an outside source. Dr. Aldwyn Stokes was chosen for the job. Stokes was director of the Toronto Psychiatric Hospital, chair of the department of psychiatry at the University of Toronto and, although never a POW, during the war this modest British-born doctor had been superintendent of the Mill Hill Hospital in England, specializing in the treatment of psychiatric war cases. Dr. Stokes found himself in a delicate position while composing his report. He did not agree on a number of points with his colleague, the famous war hero, who, he gently pointed out, was not an expert in Ethel's medical conditions. But he could see that by stressing the extent of Ethel's chronic disease, worsened by her years in captivity, and by emphasizing the horrid side effects of electric shock therapy, Jacob Markowitz was making the case that Ethel should receive a generous settlement. Stokes may have agreed with the conclusion, just not the steps taken to get there.

Unlike Markowitz, he'd had the opportunity and the time to read through Ethel's files and to gather more information before he constructed his arguments for the report. It turns out that Ethel did not have electric shock treatments while in the Toronto hospital. She was released just over two weeks after her committal, not months later as Markowitz had recalled. She was well enough to be able to return to live at Barrington Avenue with her aunt and uncle. Stokes went further back in time and wrote to Bethlem Royal Hospital to get details on the treatments Ethel had received both there and in India.

Where Markowitz had rambled on anecdotally about the inca-pacitating effects on the mind of all who had suffered imprisonment under the Japanese, Stokes made the point that Ethel had "not merely under[gone] the protracted return to health usual to all pris-oners of war but was positively and continuously suffering from a manic depressive condition." He politely disagreed with Markowitz's contention that the disease was hereditary.[17] By shifting the respon-sibility for her illness from genetics to environmental stresses, Stokes strengthened her claim before the commission. He main-tained that

> Before her incarceration into prisoner of war camp and
> despite two episodes of mental illness she was a competent
> effective outgoing person. Since her release from the prisoner
> of war camp the manifest illnesses have been at much shorter
> intervals and between them her competence has been impaired.

Working from Markowitz's description of Ethel's mania at the time of the appeal, he made the further point that it is often difficult to see that "the bouncing over-activity, 'not to be thwarted' over-confidence … is illness and representative of overcompensation of pathological hurt."[18] Citing relevant cases, he reminded the commission that the manic reaction to injury had been recently accepted as a legal defence by the courts.

The precision and orderly character of Stokes's arguments, backed up by his obvious expertise, succeeded in persuading the War Claims Commission to award Ethel just over $10,000, for personal injury, a substantial increase over the original $750 for property loss.[19] It was recommended that $7,000 of the award be put into a government annuity to give her a small stable annual income. It had taken six long years of petitioning (1953–9), letter writing, searching for receipts, gathering witnesses, and enduring trial-like proceedings—little of which dealt to Ethel's strengths—but she had won. For someone like Ethel, who could live on half a shoestring, the award from the War Claims Commission was particularly significant. But during those years of struggle leading up to the award, she had to find a way to make some money.

Bacon and Egg Pie

½ lb flour

1 tspn cream of tartar

½ tspn bicarb. soda

¼ lb lard or drippings

½ tspn salt

bacon

eggs

water to mix

Sift flour, cream of tartar, soda, and salt into a basin. Cut in lard or dripping and mix to a dough with the water. Roll onto a floured board to required thickness. Line a greased enamel plate. Lay rashers of bacon on the bottom, then break the eggs on top of bacon. Cover with pastry and bake in a moderate oven until pastry is cooked. (Enough for about 4 persons.)

Betsy Nea Barnes, Australian (b. 1907)

Changi POW Cook Book

CHAPTER TWENTY-SEVEN

TREASURE VAN

E thel desperately wanted to be able to pay her aunt and uncle something for her room and board in their home. Denis had sent her a few cheques but his support quickly dwindled then vanished. She made and sold bits of jewellery, volunteered at a day care, but it was only after her 1949 stint in the Toronto Psychiatric Hospital and her early efforts to feel forgiveness for what had happened to her, that she was able to re-enter the working world. Reading the paper one evening in Aunt Susie's living room, she saw an advertisement looking for a real estate sales agent, specifically, a woman. She thought that might be just the thing; the business was not foreign to her. She had learned something of real estate in the early 1930s when she had befriended Montreal real estate baron, J.E. Wilder. The notorious miser became smitten with Ethel when she'd had the audacity to ask him to fund a summer camp for impoverished children. She had steered clear of his advances, but stayed close enough to learn about the business.

Ethel couldn't have chosen a better time to go into real estate. With incomes growing, birth rates ballooning, homes being built, and a society that was shifting from a culture of budgeters to buyers, the housing market in Toronto was the place to be.[1] She spent her first commission of ninety-eight dollars on a used green, four-door sedan. Bustling about town in her old car with new people suited her just fine. Ethel knew just as well as the doctors that she would never be the kind of person who could work at a desk from nine to five. Once she got comfortable in the business, she went out on her own and created her own brokerage, setting up office right near one of the proposed stops on the new subway line at Yonge and Davisville.[2]

She continued to live with her aunt and uncle who would only accept ten dollars a month rent from her, so she squirrelled away the rest of her earnings, investing in mortgages, likely under the advice of her old friend. Wilder had kept track of her after she left Montreal in 1932. Even though the age difference between them was greater than that separating Ethel and her father, he kept trying to convince her to marry him, eventually resorting to bribery.

"Ethel, I'll give you a million dollars of your own the morning of our wedding." She was incensed.

"Never will I marry a wad of paper—No!"[3] Marriage without love was not for her and, besides, she had a plan brewing and it didn't include settling down.

By late 1952, the year she would turn forty-eight, Ethel had put away just enough from selling real estate that she could quit her job and bring to life a dream she had for a volunteer enterprise. Her aim was to buy arts and crafts from different countries and sell them across Canada. It was as if she were returning to finish off the job she had started almost two decades before with the Canadian Society for Literature and the Arts, only this time she would bring the arts and crafts she collected back home to Canada. On her trip through Asia in 1933, she had intended that the handicrafts she bought would be used to illustrate the lectures she gave about education in foreign lands. So too this time Ethel determined that each object would be accompanied by a story of its maker so that buyers would learn about other cultures. It had always been important to her to have "each be able to touch the other." Now her desire to bridge cultural divides had an intensity born of her own hunger and pain. She knew she couldn't stop wars from happening, but she was not going to sit back and be complacent about it.

From the start, the core of her enterprise were the manchadi seeds that had been a part of her life since the Indian Exhibition she had brought to Canada in 1935. Six years later she had held on tightly to one of these symbols of good luck while watching the Japanese bombers spread their wings over Singapore on that early morning of December 8, 1941. She had survived the ensuing battle, imprisonment, the end of her marriage, and anguishing episodes of madness. It seemed only appropriate that these tiny red seeds, each filled with a carved elephant, would be the cornerstone of her business. Along with good luck, this business venture needed a market, and Ethel happened to know that there was one for the seeds. Not long after arriving back in Canada in 1946 she had ordered a package and sold them individually whenever she had the chance, always telling the story of the craftsmen who made them. By 1951 she had raised enough money to have a well dug in the village of Hoskote, south India.

Ethel knew she could afford to volunteer her time, but she had to figure out how to cover her travel costs and find stable venues to sell her goods. Before she knew where the money would come from, she closed down her real estate business, bought a ticket on a Trans-Canada Airlines flight, and ordered her travellers' cheques. She headed off to Montreal and booked into the YMCA for the night before her departure. With a little time on her hands she decided to visit some of her old friends at the *McGill Daily* office. When she walked in the door she found a group of students there, part of an organization called the World University Service (WUS). In her usual upfront way, Ethel sat down and made herself at home. She listened barely long enough to find out that this international group had been founded by students and academics after the First World War to promote development and understanding through education.[4] Bursting with her own loosely forming ideas, she proposed that if they worked with her they could, after paying good wages to the artists, share in the profits from the arts sale.[5] WUS would have an annual fundraiser to support their scholarships for overseas students and to send Canadian students abroad on seminars, and she would be able to sell her wares at university campuses across the country, have an audience for her stories, and, as an extra bonus, she would have student helpers.[6]

With the basic structure of her plan floating into place, Ethel headed off on her first buying trip to India, the country she had once called home. The first sale with the World University Service was held at Queen's University in Kingston, Ontario, in early December 1952. Over three days the sale grossed $8,901 and set a record for a single university sale that would not be topped for nearly a decade.[7]

Ethel trademarked the business in 1953, calling it the Treasure Van. As for what treasures she would transport all over Canada in the back of her Chevrolet panel van, her dream list resembled the contents of Aladdin's cave: precious stones set in gold, rainbow-coloured mother-of-pearl pieces, streaming silk tissue scarves, aromatic incense, beaded black velvet bags stitched with gold and silver thread, brilliantly embroidered *numdah* wool rugs, showy table mats, and finely stitched cloths like the ones she had yearned for while setting her table in the sky in prison camp. Some items would be sturdy and practical: wooden trays, book ends, and leather belts. Others delicate and whimsical: clay animals, glass bangles, elephant bells, and the manchadi seeds.[8] The seeds sold so well even Ethel tired of repeating their history to each buyer. She streamlined the process by Scotch-taping each one onto a small piece of paper on which she had typed an explanation of their meaning and origin. It wasn't elegant but most importantly for her, it opened a window onto the struggles and goals of someone who lived in a faraway world.

Ethel exuded ideas for growing the Treasure Van. Why stick to university campuses as venues? Why not churches, public halls, and high schools? "Someday the Treasure Van will have a ship ... It'll be

Ethel using food to try to lure a bear out of the Treasure Van, Alberta 1955. Pioneer Museum, Mindemoya, Manitoulin.

the students staffing the ship and selling goods in stalls, as it plies the seven seas," she told a reporter.[9] Once again, she showed her flair for shaping a dream into a reality. The next year the American aircraft carrier, USS *Valley Forge*, hosted a sale, not on the high seas as Ethel had originally envisioned, but in Halifax harbour—a small concession to practicality.

Local and student newspapers across the country reported on opening events and the who's who of local dignitaries invited to tour the sale. Then prime minister Louis St Laurent was one of the VIPs who was invited to attend the 1956 Treasure Van sale at Ottawa's Carleton College, soon to be Carleton University. Ethel loved the opportunity to hob nob with celebrities but she was not shy to let on that these events were calculated to bring in the heavy financing, as she put it to one journalist. "The student isn't paying for anyone gallivanting around the world and buying. When we get back from each trip we invite the dignitaries of the university and city to a sale, and really soak them."[10]

Ethel and student whose education was aided through the sale of manchadi seeds, Bangalore (Bengaluru), India. Pioneer Museum, Mindemoya, Manitoulin.

Each year she headed off to new territory. In 1953 it was Greece, in 1954 Lebanon and Israel; 1955 Egypt, 1956 Mexico, 1957 Canada's Artic, Germany, and Peru; 1958 Ecuador, Brazil, and Chile. Toronto's *Globe and Mail* ran a story about Ethel that captured the frantic pace of her work: "She works six days a week the year long, manages a business that grosses $75,000 a year, shops for her goods in 12 countries and directs a team of sales vans that tour from the Maritimes to the prairies. And it's all volunteer."[11]

These were not easy trips for Ethel. Not only did she throw her heart into them, she faced down fears while far from the security of home. Before heading off to Peru, she was nowhere near as sure that she would survive as she had been when she had walked into Changi Jail back in 1942. Maybe it was just the sobering effect fifteen more years of living can have on a person that made her feel this way, or it could have been the panic she felt about the train ride she would be taking to the old Inca market of Huancayo high up in the Andes. It wouldn't be as terrorizing as that rail trip through France in the spring of 1940, but it had that feel about it. Trains didn't need bombs to make them tumble down sheer mountain cliffs. Then there was the air to deal with. Would the sensation of breathlessness be like what she had experienced while undergoing insulin treatments in India? Ethel was determined to go, but she was anxious enough to draw up a will before she left—just in case.

The next part of Ethel's journey began once the goods had been shipped back to Canada, sorted, and packed up in her c.1950 red Chevrolet Treasure Van. The former wartime ambulance driver then set off across the country visiting family along the way. Her cousins and nieces loved it when Ethel blew through the door at her Aunt Hanna (Rogers) Greenaway's old farm near Lindsay, Ontario. This tucked-away corner of the province rarely saw the likes of Ethel. Clothed in a swirl of exotic outfits, she always came bearing delicate glass bangles and little red manchadi seeds, and shared whatever she had with abandon, whether it be non-stop stories or the clothes off her back. However, it was not lost on any of them, even the little ones, that no matter how energized and colourful Aunt Ethel appeared, a strange sadness hung about her. Who but Ethel would sit among the trailing vines in the vegetable garden and eat every last sweet green pea yet never be able to fill the emptiness inside?

WUSC—now World University Services of Canada—had done well by its association with the tours, garnering 25 per cent of the profits.[12] But not everyone was happy with how the business was working. The biggest issue was Ethel's accounting. She could not escape her old nemesis that had plagued her work on the Indian Exhibition and her Red Cross activities in Changi.

In 1959 WUSC took over running the Treasure Van, putting into place new methods of stock control and record keeping. Ethel was retired to the role of honorary director, where she could still be active but not responsible. With less Treasure Van work to occupy her in Toronto, and maybe feeling sidelined, she took refuge on her old island home, moving in with her sister Margaret in Mindemoya. Rather than moping though, Ethel took the opportunity to resume her studies, this time at Laurentian University in Sudbury.

Through the 1960s students involved with WUSC were looking to change the world on a structural scale, far grander than what the Treasure Van aimed to do. Sales through the Treasure Van were doing very well, but to many in WUSC the Treasure Van felt too much like charity. In 1968 WUSC's relationship with the Treasure Van was severed. It was a hard financial choice for WUSC, leading to its near collapse by 1973.[13] Ethel was in turns angry and saddened, but she took back control of the Treasure Van and kept it going on a much reduced scale right into the 1980s, always with the aim of educating students about other cultures. What remained of the unsold inventory gradually settled into her niece Marion King's basement in her Ottawa home: creatures made of horn, cufflinks decorated with masks of comedy and tragedy, and hundreds and hundreds of man-chadi seeds in small brown-paper packages tied up with string. Ethel always wanted to have plenty on hand to give away to anyone who happened by, telling them "it is 10 times God's luck to own the seed; and 100 times God's good luck to give it away."

She worked hard to make her own luck throughout her life, but her next and much greater challenge was not about luck.

Mikado Pudding

1 cup self-raising flour

¼ tspn salt

¼ tspn nutmeg

¼ tspn cinnamon

¼ tspn cloves

¼ tspn mace

4 eggs

¾ cup brown sugar

2 cups raisins

1 cup cooked prunes

1 tspn brandy or lemon

1 cup soft breadcrumbs

1½ cups chopped suet or 5 ozs butter

1 cup candied peel finely cut

Combine prunes (cooked 10 minutes), raisins, peels, sugar, suet, and crumbs. Add sifted flour, salt, and spices. Add eggs and brandy. Put in well-greased pudding mould. Cover. Steam 5 hours or 3 hours if butter is used. Serve with hot custard.

Changi POW Cook Book

CHAPTER TWENTY-EIGHT

WHAT'S IN THE BOTTOM DRAWER?

Gilbert and Sullivan's comic opera, *The Mikado*, opened in London, March 14, 1885, and was an instant success, remaining popular well into the pre-Second World War era and after. This satire of British politics, set in Japan, regaled audiences with the tale of a magistrate who is both Lord High Executioner and judge all in one in charge of carrying out the emperor's decree to execute anyone found flirting. The racism of the opera is now hotly debated, but for Ethel, every remembered morsel of the libretto ridiculing the emperor and his inane bureaucrats was likely as soothing as comfort food.[1] When she had the cookbook printed up in 1946, she subtly highlighted the recipe for Mikado pudding by placing it after Melody Pudding and before Encore Pudding. A small smirk to assuage an overwhelming hatred.

During her blacker periods, Ethel knew enough to stay away from the physical focus of her pain that lay within her own home. "Don't let me open up that bottom drawer!" she warned a niece who lived with her for a time.[2] There, in the bureau drawer, she had carefully packed away intimate reminders of loss and horror, the photographs of her life from before the war, cherished mementoes of a vanished marriage, and her bible, with the spine chewed from hunger.

Eventually she was able to go back to her writing. Retrieving the notebooks Ned Pratt had given her, she marked the date, "Noon July 11, 1960" and began, "1. I get born." The handwriting is clear and elegant in the notebooks, the organization less so, but she kept at it and came up with a manuscript. At first she could not decide if she should call it "Out of the Ashes" or "The Burning of Singapore." Were these too war-like she wondered. Then she went in the opposite direction with pastoral saccharine: "The Diary of a Lass from Manitoulin." Clearly that did not reflect the content of the manuscript either, so she tried something more in keeping with the garish titles of the 1950s: "I Knew Heaven and Hell in Singapore." Eventually she returned to "The Burning of Singapore."

Ethel had likely sent some early version of her memoir to *Maclean's* magazine where it eventually ended up on Sidney Katz's desk. The experienced journalist saw something in the story and arranged a meeting with Ethel at *Maclean's*. The magazine offered to pay her for her piece, which Sid would work on with her. Their next meeting, on April 3, 1961, and all subsequent ones, were held at her place on St George Street, Toronto, apartment 1001, which in her mind was "the thousand-and-one-things-to-do apartment." From there they taped fifteen hours of interviews. Ethel was not an easy subject. Her manner seemed to fit Jacob Markowitz's description of her given at her 1958 War Claims hearing. Her "conversation [is] repeated and skipping from subject to subject, and it is very hard to know what she is talking about. She will start on one thing and it will remind her of something else, and the conversation is hard to follow."[3] Sid was remarkably patient. He tried his best to keep her on track, and when she refused to be corralled, he seldom allowed a hint of frustration to enter his voice. As he listened, he must have realized that often enough Ethel's seemingly unrelated meandering memories were in fact tangents that broadly and uniquely spoke to his questions, if not directly answered them.

It would be surprising if Sid hadn't recognized that Ethel suffered from mental health issues. His early fieldwork in psychiatric social work and his later writing showed that instead of being fearful or dismissive about diseases of the brain he was interested in understanding them. One of his most famous articles, published in the October 1, 1953, issue of *Maclean's*, eight years before he met Ethel, was "My 12 Hours as a Madman." He had agreed to take LSD as part of a research project done by the Saskatchewan Schizophrenia Research group. They believed the drug produced symptoms resembling acute schizophrenia. By giving it to an otherwise healthy subject, this was thought to be an opportunity to discover how someone with the disease perceived the world. From that point, they would try and deduce what type of therapy would be most helpful for the patient. It was a frightening experience for Sid but he felt it was important because, as he explained in the *Maclean's* article, "About half the patients in our mental hospitals suffer from some form of this terrible mental torture."[4]

Ethel's disease was, if anything at all to Sid, a side issue. She and her stories were compelling enough for him that he had hoped there would be at least one more article in the magazine, if not more. He finished off tape fifteen saying, "This is going to end our interviewing for our first two stories anyway, for *Maclean's*." The final tape, with just Ethel's voice, hints at an unravelling of this plan. She begins in a hastily dramatic voice, "Here it is April the twenty-fourth, nineteen hundred and sixty-one. Sid has just telephoned to say you know, a terrible thing has happened, Ethel. Euthanasia—the death room story—is not in our script."

If they had completed an interview about the death room, where wounded soldiers were euthanized during and just after the battle for Singapore, it was lost or erased. Whatever the case, there must have been an editorial decision to not bring up the emotionally fraught and unwieldy topic of euthanasia and to keep Ethel's story to just one piece.[5] Sid returned all the tapes to Ethel for her own use. The two of them may have spoken a few more times to clear up final details, but there were no more recordings. Sid moved on to his next assignment and countless others after that. As a writer, broadcaster, and teacher he broke new ground on the topics he covered, challenging prevailing attitudes on mental illness and gay rights and shining a light on the concerns of the aged, the youthful, and those with special needs. Ethel would never again have such a dedicated listener as she had had that April in 1961.[6]

The *Maclean's* piece came out that August. It is a powerfully edited down version of Ethel's memoir, augmented with information from the tapes. The focus is narrowly kept to her period of imprisonment with occasional glancing references to her pre-war life. For the most part she was happy with the final product, although her own copy of the magazine is decorated with pencilled-in corrections and additions. After all, it wasn't just any 1928 *National Geographic* article that she ate while in solitary confinement, "it was about ANTS!" She hadn't weighed 80 pounds when she was liberated, it was 85.

For her efforts she was paid $500 by the magazine. No matter what quibbling comments she had written in the margins, she got her story out and as a bonus, was paid for it! So unexpected was the payment, she considered it "found money." If she had saved it, it would have nicely augmented her little nest-egg. Instead, she promised the money away, perhaps thinking that like the manchadi seeds, the funds might bring more luck if they were passed on. She chose her recipient carefully but quickly.

Sago Plum Pudding

½ cup sago

1 cup milk

1 cup breadcrumbs

1 egg

1 tbspn melted butter

½ cup sugar

½ cup sultanas

½ cup raisins

Soak sago in milk for an hour or two then add breadcrumbs, butter, sugar, fruit, and beaten egg. Steam for 3 hours. Serve with cream or sauce.

Alice May Watson, Australian (b.1905)

Changi POW Cook Book

CHAPTER TWENTY-NINE

A FORGIVING SPIRIT DRAWS TWO
WORLDS TOGETHER

Ethel was an avid reader of all kinds of magazines and newspapers—national, local, political and, closest to her heart, religious. It was in one of the latter that she came across an article about a Japanese student studying theology in Toronto. Although newly married, the young man had arrived on his own, not having had enough money to bring his wife with him. The story pulled on Ethel's heart, reminding her of all that she had lost through her separation from Denis. Thoughts of the couple were fixed in her mind as she dressed for church on a chilly Easter morning in early April 1961. After the service when the members of the congregation were milling about in their new spring hats and practical winter scarves, she noticed a young man in the crowd and, as with her earlier recognition of the young man in the church gallery, she knew he was Japanese. Without hesitating, she made her way towards him.

That man, Isami Endo, now in his eighties and living in Osaka, vividly remembers Ethel and the intensity of their first meeting.

After the Easter Sunday Service ... a Canadian lady hurriedly
approached me, and spoke to me asking, "Are you Japanese?
I read an article in the magazine about an overseas student
who has left his fiancée in Japan and is having a hard time.
Is that you?"
"Maybe not. But the situation is the same," I answered.[1]

Her questions were soon followed by an invitation to tea at
her apartment. Anyone knowing Ethel had been a prisoner in
Singapore might have wondered what she was up to, just as Aunt
Susie had done that day when Ethel had insisted they sit beside the
young Japanese man in church. As for Isami, he had come to think
of Canadians as a little cold but trustworthy, so with politeness and
interest he accepted. As he and Ethel sat across from each other in
her small living room he heard about her years of imprisonment. He
was treated to as many details as Ethel could fit into a short amount
of time, coloured with all the hatred of his people that still swirled
around inside her. If it hadn't been for Ethel's exuberant personality,
the awkwardness created by her words would have flooded the space
between them, putting an end to any further discussion. But she had
not invited him into her home to harass or blame him; she wanted
him to know her story and she wanted to discover what the war had
been like for him.

Isami was just thirteen in 1945, and like other young boys and
girls in his home of Osaka, he had been conscripted to work in a
military supply factory. As a railway centre, port, and industrial
powerhouse, the city of three million was targeted for strategic
bombing by the Americans. Osaka was first hit on March 13, 1945,
with incendiary bombs aimed at civilian housing; 3,987 people died
and 678 were never found.[2] During the second round of bombings on
Friday, June 1, Isami and a friend were at work. In a language he no
longer uses on a regular basis, he remembers that afternoon.

Carpet bombing, incendiary bombing forced us to run out of
the flaming up factories. With one of my friends I run into a

manhole. However, we two were nearly choked by the smoke, but narrowly survived covering the mouth with half spittled towel for each. Few hours later, out of the manhole, passing through the fire-ravaged factories, we had to walk home for five hours without any food or water. On the very same day the parents of my friend were killed by a bomb near his home. By the time of the War ended, I suffered from tuberculosis because of malnutrition. I was not able to graduate from high school.[3]

Eventually Isami recovered from the disease that had killed Ethel's friend Euphemia. He finished high school and, with a faith undaunted by the horrors of war, decided to study theology. When he discovered that his church, the United Church of Christ in Japan, offered scholarships to Canada through its links with the Inter-board Committee (IBC) of Missionary Societies in Canada, he applied for one.[4] On a warm September day in 1960 he was welcomed upon his arrival in Toronto by Miss Wilna Thomas. The forty-three-year-old missionary had joined the army chaplaincy service in 1944, and five years later she saw the desolation of Japan for herself when she arrived as a missionary to teach in Shizouka, a coastal city south of Tokyo.[5] The city, of no strategic military importance, had been turned to rubble by the firebombing of June 19, 1945. When Wilna Thomas first met Isami, she had an idea of what he had gone through during the war.

Isami shared with Ethel what he had seen of war's destruction, the hunger and disease he had endured. He also told her about his wife Shigeko, whom he had left behind. Ethel listened with her heart. When she responded, she—unusual for her—took her time, slowly putting her thoughts together. A few years before, she had met a young man from India who had been separated from his wife for the same reason as Isami. The scholarship that T.R. Anand had won to study engineering at McGill was far too slender to cover the cost of bringing over his wife and new baby. When Ethel heard his story she had turned to her old friend James Wilder and convinced him to lend Anand four hundred dollars to bring his family to Canada.[6] Sitting in front of Isami, Ethel decided she could make an offer of assistance on her own. Even though she was terrible at numbers, she calculated that the payment she had just been promised from *Maclean's* would cover the cost of an airline ticket from Japan.

"Well then," she finally piped up, "I could help pay to bring your wife over to Canada."[7] Isami was stunned. At first he was convinced there was something wrong with Ethel's mind. All her wartime experiences that he had just heard about must have addled her thoughts. But watching as she went straight over to the phone to call the Japanese Consulate in Toronto, he realized she was serious. Why would she make this offer? Was it because he was a Christian, because he had been an innocent and hungry boy during the war? Was it that this was a face-to-face meeting with a Japanese person within the safety of her own home? He had no idea.[8] This being Easter Sunday, the Consulate was closed, but this being Ethel Mulvany, doubtless she told the operator the whole story with the aim of getting her to give up the consul's home phone number.

When Isami broke the news to Shigeko, he did not mention what Ethel had been through in Singapore or what anger she felt towards the Japanese. Maybe he thought it would make his young wife uncomfortable, and he already knew that Shigeko, like himself, felt ill at ease accepting a gift that neither could reciprocate. Both their families had been impoverished by the war. She and her six siblings had been raised by their widowed mother, and Shigeko, the youngest, had only been able to stay in school because of a scholarship from an American church. Because of their lack of money, she had intended on remaining in Japan and teaching English while Isami studied in Toronto. The couple set their misgivings aside and accepted not only Ethel's financial support but her offer of a place to live. For three months, while the Endos searched for their own apartment, Ethel gave up her bedroom and slept on the couch.

While Isami studied, Shigeko found a place for herself free from racism within the bubble of the Japanese Canadian community, the church, and Isami's Emmanuel College friends. Many of the Japanese

Ethel, Shigeko and Isami Endo outside church in Toronto, 1961. Endo Family Papers.

Canadians she met had moved from the west coast after being set free from what she called "the Concentration Camps."[9] Through the perverse legacy of war, she got a job teaching Japanese to second-generation Japanese Canadians, *Nisei*, many of whom had been imprisoned because they were not Canadian enough but who only spoke English.

By re-uniting the Endos, Ethel had stayed true to her long-time desire and efforts to bring people together. More than that, by having Isami and Shigeko in her life, she confronted her fearful hatred of the Japanese straight on and felt relief as it slowly ebbed. On a deep personal level, it gave her comfort to allow a loving couple to be together, something she and Denis had been denied during the war. The anguish over the loss of her marriage would never leave her. Years later she wrote the words that had so devastated her—*I want to be free*—for the last time on a blank page in the back of her bible, a 1971 Tyndale edition entitled *The Greatest is Love*. Beside them, she copied a letter which her niece had given her. Unbeknownst to Ethel, Marion King had written to the British Medical Records in London to find out if Denis was still alive. When the reply came she showed it to her aunt. Ethel sat down on the sofa in Marion's living room and read it.

> 7 November 1972
> Dear Madam,
> Thank you for your letter of Oct 28. I think your inquiry must refer to Dr. Denis Paul Francis Mulvany who, I regret to inform you died in March 1971.
> Yours faithfully Little,
> Membership Records Office

She turned to Marion. "Yes, I knew. I felt it and have for some time." The two sat quietly while Ethel let in the grief. Later, when she transcribed the letter in her bible she added, "My heart ached again—like that day in 1946; 'I want to be free.'"

Ethel may have previously felt that Denis was gone, but she did not know that on the morning of March 5, 1971, on his sixty-seventh birthday, Denis had taken a glass, a bottle of whiskey, and, in case that wasn't enough, one of vodka and headed out to the garage at his house in Cheltenham. With the methodical understanding of a medical doctor, he attached a green hose to the exhaust pipe on the car and trailed the other end to the rear-window where he wedged it in with a chamois cloth. He had endured too many surgeries since the end of the war, hoping to quell the constant pain he had suffered since his prison camp experiences. He started the car, then shifted into the passenger seat and let death take over from there.[10]

* * *

Just as Ethel did not know the truth about Denis's pain after their separation, it wasn't until decades after Shigeko had met Ethel that the Japanese woman discovered the truth about her benefactor's past. She'd never read the *Maclean's* article and had no idea that Ethel had been imprisoned in Singapore. When her friend, Barbara Mary Johnson, an American journalist teaching English in Osaka, heard about the Endo's time in Canada, she wrote to *Maclean's* asking for a copy of the article. When it arrived, Barbara gave it to Shigeko and witnessed her friend's astonishment. Shigeko kept trying to imagine what had been going through Ethel's mind when she first met Isami back in 1961. In the eyes of this gentle woman of faith, two miracles had happened, first that Ethel had survived Changi and secondly that she had overcome her hatred to become "a generous benefactor of a young Japanese couple in need."[11]

She knew she had to talk to Ethel. No longer having her phone number, Shigeko contacted the international operator with her request. Many voices, bleeps, and rings later she was speaking with an operator on Manitoulin. It is a small island community and Ethel was a larger than life character so maybe it wasn't so surprising that the operator knew just where to find her. But Shigeko felt she was on a roll of miracles.

In spite of being shrunken and gnarled with arthritis and living in an old-age home, Ethel was cricket-bright when the call came through. She was known to jokingly complain that her old friend "Al Zheimer" constantly followed her around, but she had no trouble remembering Shigeko and every bit of the time they had spent together in Toronto in 1961. Her frailty however, was evident even over the phone. At the end of their call, Shigeko promised Ethel she would come to see her very soon. Hanging up, the Japanese woman sobbed long and hard. Ethel was alive, but given the elderly woman's health, she knew there was no time to waste.

Back on Manitoulin word got around and the *Expositor* was put on high alert after the call, ready for an amazing story of war and resolution spanning decades and continents. In June 1992, accompanied by her sister, Shigeko set out on what she called her "pilgrimage."[12] The trip from Japan to Manitoulin was much faster than the one Ethel had taken in the reverse direction nearly sixty years before. The then twenty-eight-year-old Ethel had witnessed a whole series of dawns and dusks, first through her window as her train clattered across the vastness of Canada, and then through her cabin porthole aboard the *Empress of Japan* bound for Tokyo. During

Ethel and Shigeko on Manitoulin, published in the *Manitoulin Expositor*, June 24, 1992.

her days on land and sea, the young solo traveller had had the luxury of time to befriend strangers and in their company refine her stories and dreams for the future.

Shigeko and her sister, on the other hand, were hurried across the globe by the efficiency of flight and the sure closeness of Ethel's death. The two women flew from Japan to Vancouver, then on to Toronto and up to Sudbury without spending more than a few hours on the ground. Once in the north though, their travel slowed to the pace of earlier times. Their Greyhound bus rumbled down the Trans-Canada highway to the town of Espanola on the Spanish River. From there AJ's school bus worked overtime driving them south through the ancient La Cloche mountains, whose rocks were once used to ring out warning signals when danger threatened. The sister's route led on to Goat Island and finally across the swing bridge to Manitoulin.

Sue's Taxi took over in Little Current and drove the women on the final leg of their journey to Mindemoya.

In the weeks since Shigeko's call, Ethel had not suffered any strokes or falls or any of the myriad of small traumas that can so quickly take the life of someone her age. She was ready and eager for this reunion. Always one to attend to her looks, she had on a dress that magnified her tiny frame with its dancing patterns. Her long grey hair was braided and wrapped neatly over her head. When Shigeko walked through the door, Ethel would not have mistaken her for anyone else. The past thirty years had been kind to Shigeko's appearance. She was the same slight dark-haired woman as before. When their hugs and kisses were done, the two began the process of catching up. A photographer from the *Expositor* snapped a picture as they sat side by side, holding hands. He captured a hint of the old fire in Ethel's eyes as she smiled at her companion. The story was front page news, which Ethel would have considered appropriate, and the title was one to make her proud: "A forgiving spirit draws two worlds together."[13]

* * *

On a cool autumn morning four months later, Ethel died. She was just two months shy of her eighty-eighth birthday. At a time when she was still strong enough, she had composed a note on Laurentian University letterhead. In her elegant handwriting she explained, "This is a letter to my family" and entitled it "Death—a Graduation." She was not afraid and was happy to donate any part of her body that could be used to help others; the rest was to be buried without fuss or expense. After such a tumultuous life, Ethel was ready to let go and make peace. For so long she had striven to harness her prodigious energies and fabulous ingenuity to create a better world, and had done so under often harrowing conditions. She had faced up to demons that threatened to shred her and had won them over through acts of grace and imagination. A spirit that could have easily been crushed always stayed open to the world.

POSTSCRIPT

Characters Who Helped Tell Ethel's Story

Sheila Bruhn Allan (1924–) moved to Australia where she became a nurse, had a family and took up writing. *Diary of a Girl in Changi* (1994) is based on the secret diary she kept as a prisoner.

Lucia Bach (1898–1988) was hospitalized in England after the war and then returned to Singapore where she taught. She and Ethel kept in touch after the war. In 1982 Lucia recorded her memories of the war at the Oral History Centre of the National Archives of Singapore.

Freddy Bloom (1914–2000) and her husband Philip moved to London where he set up a medical practice and they raised two children. Their first child was born deaf, as a result of the malnutrition Freddy suffered during the war. She was awarded the Order of the British Empire (OBE) for her work with deaf children. She published *Dear Philip: A diary of captivity, Changi 1942-45* in 1980.

Katherine Mary de Moubray (1899–1979) and her husband George returned to England and lived on Jersey. Her private papers are archived in London's Imperial War Museum. Katherine and Freddy remained good friends until Katherine's death.

Isami and Shigeko Endo, now both in their eighties, returned to Japan after Isami completed his studies at the University of Toronto. Isami became a minister and the couple raised three children in Osaka.

Josephine Foss (Fossy) (1887–1983) was evacuated from Syme Rd on the same hospital ship as Ethel. She returned to Malaya to do welfare work. She became a Member of the British Empire (MBE). Fossy donated her private papers to the Imperial War Museum in London.

Audrey Katherine Goodridge (b. 1920), the most enthusiastic contributor to Ethel's cookbook, survived the war as did her daughter Penny. She was reunited with her husband Capt. R Goodridge.

Keith Greenaway (1916–2010) Ethel's much adored younger cousin from her adopted family, went on to be one of Canada's great arctic explorers.

Brenda Greenaway-Serne (1947–) Keith's daughter, was a keen and invaluable source. She offered up wonderful stories of her Aunt Ethel alongside delicious, tangible feasts.

Sidney Katz (1916–2007) after his service in the Royal Canadian Air Force (RCAF) during the war, Katz got his master's of social work (MSW) and a diploma in drug and alcohol addiction studies. He became an award winning journalist and medical columnist writing about mental illness and social issues.

Marion King (1927–) Ethel's niece from her birth family, the Cannards, is a delightful story teller like her Aunt Ethel. When she moved from her Ottawa house she donated Treasure Van stock and much of Ethel's wartime ephemera to the Pioneer Museum in Mindemoya, Manitoulin.

Tom Kitching (1890–1944) kept a detailed diary of his imprisonment until his death in Changi Jail. His diary was saved by a friend and published by his son, Brian: *Life and Death in Changi* (1998).

Dr. Jacob Markowitz (Marko) (1901–1969), Canadian physician, enlisted with the Royal Army Medical Corps (RAMC) after being rejected by the Canadian military because of his Jewish heritage. He was awarded the MBE (Military Division) for his care of the POWs on the Thai-Burma railroad. He returned to Toronto where he practised medicine, taught, and did research.

Dr. Denis Paul Francis Mulvany (1904–1971) remained in England after the war. He divorced Ethel and, in 1953, married Dr. Eileen Lawson-Matthew with whom he had three children. He saved Ethel's letters and medical files as did his family after his death.

Dorothy Forster Nixon (1896–1972) returned to England. She wrote an unpublished memoir of her time as a prisoner. Based upon this work her granddaughter, Dorothy Nixon, wrote the book *Looking for Mrs. Peel: A Story of Family and Torture.*

Iris G. Parfitt (1902–1997) returned to St George's School in Penang, Malaya, where she had taught before the war. She published her memoir of watercolours, sketches, and notes called *Jail Bird Jottings: The Impressions of a Singapore Internee* (1947).

George Peet (1902–1985) was reunited with his family in Australia but later returned to Singapore as editor of the *Straits Times*. His prison journal was published by his granddaughter, Emma Peet: *Within Changi's Walls: A record of civilian internment in World War II* (2011).

Euphemia Redfearn (1887–1944), Ethel's best friend in Changi, died June 1, 1944. Her remains, along with those of her husband, William Wyatt Redfearn, were moved to Australia after the war and buried at Fawkner, Victoria.

Joan Stanley-Cary (b.1907–19?), who painted Ethel's portrait in Changi, survived the war as did her husband, Jodie, who had worked on the Thai-Burma Railroad. Throughout the war, neither knew that the other was alive. In 1947 she mounted an exhibition of her prison artwork in Ireland called "Guests of the Emperor."

Mary Thomas (1906–2009) returned to Britain. She taught in England and retired to Wales where she translated medieval Welsh poetry. She donated her artwork and papers to the Imperial War Museum and published her wartime memoir, *In the Shadow of the Rising Sun* (1983).

Gladys Tompkins (1893–1984) took a nursing position at Jahore Hospital, Malaya, and later worked in China. At age 81, with failing eyesight, she dictated her wartime stories. Her niece, Felicity Tompkins, published *Three Wasted Years, Women in Changi Prison* (1977).

Recipe Testers' Comments

Cool Drink: Dorothy Nixon, born in Montreal, QC, the namesake of her grandmother who was a prisoner in Changi and a friend of Ethel's. "I liked it very much ... didn't need the sugar but I suspect that ginger ale has more sugar in it these days. Best drunk right away, I think the tannins in the tea get stale fast."

Palace Chocolate Cake: Laura Baskett, born in Elgin Il., USA. "The second attempt was very much a success. I did add a ½ cup more water to the recipe (to make a total of ¾ cup). I decorated the cake with pansies dipped in egg whites and sugar."

Bon Voyage Cake: Alan Cumyn, born in Ottawa, ON. "I baked in an 8 x 13 inch greased pan for 25 minutes at 350 degrees Fahrenheit. Go light on the salt. The final result was delicious. My great uncle George Cumine was captured by the Germans in 1916. Food was often in dreadfully short supply. One care package of fruitcake from his mother arrived mouldy. George ate it anyway and was terribly sick. It became one of the few stories he would tell of his POW experience."

Vanities: Julie Paschkis, born in Gwynedd Valley, PA, USA. "The recipe worked as is. They have a light cake-y texture and are not too sweet. It was odd to make the cookies in this land of plenty. All the while I was thinking about how precious all of the ingredients would have been to the imprisoned women."

Inner Secrets: Jacqueline Dawson, born in Ottawa, ON. "The first time around I quickly came to the conclusion that the proportions were off. The second time I reduced the amount of flour. It could have used more butter. I really liked the flavour of the date mixture which has lemon juice added to give it a nice zing and the pastry has a nice subtle sweetness to it."

Medical Hint: Suzanne Evans, born in Toronto, ON. This anonymous recipe uses gin in the original log book. Probably Ethel's teetotalling instincts got the better of her and she replaced the gin with sarsaparilla. The flowers of sulphur, otherwise known as brimstone, floated like yellow pollen on the gin, then sank to the bottom. The taste was repulsive. Not recommended!

Changi Macaroons: Kathryn Lyons, born in Ottawa. "I tried to be as faithful to the instructions as possible. Cracking, draining, peeling, and then finally grating a coconut with my regular cheese grater was tough! The recipe turned out well, though definitely much less sweet than our palates are used to. There are so many varieties of dates, but I opted for medjool."

Oliver Twist Cake and Jelly Foam Icing: Kathryn Lyons, born in Ottawa. "I made the recipe exactly as specified. Putting that much jam into the batter gave it an unappealing grey purple colour. The jelly foam frosting is very, very sweet, gooey, and glossy. It's unlike anything I have ever made before! The cake itself is dense and a little drier than I had expected, a little like a spice Bundt cake. The black currant and nutmeg combination is unfamiliar, but pleasant."

Toad in the Hole: Gates Cooney, born in Sudbury, ON. "It was absolutely delicious. Comfort food at its finest! The recipe instructions allowed for some creative licence. I interpreted "hot oven" to be 450 degrees (would try 400 next time). Mrs. Greig said to use a Pyrex dish so I did. My husband ate his with maple syrup and I ate mine with mustard—superb! Anything with bacon fat in it has got to be good."

Hodge Podge: Jane Allen, born in Oakville, ON. "I have never gone hungry and I am realizing how lucky I am. It is a bit overwhelming to think what others endured and are still enduring today! I didn't know what mutton was until my ninety-three-year-old Welsh-born mother—a war bride—told me. The lamb was moist and good and definitely a comfort food."

Pumpkin Scones: Louisa Murray-Bergquist, born in Iqaluit, NU. "Quite bland on their own but good with jam, brown sugar, vanilla, dried fruit, and nuts!"

Posy Pudding and Marmalade Sauce: Brenda Greenaway-Serne, born in Montreal, QC is Ethel's cousin Keith Greenaway's daughter. "Posy Pudding is a bit bland. I recommend the raisins be incorporated into the batter to add more flavour and moisture. Also, more marmalade might help. I used 2–3 tbspns of milk to moisten the batter. The marmalade sauce needs a little more cornflour to thicken it and I wouldn't strain it, the rind adds flavour."

Colcannon: Kathleen Johnson born in Aylmer, QC. "Of course it's just mashed potatoes which I love. When I was young we often had them and my brothers and I always made a crater at the top of the mound to melt butter in. Then we'd make rivulets so that the butter could flow down the mountain. The most delightful thing was hearing Mary Black sing the song Colcannon."

Stacked Hearts: Mark Fried born in Swampscott, Massachusetts, USA. "I took the Stacked Hearts to a Robbie Burns party. They were a big hit. The dough needed a little more liquid, 3 or 4 tbspns of water. They needed 10 minutes in the oven. The recipe produced a lot of cream."

Golden Glory Pudding: Mary Moncrieff, born in Trenton, ON. "The whole recipe felt like a craft project, kind of sticky and gluey. The dough part of the pudding called for only 1 cup of the flour and given the texture of the dough when it came time to roll it out I wondered if the quantity had been remembered wrong. The recipe called for 8 inch rounds and I could barely make them 6 inches. I baked them for 10 minutes at 400 degrees. I would eliminate the added salt to the dough part of the recipe. Loved the custard!"

Mint Humbugs: Bernadette Bailey, born in Barrie, ON. "I imagined Joan measuring (and then I imagined her imagining it in the jail) the soft brown sugar, the golden syrup, the heavily scented English peppermint oil, then pouring the bubbling mass onto a marble topped table and kneading it until it glistened. I think her memory was good for the candy turned out well, rich and creamy."

Ground Rice Porridge: Annie Jackson, born in Ottawa, ON. "Every breakfast while I was growing up, we would have either oatmeal, Red River, or cream of wheat. The consistency and flavour of this ground rice porridge was like cream of wheat. I used 136 grams ground rice, 95 grams crushed soya beans, salt to taste, 22 grams sugar, 22 grams peanuts, and many cups of water. I ground the rice for this recipe and did not use enough water to compensate for the water needed to cook the rice flour so the resulting porridge was a little thick. I assume that the porridge eaten in the prison camps would be very watery."

Cheesy Eggs: Brenda Greenaway-Serne, born in Montreal, QC. "The cheesy eggs recipe is very simple, although I had to guess at quantities, temperature, and timing. The eggs are much better slightly beaten. I buttered each ramekin and added ¼ tsp butter, a tbsp of grated aged cheddar cheese and a dash of salt and pepper and baked for 12 minutes at 350 Fahrenheit. They turned out puffed, moist, and slightly browned on top. I would recommend adding a stronger cheese and perhaps some hot sauce."

Damper: Kate Preston, born in Melbourne, Australia. Kate's mother, Veronica Torney, was a nurse on board the last ship to successfully evacuate from Singapore before it fell to the Japanese. Torney was a friend of Lt Col Vivian Bullwinkel, survivor of the Bangka Island Massacre. "Damper is bush food traditionally made by people in remote areas. As a girl I sometimes stayed with a school friend at her family beach house. The mum would mix up damper. We'd each wrap it around the end of a stick and cook it over a bonfire. When cooked we'd ease it off the stick and drop in a chunk of butter. I never heard of baking powder added but it is a good addition."

Sour Milk Cakes: Gwen Cumyn, born in Ottawa, ON. "I made the recipe with 2 cups of flour, 1 tsp baking powder, and 2 cups of sour milk. They reminded me of Timbits really, especially with jam. They taste a little like eating a heart-attack, but I can see how you might want that feel if you were starving."

Ambrosia Dessert: Molly Steers, born in Ottawa, ON. "The bananas I used for this easy dessert were not so ripe. Riper bananas would have better flavour and would mash more easily for a better consistency. It was quite sweet but the rinds helped to enhance the flavour. I would cut down on the amount of sugar used."

Fowl Badum or Dry Curry: Margos Zakarian, born in Baghdad, Iraq. "It was WAW [orgasmic!]. Found all the ingredients except for the white and sweet cumin. I substituted the chatty with a Peruvian clay pot."

Ragged Robins: Marina Doran, born in Derry, Northern Ireland. "Comfort food comes in all forms, but this has got to be the sweetest ever—a bit like biting into a diabetic coma! I can't imagine the pain and suffering of Ethel and the other POWs, but I can imagine her pleasure sinking her teeth into these sweet nuggets."

Peter Pans: Lesley LeMarquand, born in Vancouver, BC. "I chopped the fruit and added a cup of water and stewed the mixture until a nice syrup developed. Instead of adding the almonds to the fruit I used them for a garnish when serving the Peter Pans. My dough was a little dry so I added a few tablespoons of milk. I baked the biscuits at 400 Fahrenheit for 25 minutes and cooled them a few minutes before removing the tops."

Orange Sponge Cake: Amanda Lewis, born in NYC, NY. "Because there are no directions, I went scurrying to my *Joy of Cooking* for traditional sponge cakes. I used a basic recipe ... however, there were some ingredients that didn't fit. I've never put fruit in a sponge cake. On, but not in. Then there was the wayward egg yolk. The other thing that flummoxed me was the "corn flour." I wonder if she meant corn starch, as corn flour is not a usual ingredient for that era. The basic sponge cake was very good, although a bit denser than a regular sponge cake. Fine with fruit preserves dribbled over it."

Toronto Pie: Kathleen Johnson, born in Aylmer, QC. "It reminds me of recipes handed down from my Grandmother—instructions like 'cook 'till done' and 'use a hot oven.' I followed it exactly and the result was fabulous! I imagine those who were part of this recipe sharing group would have known how to bake."

Bacon and Egg Pie: Holly Lillico, born in Toronto, ON. "It's rich, real comfort food. I substituted baking powder, which is the present-day replacement for baking soda and cream of tartar. My old tin Bake-Ware pan accommodated 3 very large slices of bacon, and 4 large eggs. I slightly broke up the yolks, so the eggs came out as if they had been cooked 'over hard.' I added salt and pepper before covering with the top crust. I brushed the crust with a bit of cream, and baked it at 425 for 10 minutes, and 350 for 20 minutes."

Mikado Pudding: Gates Cooney, born in Sudbury, ON. "Easy to put together but not likely that I would spend 5 hours steaming a pudding in this busy day and age. Wasn't sure that I would be able to find suet, but I did quite easily. Cake is moist and full of flavour. Would have appreciated more detailed instructions about how to steam a pudding. How did they ever manage without Google in those days?"

Sage Plum Pudding: Chris Elson born in Bristol, England, and Ashleigh Elson born in Toronto, ON. The recipe worked out without changes but of the sage flavouring Ashleigh said, "It was mostly weird, a bit like having apple-jelly on turkey stuffing. Definitely needs a custard." For Chris, "It is a cross between a suet/flour pudding and a bread and butter pudding. I tried it cold with a tad of butter, not bad."

Note from Suzanne Evans: It was very late in the publishing process that I discovered the original recipe was for "Sago" Plum Pudding not "Sage" Plum Pudding, which would explain the odd review by Chris! A friend noted that Sago Plum Pudding was something she ate a lot of in England as a child. I checked my 2012 photos of the original handwritten recipes in the log book in the Manitoulin Museum and it is definitely Sago NOT Sage. However, the printed version of the cookbook (what I used for the recipes) is a different story. In the Canadian War Museum's c. 1946 copy of the printed cookbook (now scanned and available online) the "e" of Sage is more of a blob than a clear "e." There is a different recipe on the previous page for Sago Plum Pudding. The "o" in Sago is distinctly different from the "e." I think the original printer made a mistake and we have revised the recipe in the book to be "sago," but unfortunately, it was too late to redo the recipe's test.

NOTES

Prologue (pages 1–13)

[1] The 1929 Geneva Convention states that POWs are members of an armed force. Ethel would eventually be vindicated in calling herself a POW, if not all the other civilian prisoners. After the war, the Canadian War Claims Commission deemed her status as a senior representative of the Red Cross to be equivalent to that of an army lieutenant.

[2] Library and Archives Canada (LAC) War Claims File RG117, Vol. 542. Stokes Report 12 November 1958, 4.

[3] Kay Redfield Jamison, *Exuberance: The Passion for Life* (New York: Knopf, 2004), 121.

[4] Bernice Archer, *The Internment of Western Civilians under the Japanese 1941–1945: A Patchwork of Internment* (Hong Kong: Hong Kong University Press, 2008), 117.

[5] Elizabeth Driver, "Cookbooks as Primary Sources for Writing History: A Bibliographer's View," in *Food, Culture and Society* 12(2009): 264.

Chapter 1 (pages 15–27)

[1] The Society was "designated to exercise a cultural and educational influence." *Winnipeg Tribune*, 23 January 1933, 3.

[2] Library and Archives Canada (LAC) Minister 630196, Bennet, Richard Bedford (Requests for Letters of Introduction – Rogers, Ethel 1933) Letter of 27 April 1933, Rogers to McLean.

[3] Hugh L. Keenleyside, *Hammer the Golden Day: Memoirs of Hugh L. Keenleyside Volume 1* (Toronto: McClelland and Stewart, 1981), 286-7.

[4] LAC Minister 630196, Letter of 6 June 1933, Marler to McLean.

[5] Mulvany Private Papers collection (MPP).

Chapter 2 (pages 29–33)

[1] Cathie Breslin, "Cathie Breslin Meets Mrs. Mulvany," *The Varsity* 26 November 1956, 3
[2] *Globe* (Toronto), 18 June 1935, 9; *Citizen* (Ottawa), 15 August 1935, 9.
[3] *Singapore Free Press*, 16 July 1935, 11.
[4] *Globe* (Toronto), 18 June 1935, 9.

Chapter 3 (pages 35–43)

[1] Mulvany Private Papers (MPP), Letter of 17 October 1939, Dr. H.H. Lockwood to Denis's father, Dr. John Mulvany and Mulvany's reply of 24 October 1939.
[2] Articles regarding submarine sightings were frequently published in the *Globe and Mail* in April and May, 1939. Multiple pieces in the same newspaper about the accidental sinking of the American submarine, USS *Squalus* (23 May 1939) and the British submarine, HMS *Thetis* (1 June 1939) added to public awareness of submarine warfare as did articles about Germany's superior submarine strength (22 April 1939, 6; 12 June 1939, 6).
[3] Bethlem Royal Hospital Archives, London, Ethel Mulvany Medical File, April – June, 1946. Ethel told doctors in 1946 there had been six small bombs underneath her bed on the SS *Ascania* that she had thrown overboard.
[4] Transcript of Chamberlain's speech, bbc.co.uk/archive/ww2outbreak/7957. shtml?page=txt. Transcript of King's speech as read on the BBC News Network, quora. com/What-time-was-it-when-King-George-VI-gave-his-Sept-3-1939-speech-about-the-declaration-of-war-on-Germany.
[5] Francis M. Carroll, *Athenia Torpedoed: The U-boat Attack that Ignited the Battle of the Atlantic* (Naval Institute Press, 2012), 117.
[6] Martin Brayley, *The British Home Front 1939-1945* (Oxford: Osprey, 2005), 4.
[7] MPP, Letter of 29 September 1919, Lila Rose to Lt Col John Mulvany.
[8] MPP, Letter of 10 December 1939, Lt Col John Mulvany to Daniel Mulvany.
[9] MPP, Letter of 11 December 1939, Daniel Mulvany to Lt Col John Mulvany.
[10] Marg Hague, "Who's Who on Manitoulin," *Recorder* (Manitoulin), 25 October 1978, 6.
[11] Population figures vary. This conservative estimate is from *Holocaust Encyclopedia* ushmm.org/wlc/en/article.php?ModuleId=10007091.

Chapter 4 (pages 45–55)

[1] Karl Hack and Kevin Blackburn, *Did Singapore Have to Fall? Churchill and the Impregnable Fortress* (London: Routledge Curzon, 2004), 25.
[2] "Lady Brooke-Popham Criticises Singapore's Whites," *Border Watch* (Mount Gambier, S.A.) 28 February 1942, 1.
[3] Stamford Raffles as quoted in Victoria Glendinning, *Raffles and the Golden Opportunity 1781-1826* (London: Profile Books, 2013), 226.
[4] Singapore: Historical Demographic Data, populstat.info/Asia/singapoc.htm.
[5] "*More Stories and Superstitions of Old Malaya: Tales related by an old Malay to 'Yahya*,'"

Straits Times, 9 April 1939, 16.

[6] Ethel first attended the University of Toronto and then switched to McGill after having a disagreement with one of her professors over the existence of God.

[7] Lim Chen Sian, "Colonial Singapore: Archeological vs. Historical Records The Fort Serapong Case Study," (MA Thesis, National University of Singapore, 2007), 15-17.

Chapter 5 (pages 57–69)

[1] By the summer of 1941 the Japanese had a base in Indo-China for their attacks on Malaya and surrounding territories. Ian Morrison, *Malayan Postscript* (London: Faber and Faber Ltd., 1942), 15.

[2] Ethel made this comment in 1961 inferring that she was aware of the situation of the guns before the battle. Although most civilians and military personnel wanted to believe that Singapore was secure, there were some reporters who publicly questioned the city's strength. See Morrison, *Malayan Postscript*, 15.

[3] "Nip," an abbreviation of Nippon, was a racial slur commonly used against the Japanese during the Second World War. "Nippon" is the Japanese term for Japan, often translated as "Land of the Rising Sun."

[4] "Singapore Base," *Sydney Morning Herald*, 10 March 1938, 17.

[5] Bill Clements, *The Fatal Fortress: The Guns and Fortifications of Singapore 1819 – 1956* (Barnsley, South Yorkshire: Pen and Sword Books Ltd., 2016), 130.

[6] Hack and Blackburn, *Did Singapore Have to Fall?* 131.

[7] Masanobu Tsuji, *Singapore the Japanese Version* (Sydney: Ure Smith, 1960), 215, viii, 183-4.

[8] Tsuji, *Singapore*, 185.

[9] Chin Kee Onn, *Malaya Upside Down* (Singapore: Federal Publications, 1976), 4, 5.

[10] James Leasor, *Singapore: The Battle That Changed the World* (New York: Doubleday, 1968), 112-3.

[11] Anthony Bevins, "Incompetence that Led to Fall of Singapore." independent.co.uk/news/uk/incompetence-that-led-to-fall-of-singapore-1477824.html.

[12] "Leaflets on Singapore," *Liverpool Daily Post*, 29 December 1941, 1.

[13] Japan announced its policy for a Greater East Asia Co-Prosperity Sphere on 29 June 1940. See Mark R. Peattie, "Japanese attitudes towards colonialism 1895-1945,"in *The Japanese Colonial Empire, 1895-1945*, eds. Ramon H. Myers and Mark R Peattie (Princeton, NJ: Princeton University Press, 1984), 120-3.

[14] Hack and Blackburn, *Did Singapore Have to Fall?* 17.

[15] Martin Middlebrook and Patrick Mahoney, *The Sinking of the Prince of Wales and Repulse: The End of the Battleship Era* (Barnsley, England: Pen and Sword Maritime, 2014, orig.: 1977), 284.

[16] Sister Catherine P. Maudsley, *Personal Accounts by Members of Queen Alexandra's Imperial Military Nursing Service and Territorial Army Nursing Service*, scarletfinders.co.uk/177.html. British Territorial Army Nursing Sister Catherine Phoebe Maudsley, like Mulvany, was attached to No.1 MGH.

Chapter 6 (pages 71–79)

[1] Japan had signed but not ratified the Geneva Convention of 1929 stating that, irrespective of nationality, protection should be given to ambulances, hospitals, and medical personnel. *Geneva Conventions for the Protection of War Victims Report*, Washington, 27 June 1955, Convention 1 "Wounded and Sick in Armed Forces in the Field," 7.

[2] Brook Durham, "Benzedrine Sulphate Used in War Operations," *Laurier Military History Archive*, lmharchive.ca/benzedrine-sulphate-used-in-war-operations-by-brook-durham/#comments.

[3] On 15 January 1942, both the *Straits Times* (p.4) and the *Singapore Free Press* (p.1) carried the same headline, "British troops are consolidating the new positions to which they withdrew on Tuesday." On the same day even the *Globe and Mail* referred to the retreat as "orderly delaying retirement southward." 15 January 1942, 1.

[4] Mulvany noted in her unpublished memoir, "The Burning of Singapore," "Putland was put in the 'quiet room' (really the death room) – but he lived." MPP, Letter of 5 June 1946 Bombardier Putland wrote to thank Ethel Mulvany.

[5] At this time Wavell was commander of the American-British-Dutch-Australian forces (ABDACOM).

[6] Winston Churchill, *The Hinge of Fate (The Second World War Volume IV)* (New York: Rosetta Books, 2010, orig.: 1950), 88.

[7] MPP, Denis Mulvany saved his copy of this order as well as a British copy of the February 10 (2602) address of Lt General Tonoyuka Yamashita to the High Commissioner of the British Army in Malaya advising surrender of the Allied forces. He also kept Lt General Arthur Percival's order to surrender 15 February 1942 and the Selerang Special Order No.2 ordering prisoners to sign a certificate of promise not to escape, 4 September 1942. All orders were typed on the same note paper edged with Chinese characters.

Chapter 7 (pages 81–86)

[1] On the atrocities in Hong Kong see: Charles G. Roland, "Massacre and Rape in Hong Kong: Two Case Studies Involving Medical Personnel and Patients," *Journal of Contemporary History* 32:1 (1997): 43–61.

[2] Tomoyuki Yamashita quoted in James Leasor, *Singapore: The Battle That Changed the World* (Garden City, NY: Doubleday, 1968), 239. Percival vehemently disagreed with Yamashita's figures, insisting the Japanese had at least 100,000 troops in Singapore (Leasor, note 11, 239)

[3] Leasor, *Singapore*, 243-4.

[4] Dan van der Vat, *The Pacific Campaign: The US-Japanese Naval War 1941-1945* (New York: Simon and Schuster, 1992), 116-7.

[5] Yuki Tanaka, "Last Words of the Tiger of Malaya, General Yamashita Tomoyuki," *The Asia Pacific Journal* 3 (2005), 2.

[6] Denise Archer, *The Internment of Western Civilians under the Japanese*, 68, 117, 175; forces-war-records.co.uk/prisoners-of-war-of-the-japanese-1939-1945.

[7] Felicia Yap, "Prisoners of War and Civilian Internees of the Japanese in British Asia: The Similarities and Contrast of Experience," *Journal of Contemporary History* 47:2 (2012): 325.

[8] Vanessa Ong Yanqing, Stanley Tan Tik Loong, and Michelle Tay Huiwen, *Memories Unfolded: A Guide to Memories at Old Ford Factory* (Singapore: National Archives of Singapore, 2008), 88. For a more detailed breakdown of the numbers see Peter Elphick, *Singapore: The Pregnable Fortress: A Fortress in Deception, Discord and Desertion* (London: Hodder and Stoughton, 1995), 185-6.

[9] Churchill, *The Hinge of Fate*, 81.

[10] News of rapes in Hong Kong reached London within days of the city's surrender via the British Consul, J.P. Reeves in Macao. Bernice Archer and Kent Fedorowich, "The Women of Stanley: Internment in Hong Kong 1942-45," *Women's History Review* 5:3 (1996): 377-8.

[11] Chin Kee Onn, *Malaya Upside Down* (Singapore, 1976, orig.: 1946), 16, 11.

[12] On the influence of the Sino-Japanese war on Japanese military brutality see Yap, "Prisoners of War and Civilian Internees," 323. The 1937 Japanese invasion of Nanjing took on the moniker of "the Rape of Nanjing" in remembrance of the monstrosities that occurred there, including the rape of 20,000 women during the first month of the siege. This figure is from the *International Military Tribunal for the Far East* werle.rewi. hu-berlin.de/tokio.pdf.

Chapter 8 (pages 89–101)

[1] MPP Letter of 2 March 1942, Ethel Mulvany to Denis Mulvany.

[2] Imperial War Museum (IWM) Private Papers Documents 10756 de Moubray, Katherine, 15.

[3] Freddy Bloom, *Dear Philip: A diary of captivity, Changi 1942-45* (London: Bodley Head, 1980), 38, 39.

[4] IWM Private Papers Documents 10756 de Moubray, 80.

[5] Freddy Bloom, *Dear Philip*, 18.

[6] Medwyn was in theatrical productions in Southampton (1915 -1919), Leeds (1910), and Penang (1923) theatricalia.com/person/h2n/constance-medwyn; Bloom, *Dear Philip*, 18.

[7] Bloom, *Dear Philip*, 18.

[8] Bloom, *Dear Philip*, 20.

[9] Elizabeth Grice, "The Secrets of the Changi Girl Guide Quilt" *The Telegraph*, 1 June 2010 telegraph.co.uk/culture/7768593/The-secrets-of-the-Changi-Girl-Guide-quilt. html.

[10] Iris Parfitt, *Jail Bird Jottings: The Impressions of a Singapore Internee* (Kuala Lumpur: Economy Printers, 1947), 2.

[11] Yap, "Prisoners of War and Civilian Internees," 326. On 25 March 1942 camp commandant Major Kato announced to the prisoners, "When we consider the way in which Japanese internees have been treated by the British, we feel we cannot give you freedom or an easy life." As quoted in "Report of a Commission of Enquiry into the Internment of Civilians in Singapore by the Nipponese Authorities, February

1942-45," by ex-internees: S.N. King, Chairman, N.S. Alexander, and W.L. Blythe, 3 September 1942 in Eze Nathan, *The History of Jews in Singapore, 1830-1945* (Singapore: Herbilu Editorial and Marketing Service, 1986), 158. Major Kato's speech was given as he handed over the camp to Lt Okazaki. The mistreatment of Japanese in India was mentioned again to the Changi internees in April 1943 by a Japanese guard. See Tom Kitching, *Life and Death in Changi*, (Perth, Australia: Brian Kitching, 1998), 221.

[12] By the end of 1942, 106 Japanese prisoners in Purana Qila had died compared with the 29 deaths of civilian internees in Changi during the same period. Christopher Baley and Timothy Harper, *Forgotten Armies: The Fall of British Asia, 1941-1945* (Cambridge, MA: Harvard University Press, 2004), 337-8.

[13] Bloom, *Dear Philip*, 15

Chapter 9 (pages 103–115)

[1] Brooke Borel, "How do Researchers Feed Thousands of Bloodthirsty Bed Bugs,"popsci.com/science/article/2013-02/how-do-researchers-feed-thousands-bloodthirsty-bed-bugs.

[2] Thomas, *In the Shadow*, 63.

[3] IWM Private Papers Docs 10756, de Moubray, 11.

[4] Thomas, *In the Shadow*, 67. Measurements vary slightly between prisoners' records.

[5] IWM Private Papers Docs 10756, de Moubray, 12.

[6] Denise Archer, *The Internment of Western Civilians under the Japanese*, 68. Later on in the war Changi held approximately 330 children and 1,000 women. (Archer, 175).

[7] Thomas, *In the Shadow*, 70.

[8] Cicely Williams quoted in Bloom, *Dear Philip*, 26.

[9] Thomas, *In the Shadow*, 70.

[10] Myron Winick M.D., *Hunger Disease: Studies by the Jewish Physicians in the Warsaw Ghetto* (New York: John Wiley, 1979). Another famous starvation study conducted by Ancel Keys et al, *The Biology of Human Starvation*, better known as *The Minnesota Starvation Study*, was completed in 1945 and published in 1950.

[11] Winick, *Hunger Disease*, 14.

[12] Winick, *Hunger Disease*, 15.

[13] IWM *Changi Guardian* (No. 24, 1942) Private Papers, Docs. 897, Grist, D. H.

[14] IWM Private Papers Docs 10756, de Moubray, 18.

[15] Bloom, *Dear Philip*, 39.

[16] IWM Private Papers Docs 11437, Gladys Tompkins, 16.

[17] Ethel Mulvany, "The Dawn of Hope," *Guideposts* (April, 1962), 7.

[18] Bloom, *Dear Philip*, 39.

[19] Mulvany, "The Dawn of Hope," 7.

[20] Bloom, *Dear Philip*, 44.

Chapter 10 (pages 117–129)

[1] Although Mulvany did not provide specifics, Ken Wright states that Okasaki gave the order to execute four allied POWs who had attempted escape from Singapore. At war's

end he was tried, found guilty of war crimes, and on 2 September 1942 was shot on Changi beach where the four POWs had been killed. Ken Wright, "Escape and Die" cemeteries.com/ww1cemeteries/escape_and_die.htm.

2 IWM *Changi Guardian* (No. 28, 1942) in Private Papers, Docs. 897, Grist, D. H.

3 Chrissie Tate Reilly, "Food Fight: Eating and Identity in Japan During the Second World War" *International Journal of Arts and Sciences* 3(8) 188-209, 2010; "Rations" pwencycl.kgbudge.com/R/a/Rations.htm.

4 Hack and Blackburn, *Did Singapore Have to Fall?* 171.

5 Dorothy Angell, "Vivian Bullwinkel" angellpro.com.au/Bullwinkel.htm.

6 Wong Song Suen, *Wartime Kitchen: Food and Eating in Singapore 1942-1950* (Singapore: Editions Didier Millet, 2009), 19.

7 Suen, *Wartime Kitchen*, 19-20. For how the rice shortage was manufactured by the Japanese see Onn, *Malaya Upside Down*, 56.

8 Suen, *Wartime Kitchen*, 38.

9 Suen, *Wartime Kitchen*, 41.

10 Thomas, *In the Shadow*, 121.

11 See chapter 5, note 3.

12 IWM Private Papers Docs 10756 de Moubray.

13 Singapore National Archives (SNA) Oral History Centre (OHC), Lucia Bach Interview #18, 24 July 1982.

14 Bloom, *Dear Philip*, 52-7.

15 Although in the title of her newspaper, Bloom was making a word play on Prisoners of War while linking it with the Indigenous term "Pow Wow," her appropriation of that term coincided with political repression of various Indigenous ceremonies, including Pow Wows, in Canada and in the United States, where she grew up.

16 IWM Private Papers, Freddy Bloom.

17 Bloom, *Dear Philip*, 56.

18 IWM Private Papers, Docs 10756, de Moubray, 48.

19 IWM Private Papers, Docs 10756, de Moubray, 22.

20 H. Schweizer, "A Commentary" 22 April 1946 in Onn, *Malaya Upside Down*, xiv.

21 Thomas, *In the Shadow*, 96.

22 Lizzie Collingham, *The Taste of War*, (Penguin: New York, 2012), 246; Suen, *Wartime Kitchen*, 57.

Chapter 11 (pages 131–141)

1 C. Sleeman and S.C. Silkin, eds., *The Double Tenth Trial* (London: William Hodge, 1951), xvii.

2 Sleeman and Silkin, *The Double Tenth Trial*, xxvi.

3 MPP, Anne Courtenay explained this procedure and its impact on the internees in her letter to Denis Mulvany, September 1945.

4 This is the figure Mulvany mentions on the tapes, although the one given in the *Maclean's* article was thirty thousand dollars. Sidney Katz, "Miracle at Changi Prison: A study in survival" *Maclean's* 12 August 1961, 40.

[5] Thomas, *In the Shadow*, 139. Many prisoners had stashes of money in the jail. During the search of the jail on October 10, 1943, the Double Tenth, large sums of money were discovered. Ethel never mentions whether or not her cache was confiscated. So much was found that Lieut.-Colonel Sumida Haruzo, who was in charge of the search, became suspicious that the funds were intended for seditious activities. Sleeman and Silkin, *The Double Tenth Trial*, xxv.

[6] Bloom, *Dear Philip*, 37, 64.

[7] Pioneer Museum, Mindemoya, Manitoulin Island, ON, Mulvany Collection.

[8] Thomas, *In the Shadow*, 120.

[9] IWM Private Papers Docs. 11437 Tompkins, G., 4 January 1943.

[10] For references to Maurice Johns, see Kitching, *Life and Death in Changi* and "Vile Jap Tortures in Singapore Camp," *Sydney Morning Herald*, 26 September 1945, 3. Johns was not alone in his views of women's abilities. George Peet was clear that "women cannot get along together as well as men. They are far less tolerant, less accustomed to mixing with all types and adjusting themselves to different types. Peet, *"Within Changi's Walls,"* 159.

[11] IWM Private Papers Docs. 11437 Tompkins, 4 January 1943.

Chapter 12 (pages 143–153)

[1] IWM Private Papers Freddy Bloom, 66/254/1 *PowWow*, 17 June 1942, 3.

[2] IWM Private Papers Bloom, 66/254/1 *PowWow*, 9 December 1942, 1.

[3] IWM Private Papers Bloom, 66/254/1 *PowWow*, 17 June 1942, 3.

[4] Thomas, *In the Shadow*, 71.

[5] Kurt Vonnegut, "Guns Before Butter" in *Armageddon in Retrospect* (New York: Penguin, 2008), 74.

[6] Ruth Kluger, *Still Alive: A Holocaust Girlhood Remembered* (New York: Feminist Press, 2001), 117.

[7] Cara De Silva, "Introduction" in *In Memory's Kitchen: A Legacy from the Women of Terezin*, trans. Bianca Steiner Brown, ed. Cara De Silva (New Jersey: Jason Aronson Inc., 1996), xxix.

[8] Halstead C. Fowler, *Recipes Out of Bilibid* (New York: George W Stewart, 1946), 30.

[9] Fowler, *Recipes Out of Bilibid*, 30.

Chapter 13 (pages 155–160)

[1] Nick Enoch, "'Oh, for a house, a garden, seclusion': How English couple kept apart in brutal Japanese WWII POW camp for three years kept spirits up with secret letters about their dream cottage," *Daily Mail*, 6 March 2012.

[2] W.S. Gilbert, *The Mikado*, Act 1 archive.org/details/mikadolibrettoof00sulluoft.

[3] Michiko Nakahara, "The Civilian Women's Internment Camp in Singapore: The World of Pow Wow," in *New Perspectives on the Japanese Occupation in Malaya and Singapore, 1941-1945*, eds. Y. Akashi, M. Yoshimura, (Singapore: NUS Press, 2008), 197.

Chapter 14 (pages 163–171)

[1] Nathan, *The History of Jews in Singapore*, 160.

[2] Bernice Archer has written extensively on the quilts. Sheila Allan has included a section on the quilts in her memoir, *Diary of a Girl in Changi (1941–1945)* (Australia, 2004, orig.: 1994). Also of interest, *The Changi Quilt*, Victoria and Albert Museum, London (2010) Video and "Time Flies," a song by Cathy Miller (2004).

[3] British Red Cross archives, London, Changi Quilt.

[4] Australian War Memorial (AWM) REL/14235 Australian quilt. This block was signed by Iris Parfitt and Joan MacIntosh-Whyte.

[5] IWM Private Papers Documents 10756, de Moubray, 22.

[6] AWM Changi Quilts, awm.gov.au/collection/RELAWM32526/.

[7] Comment made 6 September 1942. Kitching, *Life and Death in Changi*, 144. Kitching died in Changi Jail 14 April 1944.

[8] IWM *Changi Guardian* (No. 117, 1942) in Private Papers, Docs. 897, Grist, D. H.

[9] At Christmas 1942, most of the military wives were allowed to see their husbands for thirty minutes. The men and women on either side of the jail were also allowed to meet on Christmas day. The only other meetings between male and female prisoners at Changi jail and Sime Rd camp occurred on 11 February 1943, June to September 1943 (thirty minutes every two weeks), 13 September 1943 to 10 October 1943 (thirty minutes each week), 25 December 1943 (one hour), 1 January 1944 (one hour), 7 April 1944 (one hour), 4 June 1944 to liberation (weekly meetings). Nathan, *The History of Jews in Singapore*, 158.

[10] "Threads of Hope" BBC Radio 4, Broadcast 13 September 2001. All three quilts are now in national archives. The British one in the British Red Cross museum, London, while the Japanese and Australian quilts are in the Australian War Memorial, Canberra.

[11] Ethel Mulvany to Sidney Katz, as recounted on tape, 1961.

[12] Charles G. Roland *Long Night's Journey into Day: Prisoners of War in Hong Kong and Japan, 1941–1945* (Wilfred Laurier University Press, 2001), 192.

Chapter 15 (pages 173–181)

[1] Thomas, *In the Shadow*, 65.

[2] Peet, "Within Changi's Walls," 117, 121.

[3] See Thomas, *In the Shadow*, 93; Bloom, *Dear Philip*, 40, 73; IWM Private Papers, De Moubray, 23; IWM Private Papers, Tompkins, 20.

[4] MPP, Anne Courtnay described the management of the Silence Hut in her undated letter to Denis Mulvany upon liberation.

[5] Sheila Allan, *Diary of a Girl in Changi*, 78–9.

[6] IWM *Pow Wow* (24 February 1943), Private Papers, Freddy Bloom. The *Pow Wow* recorded the opening date as Wednesday 17 February 1943 four days after the date given by Allan.

[7] IWM *Pow Wow* (26 August 1942), Private Papers, Freddy Bloom.

Chapter 16 (pages 183–187)

[1] Allan, *Diary of a Girl in Changi*, 57-8.

[2] Bloom, *Dear Philip*, 80.

[3] George Eisen, *Children and Play in the Holocaust: Games Among the Shadows* (Amherst: University of Massachusetts Press, 1988), 72-3, 82, 91. Eisen briefly addresses the controversy among historians over what constitutes "resistance" during the Holocaust, see also note 2, 134.

[4] "Cosmopolis at Sime Road," *Straits Times* (Singapore), 8 September 1945, 2. At the time of liberation there were 328 children, 1,023 women, and 3,156 men.

[5] Mulvany did not give a surname for John and there were a number of boys named John in Changi.

[6] Peter Thompson, *The Battle for Singapore: The True Story of the Greatest Catastrophe of World War II* (London: Portrait Books, 2005), 399.

Chapter 17 (pages 189–193)

[1] Peet, "*Within Changi's Walls*," 76.

[2] M.R. Smallman-Raynor and A.D. Cliff, *War Epidemics: An Historical Geography of Infectious Diseases in Military Conflict and Civil Strife, 1850-2000* (Oxford: Oxford University Press, 2004), 640.

[3] Sleeman and Silkin, *The Double Tenth Trial*, 77- 81.

[4] In 1946, twenty-one Japanese officials were tried for war crimes, eight were condemned to death. Sleeman and Silkin, *The Double Tenth Trial*, 297.

[5] Thomas, *In the Shadow*, 151.

Chapter 18 (pages 195–205)

[1] Barbara Glanville in Nicola Tyrer, *Stolen Childhoods: The Untold Story of the Children Interned by the Japanese in the Second World War* (London: Weidenfeld & Nicolson, 2011), 186. IWM Private Papers Documents 10756, de Moubray, 94. De Moubray never mentions that Ethel underwent torture but did say that Ethel "survived her gestapo questioning."

[2] SNA OHC Lucia Bach Interview # 18.

[3] See chapter 5, note 3.

[4] IWM Private Papers Documents 10756, de Moubray, 95.

[5] IWM Private Papers Documents, 10756, de Moubray, 94.

[6] Sleeman and Silkin, *The Double Tenth Trial*, xxiv.

[7] A description of electric torture resembling what Ethel described can be found in Sleeman and Silkin, *The Double Tenth Trial*, 293. A post-war medical report attributes Ethel's scars on her back over the ninth and tenth vertebrae to her handling by the Japanese. LAC War Claims Report RG117 vol. 542. Stokes Report 12 November 1958, 2.

[8] Dr. Jacob Markowitz, Ethel's doctor after the war, stated that her scar "was on the flexor aspect of the left arm three inches long by three-quarters of an inch wide on average. It has a serpiginous border. Her scar is consistent with her statement that the number was printed here by the Japanese, rather than tattooed (the German practice),

and that the number was removed by caustics medically applied." LAC War Claims Report RG117 vol. 542. Report 10 September 1958, 20.

Chapter 19 (pages 207–210)

[1] Barbara Glanville in Tyrer, *Stolen Childhoods*, 186.

[2] MPP, quote from notes by Kathy Mulvany, Denis's daughter from his second marriage, on Ethel's medical records some of which were later destroyed.

[3] Thomas, *In the Shadow*, 121.

[4] Nathan, *The History of Jews in Singapore*, 121.

Chapter 20 (pages 213–225)

[1] Peet, *"Within Changi's Walls,"* 205.

[2] Thomas, *In the Shadow*, 181.

[3] Peet, *"Within Changi's Walls,"* 206, 213, 219.

[4] Bloom, *Dear Philip*, 147.

[5] Thomas, *In the Shadow*, 183.

[6] "Emperor Hirohito, Accepting the Potsdam Declaration, Radio Broadcast." https://www.mtholyoke.edu/acad/intrel/hirohito.htm, accessed 28 November 2014.

[7] Robert Guillian, *I Saw Tokyo Burning*, trans. William Byron (New York: Doubleday, 1981), 265.

[8] Thomas, *In the Shadow*, 183.

[9] Richard Gough, *The Jungle was Red* (Singapore: SNP Panpac, 2003), 148.

[10] Gough, *The Jungle*, 148.

[11] "The Real Japanese Surrender," *The Sunday Times*, 4 September 2005; Romen Bose, *The End of the War: Singapore's Liberation and the Aftermath of the Second World War* (Singapore, Marshall Cavendish, 2005), 68.

[12] Thomas, *In the Shadow*, 184.

[13] Peet, *"Within Changi's Walls,"* 243.

[14] H. Miller, "An End to 1,318 Days of Terror," *The Telegraph*, 12 August 1985, 12.

[15] Pacific War Online Encyclopedia, pwencycl.kgbudge.com/S/a/Saito_Masatoshi.htm.

[16] MPP, Letter of 1 September 1945, Ethel Mulvany to Denis Mulvany.

[17] MPP, Letter of 6 September 1945 Lucia Bach, at the request of Sue Williams, to Major Mulvany.

[18] Denis correctly connected the name of Collins with the quilts but Lt Col J.C. Collins, of the Royal Army Medical Corps was not responsible for transporting the British Red Cross quilt out of Singapore. Collins, who had commanded the combined British Australian General Hospital in Changi, was given the Japanese and the Australian quilts by the Japanese. He in turn gave the quilts to Lt Col Robert Marriott William Webster, who had been captured by the Japanese while serving with the 2/9th Field Ambulance. Webster brought the quilts to Australia and presented the Australian quilt to the Australian Red Cross and gave the Japanese quilt to his wife who donated it to the War Memorial in 1968. The Australian quilt has been permanently lent to the Memorial by the Red Cross. How the British Red Cross quilt arrived in England after

the war is undocumented. Australian War Memorial site, awm.gov.au/collection/
RELAWM32526/.

Chapter 21 (pages 227–231)

[1] Myron Winick, "Hunger Disease: Studies by the Jewish Physicians in the Warsaw Ghetto, Their Historical Importance and Their Relevance Today," columbia.edu/cu/epic/pdf/winick_lecture_2005.pdf.

[2] Thomas, *In the Shadow*, 186.

[3] Bedford's article, of 15 September 1945 was written for his hometown newspaper in Middlesbrough, UK. Guy Howard Bedford, "The Liberation of Singapore," britain-at-war.org.uk/WW2/Liberation-of-Singapore.

[4] F. Lopez-Munoz, R. Ucha-Udabe, C. Alamo, "The history of barbiturates a century after their clinical introduction" in Neuropsychiatric Disease and Treatment, 1 (2005): 329-43.

Chapter 22 (pages 233–239)

[1] IWM Private Papers Docs 20417, Foss, Josephine.

[2] "Mulvaneys [sic] are freed from Japs." *Manitoulin Expositor*, 25 October 1945, 1.

[3] MPP, Ethel Mulvany's medical file from the #41 British General Hospital, Bangalore; Kingsley Jones, "Insulin Coma Therapy in Schizophrenia," *Journal of the Royal Society of Medicine* 93 (2000): 147.

[4] LAC War Claims RG117, Vol. 542. Report, 10 September 1958.

[5] Kingsley Jones, "Insulin Coma Therapy," 147.

[6] MPP, Ethel Mulvany's medical file from the #41 British General Hospital, Bangalore. Ethel's views were remarked upon on the first day of her treatment, 20 September 1945 and then again upon her discharge on 15 October 1945.

[7] Bethlem Royal Hospital Archives (BRH), London, Ethel Mulvany Medical File, April – June, 1946.

[8] MPP, Letter of 5 June 1946, Ethel Mulvany to Denis Mulvany.

[9] BRH, E. Mulvany Medical File, April–June, 1946.

Chapter 23 (pages 241–245)

[1] MPP, Original letter From Ethel to Denis of 30 July 1946 disposed of, but careful notes on Ethel including quotes from letters not saved were made by Denis's daughter, Kathy Mulvany, 1 January 2009.

[2] All the letters quoted in this chapter are from MPP, except for the words "I want to be free" which are found in Ethel's papers.

[3] The British Red Cross Museum in London, where the quilt is now held, merely hints at the controversy without naming names. "Three quilts are known to exist and it is probable that there was a fourth, as the quilts were intended to be presented to the Red Cross Societies of Britain, Australia, Canada and Japan at the cessation of hostilities." Changi Quilt, redcross.org.uk/About-us/Who-we-are/Museum-and-archives/Historical-factsheets/The-Changi-quilt.

Chapter 25 (pages 253–257)

[1] Although Ethel claimed to have been the only Canadian woman imprisoned in Singapore there are two other Canadian women listed on the Civilian Internee Database of the Changi Museum; Sarah MacKay and Edna Rebecca Howland or Holland. Civilian Internees, changimuseum.sg/civilian-internees-database/#formmm.

[2] 1 Kings 19:12.

[3] Mulvany, Foreword, *Prisoners of War Cook Book*, 1946.

Chapter 26 (pages 261–271)

[1] Stories that might have had a particularly negative influence on opinions across the country concerned Japanese individuals with Canadian connections such as the Canadian born Kanao Inouye, known as the Kamloops Kid, who went to Japan before the war and by war's end had the reputation of being one of the most malicious guards Canadian POWs had experienced. "Daddy of All Tortures, Canadian Jap Arrested," *Globe and Mail*, 11 September 1945; "Remember Canadian-Born Jap for Cruelty in Prison Camp," *Globe and Mail*, 25 September 1945. Kenneth Yunone, who had studied in Winnipeg, was infamous for beheading an Australian airman. "Jap who beheaded flier betrayed by his diary," *Globe and Mail*, 13 October 1945.

[2] In mid-March 1945 the Canadian government announced to the British Columbian Japanese that they had to either sign up for voluntary repatriation to Japan or move east. Patricia Roy, *Triumph of Citizenship: The Japanese and Chinese in Canada, 1941-67* (Vancouver: UBC Press, 2007), 141. The first ships carrying deportees left in May 1946. The Chronology of Key Events in Japanese Canadian History, japanesecanadianhistory.net/ReferenceTimeline.pdf.

[3] Roy, *Triumph of Citizenship*, 146.

[4] LAC War Claims File, RG117, Vol. 542. Report, 10 September 1958.

[5] LAC War Claims File, RG117, Vol. 542. Report, 10 September 1958.

[6] Jonathan Vance, *Objects of Concern: Canadian Prisoners of War Through the Twentieth Century* (Vancouver: UBC Press, 1994), 237.

[7] LAC War Claims File, RG117, Vol. 542 Review Report, 2 December 1958.

[8] This amount covered the period 8 March 1942 to 25 August 1945.

[9] LAC War Claims RG117, Vol. 542 Letter of 29 August 1955 Ram Bharose to Ethel Mulvany.

[10] LAC War Claims RG117, Vol. 542 Letter of 1 March 1956 Ethel Mulvany to Mr. Batt.

[11] LAC War Claims RG117, Vol. 542 Recommendation Report, 14 September 1956.

[12] LAC War Claims RG117, Vol. 542 Letter of 5 October 1956 Ethel Mulvany to Judge Thane Campbell.

[13] LAC War Claims RG117, Vol. 542 Report, 10 September 1958.

[14] The publicly available information and Ethel's own statements on the subject show that she only had six treatments at a time.

[15] LAC War Claims RG117, Vol. 542 Report 10 September 1958.

[16] LAC War Claims RG117, Vol. 542 Report 10 September 1958.

[17] Subsequent research would prove that genetics do play a significant role, but the precise interaction between genetic predisposition and the environment is still in doubt. nature.com/mp/journal/v13/n2/abs/4002012a.html.

[18] LAC War Claims RG117, Vol. 542 Stokes Report, 12 November 1958, 4.

[19] The award for personal injury amounted to $6,600 bearing interest of 3 per cent per year from 1945. In addition, Ethel received $1,274 for each day in prison and $750 for property loss. LAC War Claims RG117, Vol. 542 Final Report 19 January 1959.

Chapter 27 (pages 273–281)

[1] See John R. Miron, *Housing in Postwar Canada: Demographic Change, Household Formation, and Housing Demand* (Montreal: McGill-Queens University Press, 1981).

[2] The Mulvany brokerage was situated at 1300 Yonge St at Davisville and was active throughout 1950 and 1951.

[3] Ethel wrote these words in her Tyndale bible beside 1 Timothy 5.1.

[4] The organization was first named International Student Service, renamed World University Service in 1950 and in 1957 the World University Service of Canada was incorporated.

[5] Treasure Van was also sponsored by church groups, YMCAs, the UN Association, and the Jaycees. unbhistory.lib.unb.ca/index.php/World_University_Service_of_Canada_(WUSC).

[6] Cathie Breslin, "Cathie Breslin Meets Mrs. Mulvany," *The Varsity* 26 November 1956, 3; 1987 tapes.

[7] Wilfred Laurier University Archives (WLU), Robert Langen Fonds, WUSC 1958-66, Business Report 1961.

[8] Treasure Van Trademark, ic.gc.ca/app/opic-cipo/trdmrks/srch/viewTrademark.html?id=220641&lang=eng. The list of items Ethel collected for her trademark application is almost an exact duplication of the handicrafts she brought to Canada for the India exhibit as described in newspaper articles such as the *Citizen* (Ottawa) 15 August 1935, 5.

[9] Janet MacDonald, "Peruvian Trip Yields Treasures" *Globe and Mail*, 19 November 1958, 13.

[10] MacDonald, "Peruvian Trip," 13.

[11] MacDonald, "Peruvian Trip," 13.

[12] WLU, Robert Langen Fonds, WUSC 1958-66, Business Report 1961.

[13] Kathy Blacklock, "Managing Linguistic Practices in International Development NGOs: The World University Service of Canada" in *Language Matters: How Canadian Voluntary Associations Manage French and English*, ed. David R. Cameron and Richard Simeon (Vancouver: UBC Press, 2009), 136.

Chapter 28 (pages 283–287)

[1] See Michael Cooper, "Reviving 'The Mikado' in a Balancing Act of Taste," *New York Times*, 25 December 2016.

[2] Personal communication with Brenda Serne, April 2013.

[3] LAC War Claims Report RG117 vol. 542. Report 10 September 1958.

[4] Sidney Katz, "My 12 Hours as a Madman," *Maclean's*, 1 October 1953.

[5] Shigeko Endo remembers that there was to be a second article that did not get written "because," she wrote, "it was too awful and too terrible to recall for Ethel." (Personal communication, 15 July 2014.)

[6] Sidney Katz did not keep files on Ethel Mulvany. (Personal communication with his son Jeremy Katz, June, 2013) Continuing on with his interest in mental health, Sidney co-authored *The Divided Woman* (Toronto: General Publishing Co., 1973) about a woman with multiple personality disorder.

Chapter 29 (pages 289–297)

[1] Personal communication with Isami and Shigeko Endo, 15 July 2014. Although the article that Ethel read about a young Japanese student might have been about another student, Isami Endo published an article about being in Canada two months after he and Ethel first met. Isami Endo, "Canadians are Trusting Folk," *United Church Observer*, 1 June 1961, 18.

[2] "10 Most Devastating Bombing Campaigns of WW II," onlinemilitaryeducation.org/posts/10-most-devastating-bombing-campaigns-of-wwii/.

[3] Personal communication with Isami and Shigeko Endo, 15 July 2014.

[4] The Inter-board Committee was created in 1925 by the Women's Inter-Church Council of Canada.

[5] United Church of Canada Archives, Wilna Thomas Fonds. Thomas was one of the first two Canadian women to join the army chaplaincy service. The Shizuoka Girls School had been founded by Canadian Methodist Church missionaries in 1887.

[6] T.R. Anand, "A Passage from India," *The Gazette* (Montreal), 5 September 1992, B3.

[7] Personal communication with Isami and Shigeko Endo, 15 July 2014.

[8] Personal communication with Isami and Shigeko Endo, 15 July 2014.

[9] Personal communication with Isami and Shigeko Endo, 15 July 2014. Shigeko's use of the phrase "Concentration Camp" highlights the debate over terminology. Patricia Roy notes that "under international law, internment refers to the detention of enemy aliens, whereas most Japanese Canadians were Canadian citizens." See: thecanadianencyclopedia.ca/en/article/internment.

[10] "Cheltenham doctor took own life," *Cheltenham Echo*, 9 March 1971.

[11] Endo, "Barrier-Breaking Miracles,"2.

[12] Endo, "Barrier-Breaking Miracles,"6.

[13] "A forgiving spirit draws two worlds together," *Manitoulin Expositor*, 24 June 1992, 1.

INDEX

Photograph by Alan Cumyn

Dr. Suzanne Evans holds a PhD in Religious Studies. After working, studying, and living in China, Indonesia, India, and Vietnam, she now lives and writes in Ottawa. She is the author of *Mothers of Heroes, Mothers of Martyrs: World War I and the Politics of Grief.* Her writing, which has appeared in academic and literary journals, newspapers, magazines, and books, has a strong focus on women and war.